I Don't Feel Old

The Experience of
Later Life

I Don't Feel Old

The Experience of
Later Life

Paul Thompson, Catherine Itzin,
and Michele Abendstern

Oxford   New York
OXFORD UNIVERSITY PRESS
1990

Oxford University Press, Walton Street, Oxford OX2 6DP

Oxford New York Toronto
Delhi Bombay Calcutta Madras Karachi
Petaling Jaya Singapore Hong Kong Tokyo
Nairobi Dar es Salaam Cape Town
Melbourne Auckland
and associated companies in
Berlin Ibadan

Oxford is a trade mark of Oxford University Press

British Library Cataloguing in Publication Data
Thompson, Paul, 1935–
I don't feel old: the experience of later life.
1. Adults. Ageing. Social Aspects
I. Title   II. Itzin, Catherine, 1944–   III. Abendstern, Michele
305.2'6
ISBN 0–19–820147–8

Library of Congress Cataloging in Publication Data
Thompson, Paul Richard, 1935–
I don't feel old : the experience of later life / by Paul
Thompson, Catherine Itzen, and Michele Abendstern.
p. cm.
Includes bibliographical references.
1. Aged—Great Britain—Biography.   2. Old age—Great Britain.
I. Itzin, Catherine, 1944–   , II. Abendstern, Michele.
III. Title.
HQ1064.G7T46 1990   305.26'0941—dc20   89–27976
ISBN 0–19–820147–8

Typeset by Graphicraft Typesetters Ltd.
Printed in Great Britain by
Biddles Ltd, Guildford and King's Lynn

*To Marion, Tilli, Lenore, Mary Ellen,
Ada, and Hannah,
grandmothers in our own families*

Acknowledgements

We are grateful for many different kinds of help on which we have drawn in writing this book. Our greatest debt is to the men and women who allowed us to record the stories of their lives. Chapter 4 depends partly on interviews from our earlier project on 'Family Life and Work Experience' funded by the Social Science Research Council, for which the full acknowledgements are in my *The Edwardians* (1975). The new set of interviews was carried out for our project on 'Life Stories and Ageing' (G01250010) funded by the Economic and Social Research Council. The interviews were carried out by Catherine Itzin, Michele Abendstern, Graham Smith, Sandra Lotti, Marion Haberhauer, Kay Sanderson, and Bob Little, and were transcribed by Sue Newton, Pat Debenham, and Shirley Millar. We should also particularly like to thank Lenore Davidoff for help with autobiographical sources and Richard Wall with statistics; Terry Tostevin for tracing many obscure books; Bie de Graeve and Peter Moorhouse, who provided especially congenial places for writing; Joanna Bornat, Bob Little, Graham Smith, and Natasha Burchardt for comments on the manuscript; and Margot Jefferys and David Attwooll not only for comments at that stage, but for much earlier advice and encouragement.

Finally we wish to note that while *I Don't Feel Old* is the outcome of working and talking together both in fieldwork and on the book itself, and its shape and message are our joint responsibility, 'As Old As You Feel' was written by Catherine Itzin, 'Grandparenthood' by Michele Abendstern, and the remaining chapters by myself.

P.T.

Contents

1

Introduction

THIS book is about later life from the inside. The heart of it is about later life today, as told to us by 55 older men and women who are all grandparents. We have reached out in two directions. For each of them we aimed to speak to one of their children and if possible one of their grandchildren too, in order to have more than one perspective from inside each family. We have also reached back in time, using memories of grandparents from more than 600 interviews and autobiographies, to try to sense how later life may have changed over two or more centuries.

Listening to all these personal accounts has had a profound effect on us. The fundamental message is in our title. In terms of chronological years, our 55 grandparents are aged from around sixty to over eighty. But unless they are ill, or miserable, they do not feel, in their real selves, that they are old. And considering how most of us think about old age, they are absolutely right.

Contrary to the all too common belief that ageing is essentially an unavoidable process of retreat, of withdrawal into passivity and dependence, the truth is that for most men and women later life is a time of active challenge: a time when perhaps more than ever they need to be able to respond imaginatively to change. To succeed, they have to be able to draw on their full resources, built up over a lifetime. They need not to feel old, but to feel themselves. We have been able to explore, through what they told us, the many different ways in which they respond to this challenge. Revealing the roots of their resilience through their own accounts is the essential purpose of this book.

A century ago, later life was a privilege reached only by a fortunate minority: average life expectancy was under fifty years. Today it has risen by more than twenty years, to 72 for men and 77 for women, and it is still rising. The proportion of our population aged over 65 has swollen from one in twenty to one in five. The once tiny fringe of retired men and women has broadened to a band of ten million. This dramatic alteration in the pattern of human life is part of a still-continuing worldwide change. More men and women are not only living healthily into their seventies, but into their eighties and nineties. By the early twenty-first century there will be two million eighty-year-olds in Britain; seven million in the United States; 25 million in China. For the first time in history, later life has become a normal human expectation.

Yet for all that, it remains a strangely secret and much misunderstood world. In writing this book we have had a double objective. The first is to convey a picture of ordinary later life and its diverse patterns and meanings as older men and women have expressed it to us. The second is to place that direct experience of a particular generation against the longer perspective of time. We shall turn to the dimensions of historical change in our next chapter. Let us begin here with a few facts—and also some fallacies—about the present.

They bring us immediately up against the complex and fundamental issue of how the images we hold of later life and ageing are put together. Why do we take some things as natural, unavoidable, and others as socially shaped and changeable? Take health. The image of natural decay is very deep-seated. Nor should we underestimate the health problems of later life. In middle age a quarter of the population report some kind of ill-health or disability; at seventy, two-fifths; beyond 75, half. Of those over 65, 15 per cent are seriously incapacitated or housebound; 5 per cent are psychiatrically ill, and depression is much more widespread. Nevertheless, looked at the other way round these figures show that most older men and women enjoy reasonable if not perfect health. Only one in twenty of them is reduced to a dependent life in a hospital or home: considerably more, in fact, are carers for others. The transformation in earlier health patterns brought about by social and medical change is obvious, and can be expected to continue. The most recent Scandinavian and American research suggests that however long you live, serious ill-health is most likely to be compressed into the last three or four years before death. Contrary to common belief, in short, 'longer life means longer healthier life.'[1]

What of the association of old age with poverty? Some older men and women have very comfortable incomes, and the recent spread of advertised facilities for them such as sheltered home developments suggests their numbers are far from insignificant. On the other hand, a third of the retired today live at or below the poverty line. Such sharp contrasts are partly the consequence of inequalities of income earlier in life. But poverty is also the direct result of a new historical disadvantage: the exclusion of older men and women from work. In the past they worked as long as they were able: it was illness rather than age as such which placed them in need. This may be one reason for the relative generosity of earlier community help. We falsely congratulate ourselves on the progressiveness of contemporary welfare provision, ignoring not only its insufficiency but also the fact that much of the need itself is an artificial creation of contemporary social prejudices against people continuing at work.

How about the differences between older men and older women? Beyond 75, women outnumber men by almost two to one. Not surprisingly, the contemporary image of an old person is typically of an old woman, and of the loneliness of widowhood. But again, this imbalance is a new historical phenomenon, brought about by the uneven advances in medicine and the lesser exposure of this particular generation of women to health hazards such as smoking or industrial injury. We need to remember that it is no more natural for women to live longer than men than it is for them to have lower incomes, to expect to give up work if their men wish it at marriage or in later life, to be the keepers of family memory, the main carers of those in need, the main sufferers from the empty nest as children leave home. This may have been their experience in a particular historical era. But even within it, we can see plenty of seeds of possible change: older women intensely committed to a work calling, older men who become housekeepers or carers.

The danger, however, lies not only in swallowing false generalizations, or in forgetting how far the realities of later life are shaped by social pressures which may be quite new or open to future change. We should be equally sensitive to the pervasive and often demeaning influences of some of the common images of old age on older men and women themselves. These images build up into stereotypes; generalizations about what is to be expected of older people, which are based at best on partial information rather than the full diversity of their real lives.

The process of stereotyping is complex and only partly conscious. Behind it seems to lie a powerful public need to provide a justification for social inequality by blaming those who have the rawest deal for their own fate; hence the stereotyping of immigrants, and of women, as well as of older people. Stereotyping takes place partly through splitting, and partly through discarding. Splitting creates idealized images as well as vilification: the quiet, kindly grandmother, the benevolent granddad, the wise elder, set against the dried-up spinster, the interfering granny, the miser, the dirty old man, the bedsoiler. But it is the derogatory, spoilt image which sticks as the group image. The typical old person is transformed into a patronized welfare recipient, only one step removed from the 'poor dears' in nursing homes: not to be listened to very seriously, if at all, 'not quite whole people, not people like us'. But everyone knows real old people who do not fit the stereotypes: so discarding follows. The active next-door neighbour, the national political leader, artist, or intellectual, the well-to-do couple on their constant travels, are defined out of the frame. 'They are not a problem, they have no obvious needs, hence they cannot really be elderly.'[2]

The real lives of ordinary men and women described here give the lie to such false images of later life. But we must not forget the shadow which they cast, particularly on older women, who bear the double burden of sex as well as age prejudice. Some of the attitudes and strategies which we shall find—defining only others as old, for example—are ways chosen, sometimes consciously, sometimes not, to avoid the humiliations of a spoilt identity.

Later life, in short, demands courage; and as we shall see, imagination too. But both prove abundant.

It may seem odd that what we heard was such a revelation. After all, interviewing old people is no new idea. How is it that the sociologists and oral historians who interview and record the elderly have not already countered the derogatory myth of old age as helpless degeneration? In part it is because they too have unknowingly taken in the prevailing stereotypes. But it is also because their own specialist interests have led them in other directions.

Thus the most influential sociologists researching on later life in the last thirty years have been first and foremost concerned with documenting poverty and need among the old, rather than looking at their present lives as a whole, or how they reached where they are now. For the same reason they have focused on the groups who seemed most likely to be needy: the working class in the inner city, the isolated and the institutionalized. Peter Townsend's classic *The Family Life of Old People* (1957) still remains in many ways the most sympathetic and sensitive portrait of ordinary old people's lives published in Britain. It takes us into their homes, gives space for their voices; and Townsend powerfully attacked the widespread myth that the family was no longer providing most of them with social support or practical help. But even then the East End of London could not have represented the rest of the country; and even he plays for our pity, opening with a classic portrait of poverty and deprivation. The emphasis in his own later work, and of others who have followed him, has been increasingly on the most vulnerable. For the study of social need and welfare policy this is clearly right; yet it unwittingly helps to reinforce the stereotypes.[3]

Oral historians had meanwhile begun to record the earlier memories of ordinary old people, working right across the country. But as historians they were more concerned with the past than the present, so they only gradually came to realize that the two were in many ways inseparable: both that remembering itself could be a help to the present lives of those telling their story, and also that the memory could be profoundly shaped by subsequent experience and this needed to be known to interpret it more effectively.[4] Hence oral history interviews were typically truncated. Sociologists chopped off childhood and most of adulthood from their interviews, and oral historians neatly matched this by chopping off the whole later life.

More than this, even with earlier memories they rarely made any systematic attempt to gather evidence of later life from childhood memories about grandparents or old people in the neighbourhood.[5] In this they were simply reflecting the typical disinterest of historians. Indeed, even today, the social history of ordinary ageing in this country has barely started. We have tried to sum up the fragments of information which we have for the last three centuries in our second chapter, 'Glimpses of a Lost History'. There has been no British work to match the attempts of pioneering European and American historians to provide an overview. Although we have a clearer picture than we did of long-term changes in demography and household structure, little has been done to fill out the picture in terms of living experience. More than ten years ago Peter Laslett complained that 'we can say little yet about the everyday relationship between old people and their grown-up, independent children for any period earlier than recent times.'[6] That remains true: and the recent past, which is the one period open to direct study through life story testimony, is the least subject to research by either historians or sociologists because it falls uneasily between their concerns.

For these various reasons our own use of full life stories for understanding later life both in the past and today remains exceptional. But its context has been a general quickening of interest in research on ageing not only among sociologists and historians, but also from other disciplines such as psychiatry and anthropology. Our research itself gained from its context as part of the recent Economic and Social Research Council 'Ageing Initiative'. The work of other researchers has in many different ways helped to shape our work, to influence what we have asked and to make us more sensitive to what we have heard. There are four ways in particular which we wish to mention here.

The first is the 'life course' approach which was first developed by sociologists, but has recently been taken up by some historians. Ageing has to be recognized as a *process*, a gradual transition, rather than a once-for-all event. In the crudest sense, there are indeed 'young old' and 'old old'; and although you can be either younger or older at any age, physical and mental disabilities do slowly cumulate on average with increasing years. Some of the first life course sociologists assumed that this gradual ageing process was also socially unidirectional, towards 'disengagement', as if in acceptance that life itself was ebbing away. This was the approach of M. E. Cumming and W. H. Henry's influential book, *Growing Old* (1961). But it was soon followed by another American study of the elderly, Margaret Clark and Barbara Anderson's *Culture and Ageing* (1967), attacking the idea that disengagement was typical or commendable. On the contrary, they saw their San Francisco elderly as fighting for survival and self-esteem through a remarkable variety of strategies. What was most striking was 'the rich and wide variety of adaptations to ageing' which they had encountered. 'The clearest, most unequivocal finding to come out of our social analysis is the singularity of the subjects in it.' And their telling portraits of their subjects vividly brought this home.[7]

Although earlier crude categories survive in some influential textbooks on ageing, a subtler stance has gradually emerged from this controversy. It is recognized that there are many valid ways of growing older. Social workers in training are now encouraged to accept that 'older people are entitled to select their own destiny, within given limits.' This in itself means that it has become more important to understand what their lives mean to them. Even at the most practical, simple level, those concerns and aspects of their lives 'which are not highly valued by external observers may well be amongst the most significant.' Equally important, the interest and wishes of the old are not created spontaneously in the present. They are the culminations of a whole life which, as Malcolm Johnson puts it, 'sculpted their present problems and concerns'; a life itself built around many different 'life-threads'— education, work, marriage, children, hobbies, and so on—so that it is best understood, both in psychological and social terms, 'as a complex of strands running for different lengths of time throughout a life biography and moulding its individuality'.[8] Only a life history approach can allow us to follow these threads to a fuller understanding of each person's singular present. It has been fundamental to our own work here.

A second influence has been the developing interest in the differences in later life experience between men and women. The fact that men are likely to die earlier, and far more women experience many years of widowed life, is well known. Sociologists have also frequently documented the peculiar strength of the tie between married daughters and their mothers in many communities, and how women are more likely both to be cared for by their families in old age, and to be the carers.[9] Relatively recently, feminist scholars, now drawn closer through common experience to an older generation many of whose values they had challenged, have extended their concerns and pushed forward a more subtle questioning of women's experience of ageing and how it might differ from men's as a result of inequalities right through the life cycle. In what special ways, Sarah Matthews asks, could a group of American widows maintain their sense of self-identity? Or following closely from this, what do physical changes in their bodies imply for men and for women? Is there a 'double standard of ageing', Susan Sontag asks? Getting older may be 'less profoundly wounding for a man', because throughout life being physically

attractive counts more in a woman's life than in a man's, and for
women especially beauty is identified with youthfulness. Or perhaps, on the contrary, it is a release for older women no longer to
have to be so concerned with sexual appearances. It can give them a
chance—certainly often seized by widows in the past—to assert
themselves with genuine dignity and authority in the public
world.[10]

What of the implications of the traditional division of roles in the
home and at paid work? The unthinking equation of widowhood for
women with retirement for men has been challenged. So has the
common assumption that retirement from paid employment is 'far
less drastic' for women than for men. The majority of women do
undertake paid work in their later middle life, and it can be just as
wrenching for them to leave it as for men. Hence the social
acceptability of earlier retirement by women can prove a mixed
blessing: it gives them more chance to leave paid work at a time of
their own choosing, but also leaves them more open to pressure
from others to retire. Similarly, the changing of domestic roles
proves complex: while some wives may welcome more domestic
help from their retired husbands, others will resent it as an intru-
sion into their sphere of control in daily life. Françoise Cribier
finds one reason for the remarkable exodus of retired couples from
Paris is that both man and wife need the husband to get out of the
house. In the city they are cooped up together all day in an
apartment. In the country or on the coast they can re-create their
routine of earlier days. They rise early by the alarm clock, so the
husband can go out to work—cultivating vegetables, rearing rabbits and poultry in the garden, and mending things in his shed.
British couples have less need to leave the city to find a garden.
But perhaps more generally women find their own retirement
easier because they have had to organize their own time for most
of their lives and have relied more on the small pleasures of
domestic life. And what were the implications of these traditional
roles for grandparenthood? Sarah Cunningham-Burley finds Aberdeen grandfathers much more uncertain than grandmothers of
what their role should be. But could that not be a new chance for a
man to find in later life 'an emotional experience that he missed
when his children were young'?[11]

Beyond that, how are the implications of widowhood different
for women and men? Sheer numbers mean that widows are much
less likely to remarry than widowers: there simply aren't enough

men of their age around. It has been suggested that the shock of widowhood for a woman is like compulsory redundancy for a man; and for a woman whose career has been as a housewife this might certainly be the case, even though for others it could prove a relief from the narrow constraints of their domestic role. But if widowhood is such a double shock for many women, why do widows survive much longer than widowers? Is it that men are simply less used to looking after themselves, less adept at creating the new social relationships they need? But if older women do have special survival skills, evaluating them is not a simple matter.

Throughout their lives most women play less prestigious social roles than men, and their paid work is generally worse paid, less secure, and of lower status. They also take the primary responsibility for the care of children. The unbalanced responsibilities which they bear as carers continue in middle and later life. In Britain, three times as many women as men care for elderly or handicapped relatives: most typically women in middle age, but many themselves older. They look after parents most often, but also neighbours, friends, and other relatives. Men in middle age do this much less often, although surprisingly, in later life those who survive are as likely to be carers as women. A notable group of recent feminist studies has focused on these women carers, bringing home in no uncertain measure the cost they pay, financially, in time, and emotionally: 'the claustrophobia, to the point of being suffocated, of living with the situation and, of course, the exhausting conflict of mixed emotions . . . the love, anger, frustration and guilt.'[12]

At the same time there is a real personal value and satisfaction to be gained from the caring and nurturing work of women in the family. Barbara Myerhoff's notably thoughtful study of a seafront Jewish old people's centre in Venice, Los Angeles, conveys this well. Observing the men and women here, she came to suspect that appearances were deceptive. The men had won their prestige from work, from scholarship, in the public arena; and they sat outside on the pavement benches, publicly debating politics, theology, and history. But did the women really feel that their own work had been less important? She had her doubts:

Perhaps it is true that women are kept humble by the nature of their everyday activities. They spend so much time immersed in unglamorous stuff—transient and trivial details that vanish and reappear to be done again the next moment. But does this necessarily mean that a woman is not fully aware of the enormous importance of offering food, producing and raising children, shaping the atmosphere of the home? Considering again my grandmother and the Center women, I suggest there is a set of understandings shared among women, concerning the meaning and value of the conventional functions....In caring for others, in serious, dedicated friendships, in constructing individual careers made of personally discovered projects, in arranging lives of self-care and attentiveness to others who are needy... These understandings are a kind of underground culture, quietly transmitted... Real but rather easy to overlook, they continue through the life cycle, and may reemerge as essential aids in later life.[13]

Certainly the importance of such roles, and the strengths won from them, need to be taken seriously; but not at the price of romanticization.

A third way of distinguishing experiences in later life is in terms of community, class, and conflict. This has been a traditional starting-point for both historians and sociologists. The Americans have again gone ahead, with books on retirement communities like *Idle Haven* and *Fun City*, documenting their way of life and internal struggles for leadership. The same can be done in miniature by looking at a sheltered housing group or an institutional home.[14] Chris Phillipson has contrasted retired men from different work backgrounds in different British communities. He found that both class and community mattered. Birmingham architects had the continuing energy, self-confidence, and material means to create a comfortable and interesting retirement for themselves. Former Midland carworkers and Tyneside shipbuilders seemed by contrast worn out, despairingly lost, cut off from former workmates in their conurbations. They wept on their last day of work: 'I felt terrible'; 'it seemed as though you were suddenly cut off from life.' They lay in bed in the morning, 'puzzled about how to fill me time in.' Yet in a former Durham pit village, although all had either been made redundant or been forced out of work by ill-health, a group of miners were so sustained by the community network of neighbours and relatives that giving up work seemed a positive blessing. 'When a person has been underground for so many years it's a new lease of life'; 'it's just a grand feeling.'[15]

In practice, although this way of thinking was one perspective from which we looked at our material, it proved much less useful than we expected. This was partly because our people were all scattered, rather than concentrated in particular communities. The material therefore only hinted at differences in social life between them. But it was a good deal more surprising to find that class patterns were not more obvious. Judged in terms of former occupations, there seemed to be much more variety within than between classes.

There are in fact good reasons for this. Occupation is never more than a shorthand for allocating social class, which leaves out other key dimensions: your education, or the house you live in, for instance. It works particularly awkwardly for married women at any age, since they may be employed at quite a different level from their husbands, or not at all. But in later life these difficulties apply equally strongly to both men and women. If they carry on working, it may be in a lower status occupation: should they be classified by this, or by their earlier main job? And as the years from retirement lengthen, it seems more and more tenuous to group men in terms of long-past work, let alone women who since marriage may never have been in paid work at all. What must count is their present resources: their home, their pension, their health, their family, their friends, their psychic energy. In terms of class background, some of these factors are more sharply tilted than others—and not all the same way. Thus those who were in middle-class occupations will almost certainly enjoy larger pensions and more comfortable houses, and they can expect to suffer fewer disabilities, and live longer too. But they are less likely to benefit from family living close by to support them.

On the other hand, what older people have in common is in some ways more striking than the class differences between them. Except for a very few rich people, they are all financially much less well off than they were. As a whole group they are in relative or absolute poverty, in contrast to the general adult population of working age. Nor can they hope to earn more in the future. Systematically pushed to the margins in the labour market, past the household power of active parenthood, soon deprived of all but the trimmings of public influence, are they not all victims in the age-bound society of the contemporary West? Anthropologists, like Nancy Foner in *Ages in Conflict*, have shown how in non-Western societies this struggle for rewards and power may be openly organized through recognized age-sets. It is this perspective, drawn from both anthropology and history, rather than class conflict, which provides the deeply pessimistic theme of Simone de Beauvoir's *Old Age*.[16] We reject her pessimism. But the discrimination is undeniable.

More positively, older people share a degree of freedom. Just because their lives are no longer structured by employment or education, there is more space for a variety of life patterns among the elderly of any class background. They are distinctive, 'because they *must* choose; responsibility for structuring their lives is uniquely their own.' Rex Taylor and Graeme Ford found a 'seemingly endless' diversity of life patterns through interviewing old people in Aberdeen. They could focus on their wider family, or their spouse, or a continuing job, or a social cause or hobby, or their own physical health. 'Some lead such active lives that we found it difficult to arrange a time for interview, while others are so isolated and lonely that our interviewers felt guilty about terminating the interview and leaving them to themselves.' This certainly fits with our experience. And the overall groupings which we finally evolved for this book in terms of life focus also turn out to be remarkably close to the clusters of life styles picked out in an earlier American study taking just this perspective, Robert Williams and Claudine Wirths's *Lives through the Years*.[17]

This brings us to the last perspective which has influenced us: the study, in the broadest sense, of personality. Older people may have the scope for choice, but how they use it depends on the resources which they have built up over their lives. Partly this is a question of class. We have also been impressed by the independent influence of family relationships over the generations, an approach which has been brought home to us through discussion with family therapists.[18] But the individual variety in resilience, energy, and adaptability remains remarkable. Sometimes it is clearly the outcome of a lifetime. There are also others whose unrealized creativity only flowers in later life. These personal responses and strategies build the sense of individual meaning and self-identity essential for survival. They will remain fundamental to our concern, and a basic issue to which we shall return at the end.

How typical of the ordinary experience of later life are the accounts which we present here? Two kinds of caution are needed:

about the nature of the evidence, and about the people who gave it.

One chapter of this book is based on written autobiographies, and almost the whole of the rest on tape-recorded life story interviews. Typically these interviews lasted three or more hours and were recorded over two or three visits. They were all transcribed, to produce 50 to 150 pages of transcript each. This gives our evidence great strength. Telling their own story from childhood to an interviewer is for most people an intimate experience which encourages them to be remarkably open about themselves. Not uncommonly, indeed, they will speak of things which they have never before told anyone. They have the time and space to explain themselves. We have the exact record of their words, rather than an interviewer's summary interpretation. And we can look at the interview as a whole to understand what particular comments mean. These are all significant advantages when compared with the evidence of most social surveys.[19]

We use this evidence in two different ways. The first is retrospective. It is therefore subject to the omissions and confusions of long-term memory, which have been discussed in considerable detail by both social scientists and oral historians.[20] It will suffice to say here that while most people retain quite substantial and reliable memories of their own everyday lives in childhood and young adulthood, and also of the key turning-points in middle and later life, both fleeting and peripheral experience is much more rarely remembered. Memory of life in middle age tends to be sketchier. Dates are never reliable, and similar events can easily be confused or telescoped into one. And most important of all, although past feelings—often encapsulated in vivid stories—can certainly be remembered, we all go on reinterpreting our lives in emotional terms at every stage. We feel differently about our parents when we are children than we do as adults, and while this may not alter our recollections of everyday family life, it will affect what we choose to highlight, and how we sum up our relationship with them. In a similar way, as we shall find later, although the widowed and still married give similar pictures of the practical division of roles in their married lives, the widowed tend to interpret these apparently similar marriages differently, remembering themselves as having been closer couples than do those who are still married.

In Part One the life stories are used only retrospectively, drawing on childhood memories of grandparents. A child's view of the older generation is clearly very partial. It is most intrinsically valuable as an indication of the quality of relationships between the generations, and we have primarily interpreted it in that way. We also believe that these intimate, naïve glimpses of a lost past have a wider interest just because what we know of the history of later life from inside is so meagre. The impressions conveyed, however, need to be taken within the frame which historians have put together from other sources, with which we therefore begin.

In the remainder of the book the focus is on activities, feelings, and relationships in the present. For this purpose the type of interview was particularly suitable, with accounts of present-day life coming towards the end of a now intimate interview. We wanted both detailed accounts and subjective interpretations, and we were given both. It is important to re-emphasize, however, that just because we are presenting an account of later life from the inside, rather than as judged by outsiders, this book does not attempt to present an objective measure of disadvantage. If we had wanted that we would have used medical questionnaires to evaluate physical and mental health, listed the facilities and defects in each house, and asked for income and expenditure budgets. Many very thorough and valid surveys of this type have been carried out. Our objective was different: not so much to plot the difficulties of later life, as to discover how people find a path through them.

What about the people who wrote or told us life stories: how far can they be taken as typical? For Part One we used two separate samples, which we explain in detail. The 142 written autobiographies from the nineteenth century are a cross-section of the social classes, but in no sense representative. Autobiographers are clearly special people—even though many may come from quite typical families. But once we try to reach beyond living memory this constraint is inevitable. Our other main sample, however, the 444 life stories recorded for an earlier project, had been deliberately chosen on the basis of a quota sample to be representative of the British population as a whole in the early twentieth century. We are confident that these are a broadly reliable cross-section.

The remainder of the book is based on the 55 interviews with contemporary older men and women. This is too small a number to make any claims to statistical representativeness. We nevertheless ensured that as individuals they were selected in a random way, by using an earlier sample survey as our starting list. Through that we obtained a middle generation, who then passed us on to the older generation of the family. As a result there was a double filter, in terms of willingness to be recorded. Since we wanted to record long, in-depth interviews, this was inevitable, but it is a difficulty which must bring caution. For example, we know that some people eventually decided not to be recorded because of painful secrets in their lives, while there were others who for just this reason found it helpful to talk: but how far these two groups balance out can only be guessed.[21]

Fortunately it is possible to check how far—in terms of occupational background, type of housing and main income, and general health—these grandparents match the general population of their age. One qualification must be that because the sample is small, there is only one immigrant family among them, which excludes any consideration of the special features of later life in ethnic minorities. Another crucial difference is a direct result of our research design: among the population as a whole, only two-thirds of those over 65 have children and grandchildren. We have therefore missed two important minorities: those who never married, and those couples who had no children. In terms of needing help, these are precisely the most vulnerable groups, and for good reasons they have therefore received more attention in earlier work on the elderly. We have to remember this in considering how far the experience presented in this book is typical. On the other hand, the elderly with descendants are the majority. It is worth noting too, that with higher marriage rates and less involuntary childlessness, they will constitute a rising proportion of those entering later life. In all other respects, however, our group seem to present a typical spread, excluding only the very small minority too seriously ill to be interviewed. We cannot claim these life stories to be 'representative' in the strict social scientific sense, but we do believe them to be 'valid'.[22] What they have to tell us fully demands our respect.

We must add one final personal note. It did not feel right, in a project on latter life from the inside, to stay on the outside ourselves. So early on we recorded our own life stories and our own reflections on the personal experience of getting older: at around thirty, around forty, and around fifty. We have also recorded the older generation in our own families—noticing how some things we knew went unmentioned, but also making some surprising new discoveries of our own family secrets. And as family members we have seen and felt at close hand some of the most intense pains and also pleasures of later life: on the one hand, bereavement and loss, but on the other, the continued mastery of old skills, the creation of new pursuits and interests, the discovery of new friends and of new ways of contributing to the wider community. In dedicating our book to six grandmothers in our own families, we mark the special inspiration which each in different ways has given us.

Part One
Then

2
Glimpses of a Lost History

WHAT was it like to grow old in the past in Britain? For the moment we can only piece together fragments of evidence. The history of ageing in this country has still to be written. Much of it is now irrecoverably lost; for the lack of interest in the experience of ordinary old people shown by historians is mirrored in the scanty documentation which survives from the past. Like ordinary people in general, old people usually show up vividly in the record only when they become a problem. At death, in the moment of passing, all secure an entry, and some a lasting monument; but of most people's later life little is ever known, or now knowable. Such a silence is itself significant. It reflects powerlessness. It also reflects ambivalence.

A rounded picture of later life over the past two or three centuries is thus impossible. But we do know enough to be able to pick out some clear changes, and continuities too, by tracing particular themes. Let us begin with social attitudes to ageing. How different were they in the seventeenth century from today? 'In early modern England,' Keith Thomas has written, 'the prevailing ideal was gerontocratic: the young were to serve and the old were to rule.' It was assumed that wisdom, as the sum of experience and self-control, grew with age. The image of God as an old man was echoed throughout society. The church itself was headed by elderly archbishops and the law by aged judges. In the printer's workshop the oldest workman would be 'father' of the chapel. Children were taught to show their parents obedience, duty, and respect, taking their hat off to their father as a matter of manners, and at solemn moments kneeling to receive his formal blessing. Communities were typically run by the 'ancientry of the parish.' Often this was reflected in the village church, where the old sat in the best seats and the young at the back.[1]

Yet alongside this ideal—perhaps in part provoked by it—ran strong counter-currents. In reality the key positions of power in

both politics and the law were normally held by men in their
forties and fifties. The elderly could not sustain the more strenuous
manual work in agriculture or the crafts. Respect did not prevent
children from rebelling against their parents. And the grave, sober
image of old age was a constraint on social behaviour. The elderly
who expressed continuing sexual interests would be mercilessly
ridiculed by the youth groups of their village. There was a widespread mocking of 'old fools.' 'Old people commonly are despised,'
observed Richard Steele, 'especially when they are not supported
with good estates;' while another commented in 1621 how, in
contrast to the common 'pleasure in infants' shown by women, 'old
people are burdensome to all; neither their talk nor their company
is acceptable.'[2]

This ambivalence towards the old is clearly shown in the traditional seven stages of life. These stages, linked to the known
planets, can be traced back through medieval literature to the
ancients. From the middle years onwards the phases were Man-
hood, under the control of Mars, Old Age under Jupiter, and
finally Senility under Saturn. The idea of an important division
between the 'young old' and the 'old old' in today's terms was thus
already accepted. One respected writer, Dr John Smith, went
further in his *Portrait of Old Age* (1666) in suggesting a triple
division between 'green' old age when men could still work well,
the 'full, mature' or 'good old age' of the retirement years, and a
last stage of extreme, 'sickly, decrepit, ever growing old age.' But
most of his contemporaries did not share his hopeful vision of 'good
old age.' They preferred to contrast the typically active and widely
powerful young old with the pathetic senility of old old age, the
'Crooked Age,' summed up by Shakespeare as 'second childish-
ness . . . sans teeth, sans eyes, sans taste, sans everything.'[3] There
were thus two concurrent stereotypes of the old. One was as
strikingly negative as the other was positive. Either could be
drawn on, to support respect or scorn. And the balance of early
modern attitudes to the old looks a good deal less favourable when
we realize that the terms of chronological age used then were quite
different from those in use today. Their Old Age, from fifty to 62,
we now see as part of Middle Age. Our Young Old Age they saw as
Senility; our Old Old Age was beyond the focus of their conventional wisdom.

This pushing onwards of the chronological stages over the centuries partly reflects a second, more fundamental transformation: the cumulative impact of changes in health and demography. The direct impact of improving health in later life has been relatively recent. But the position of older people is also shaped by general birth and death rates. Thus in a rapidly growing population there will be relatively few older people, as in many contemporary Third World countries; while in a stagnant population they will be relatively more numerous, and more of them will lack the support of children. Hence in late nineteenth-century France the aged were already a more prominent group, almost twice the proportion in England at the same time: indeed, there were proportionally somewhat fewer old in booming Victorian England than in 1700. But these changes through the birth rate remained relatively modest in this country until the present century. Right through from the seventeenth until the early twentieth century those who reached the age of sixty years remained a small but quite steady 5–7 per cent of the English population.[4] By 1900 however, the birth rate was plunging as couples chose to have fewer children, just as improved health had also begun to have a marked impact; and it is the *combination* in the twentieth century of a now almost stagnant population of small families with a new fall in death rates which explains the striking rise of over-sixty-year-olds to form over 20 per cent of our population today and why, more than in any previous generation, such a high proportion of them are without children.

It is partly that old people themselves are living longer. A late Victorian at sixty could look forward to scarcely a dozen more years of life; a contemporary sixty-year-old man can expect almost twenty more years and a woman even more. But the impact of the fall in death rates among younger age groups (which began earlier, in the mid-nineteenth century) has been still more dramatic. In the past, death struck right through the life cycle. Children were especially vulnerable, but many also died in young or middle adulthood. By fifty a married man or woman was as likely as not to have suffered widowhood, and would have already lost half his or her contemporaries: in contrast to a mere twentieth today. Hence far more people *enter* old age. But they pay an unexpected price, which is itself one of the underlying differences between old age in the past and in the present.

The withdrawal of earlier death has been so marked that today most English people will have no direct experience of the grief of bereavement until they lose their own parents, when they are themselves well into middle age. For the young, death is so unreal that it has become a pleasure to play with, part of the fantasy of violence. Then suddenly, unprepared by experience, as they become old they are struck by the unfamiliar, relentless impact of death combing out their social world, remorselessly striking down their family and friends.

Today it is only the old who regularly die, so only the old who have to deal with the universality of death. Funerals were within living memory ceremonial rites engaging whole communities— blinds drawn down across the street, the pomp of plumed horses and the procession of followers, traffic momentarily halted, the bereaved publicly showing their sorrow for months in the long wearing of black afterwards; monuments and cemeteries were focuses of family and civic pride; fear of a pauper grave was so powerful that death insurance was by far the most widespread Victorian insurance policy. Ironically, just because death was such a central concern in the past, the history of death is much more fully studied than the history of living old people.[5] Today, by contrast, funerals are diminished, cemeteries deserted, even sold off. Once loudly and publicly proclaimed, death has become private, secret, almost shameful: so much so that nobody of any age wants to talk about it. That makes facing one's own death, and the crushing pain of bereavement through the death of others, even more bewildering. The very changes which have lengthened life have made the coming of death feel stranger and harsher from its new unfamiliarity.

It is above all women who are living longer. In 1800 there were roughly equal numbers of older men and older women, but today there are three women to every two men. Since women in general have less social prestige than men, this in itself tends to reinforce negative attitudes to the elderly. But the imbalance affects women more directly. The majority of men who survive can expect to have the support of a wife up to the age of 85, but any woman over 72 is more likely to be a widow left on her own. While men today enjoy later life as one of a couple, for women the experience is most often solitary. There was no such sharp contrast in the earlier past.[6]

Less dramatically, the health of the surviving has improved.

Doctors in early modern England had developed no special skills for dealing with the health of older people. Probably most of those surviving were reasonably active, as they would die rather quickly when they succumbed to their first serious illness at this stage of life. However they would have been commonly toothless, since false teeth were a luxury until the nineteenth-century. And enough elderly people did survive as chronically sick, physically maimed, or mentally impaired, to sustain the most negative seventeenth-century images of old age as 'a perpetual sickness,' 'a disease,' a time of impotence in the widest sense, 'the dregs . . . of a man's life.'[7]

One very early sign of a more positive attitude, arguing that physical ageing could be delayed through a plentiful diet, regular sleep and short naps, and moderate exercise including riding and dancing, is Francis Bacon's *History of Life and Death* (1623). Possibly the earliest attempt at a scientific study of ageing, he wrote it when he was himself 62. Bacon's fundamental concept was of 'age as a great but slow drier.' By comparing different plants, animals, and human physical types and ways of life, he suggested defences against this drying-out. These were mainly from changing daily habits, but included some medicines. He claimed that there were places in the past where 'men's lives were longer, when plain homely diet and bodily labour were much used, and shorter when more civiliz'd times delighted in idleness, and wanton luxury.' In the countryside you could still find 'in every populous village a man or woman of three-score years of age. And at a wake in Herefordshire, a Dance was performed by eight men, whose *age* added together, amounted to eight hundred yeeres.' A shift to simple wholesome living could bring long life to many more.[8]

The sustained development of the study of the diseases of later life had to wait until the nineteenth-century. It was led by French physicians and at first it simply confirmed the most pessimistic of common views. Old age was a phase of irrevocable and inevitable decline. The external signs of ageing, as at different points eyesight blurred, menstruation ceased, hair and teeth fell out, were seen as linked to signs of internal degeneration such as sclerosis which were being discovered through post-mortems. Decay was seen as mental as well as physical: 'the faculties of intelligence share equally in this universal deterioration.' Loss of memory and progressive senile dementia were all part of 'normal mental deterioration.' Even genius disappeared in old age. Texts in English such as George Day's *Practical Treatise on the Domestic Management and Most Important Diseases of Advanced Life* (1849) soon took up this thinking. Old age was a disability in itself. The elderly were advised to put themselves 'under the immediate and constant care of the physician.' Physical exertion was dangerous, sexuality inappropriate and obscene, and even overworking the mind 'might bring on mental exhaustion.'[9]

In France itself this stifling view was still being propagated up until the 1950s. It was only with the American-led development from the 1900s of geriatric medicine as a new specialty, followed in the interwar years by self-help books and clubs encouraging older people to keep fit, travel, keep working, and—at least from the 1950s—stay sexually active, that informed European opinion began once more to swing towards a positive view of ageing. Changed attitudes, rising living standards, and more effective health care have together resulted in not only a longer, but a fuller life expectancy. The new conventional wisdom which divides the young old from the old old at 75 marks a boundary for entry into the last stage of life which has now been pushed back by a dozen years. While the ancient ambivalence in attitudes to ageing, symbolized in this division, undoubtedly survives, the targets have shifted. The young old now keep one foot in the full humanity of middle age.

Our understand of the quality of later life before this revolution in attitudes is severely constrained by the kinds of information which have survived. Most of this information is disconcertingly dry: we have to squeeze it hard to make anything of it at all. But let us look more closely at what the archives can yield.

There is only one type of personal family document which survives right through the last three centuries in really significant numbers. This is the last testament, will, or contract through which the elderly transmitted their material possessions and land to their heirs. In fact, because most older people had nothing significant to leave, only a minority wrote wills. But they were a substantial minority, and those historians who have recently been studying inheritance have reached some interesting conclusions.

It was a general principle of English and also Scandinavian medieval law that relatives who inherited land were responsible for supporting its former owners, including widows. But this operated in very different forms between countries and regions, and even at the level of a single English county. Nor is it really clear what the documents tell us. Thus before the 1833 Dower Act, the principle under English common law was that a widow had a life entitlement to one-third of the income from her husband's former property. Some wills assumed this as an inexcludable entitlement and did not even mention it. Others attempted to alter it, or to enforce it when land was left by the will to the children alone, rather than as more usually to the widow or the widow and children jointly. Historians have found some manors where the local custom was for the widow to receive a half proportion, or even the whole, and yet in others apparently none—although in these cases it is more likely that the documentation is being misconstrued. But normally either the land was eventually to be divided equally between the children or, more typically where land was scarcer, the land itself would go to a single son and provision be made for the other children in cash—very often advanced earlier in life, on marriage or to set up in a trade. In some parts of Scandinavia where the land was divided equally, the old person would move between the heirs, receiving food and lodging from each in turn. More usually, as for instance in Scotland, one heir took on the duty. In England, by contrast, although there were some villages where having a widowed parent in the house 'was very much the ordinary, expected thing' at a certain stage in life, already by the late middle ages it was not the normal pattern.[10]

It was a part of folk wisdom that providing houseroom for a widowed parent could lead to intense family friction. The Bethnal Greeners of the 1950s who believed that to live together was an invitation to 'open conflict' belonged to a long tradition. One Scots proverb ran:

> Here is the fair mall [mallet]
> To give a knock on the skull
> To the man who keeps no gear for himself
> But gives all to his bairns.

There are English law cases of the late fifteenth-century for not providing meat, drink, and lodging to a retired father-in-law, while Swedish High Court disputes of two centuries later show grievances ranging from poor food to cursing and physical violence.

The Swedish priest who advised, 'He wrongs himself who turns over his farm to his children, if they are badly brought up,' was echoing the ancient Biblical warning in *Ecclesiasticus*: 'As long as thou livest and hast breath in thee, give not thyself over to any. For it is better that thy children should seek to thee, than that thou shouldest stand to their courtesy.' One Jacobean preacher vividly elaborated on just this text.

> Hath any man ever seen a poor aged man live in courtesy in the house of his son with his daughter-in-law? . . . Doth not the good father in short time, either by his coughing or spitting or testiness . . . become troublesome either to his own son or to his nice daughter-in-law, with continuing so long chargeable and so much waited-on, or to the children, with taking up their room at the fire or at the table, or to the servants, while his slow eating doth scant their reversions?

And the grumbling was unlikely to be one-sided. One retired Somerset man told a visiting kinsman, 'You are likely to have but a short feast here, but I pray you if you have not good cheer blame my sonne John Webb and not me, for of my troth I have made him master of all.' As Daniel Rogers warned in 1642, 'No prison can be more irksome than a son or daughter's house.'[11]

In Scandinavia living space was cramped. Whole farm families normally shared a common bedroom well into the nineteenth-century. By the mid-seventeenth century it had become normal for the wealth of the old people to be transferred to the next generation when they retired, perhaps in their sixties, but for the retired couple to retain houseroom in the family home; and in order to make disputes less likely, these retirement arrangements were increasingly recorded in deeds. Only in the late nineteenth century did these contracts generally disappear and instead the land was sold or let and the old people lived off the cash proceeds. In the far west of Ireland retirement contracts were still quite common in the 1930s. Both the practice and the tensions associated with it were meticulously described by the American anthropologists Arensberg and Kimball. Families in this still Gaelic-speaking region were classically patriarchal. Even when the sons were carrying out all the farm labour, the father would continue to control all their tasks and all money matters, to the extent of walking to collect a son's wages for work off the farm. So long as the old couple had not made over the farm, their middle-aged son remained a 'boy': 'You can be a boy here forever as long as the old fellow is still alive.' Inside the farmhouse the warmest seats by the fire belonged to the old couple 'by right.' Significantly, the form of written agreement by which the father handed over the farm would make explicit not only his right to a room in the house, a place at the hearth, food, and the yield of a potato-patch and 'grass of a cow,' but also clear financial compensation if the arrangement broke down. Inharmonious transitions were evidently far from rare, with not only violent arguments, but 'the young woman and the old woman slashing each other with tongs, the doors broke, and it would be two dwellings in one house.' Custom, in short, was no guarantee of harmonious relationships in three-generation households. On the contrary, one sees how greater physical distance could well help to bring emotional relationships closer.[12]

In England, however, written retirement contracts are historically 'very rare indeed.' But this is probably because such retirement arrangements died out before formalizing them became the normal custom, rather than because they were never common. Certainly, already by the thirteenth century the building of a separate cottage for a widow was as often stipulated in wills as the provision of houseroom. Nor was this simply because the land market was developed earlier.[13] Already by the late middle ages the English were beginning to expect more space and more privacy in their houses than was to be normal in Scandinavia for another three centuries.

England's very unusual system of inheritance is of particular interest because of its continuing influence in later centuries, both on the fate of older people and also more generally on the English class system. The English aristocracy pursued the principle of independent homes for the older generation to its ultimate conclusion. Despite the vast size of their houses and the numerous servants surrounding each aristocratic family, on the death of a Victorian head of household 'his or her resident family was expected to leave to make way for the incoming heir and his or her family. The widowed mother and any unmarried siblings living at home usually had to move out.' As an American commentator put it, 'a duchess abdicates when her son comes to his title; she is turned out of the mansion where she once presided....'[14] It was especially through this single-minded concentration of resources through inheritance on a principal heir that the English aristocracy were able to tighten their grip on the land. Farm families by contrast increasingly sold off their holdings, in order to secure their own last years and at the same time allow equal treatment of their children.

The farmers' descendents, moving over the generations into commerce and trade, stuck to the old peasant form of succession, if the picture given by Leonore Davidoff and Catherine Hall of *Family Fortunes* in early nineteenth-century Birmingham and East Anglia is representative. The system was still one of equal division between the children. As with the land, if division was difficult the business or the family home would be sold to allow it. Lifetime gifts such as apprentice premiums or partnership capital or lump sums on marriage were treated as advances on inheritance portions. There were also some devices which counterbalanced this continual splitting of family resources, such as the partnership system of the family firm, marriage between cousins, and setting up trusts to provide income for daughters and wives which at the same time allowed the trustees, who were always men, to use the trust capital for the business. A widow without sufficient means was still expected to work. Some carried on the family business, as had been typical in the past. But the development of trusts and the final disappearance of common law dower rights in 1833 meant that until the late nineteenth-century reassertion of women's independent property rights, a wealthy widow was much more dependent on her male kin than either in the past or today. Her fortunes were in the control of men who could candidly say, like one Essex trustee, that her 'present views are of entire indifference to me.'[15]

Those with significant property to leave were of course a minority. But it seems to have been equally rare for young couples in the poorer classes to help their ageing parents by providing them with houseroom. Thanks to the recent statistical work of demographic historians we now have quite detailed information on with whom the old lived in England from early modern times onwards. These statistics can easily seem impenetrable and tedious, but they have important light to throw if we can tease out their implications.

Studies of household listings reveal comparatively few three-generational homes in England from the sixteenth century onwards: a mere 5 per cent on average. This is half the typical findings for France, and far less than the third or more often reported from eastern Europe or from Japan in the same centuries. The English figure climbed briefly to 9 per cent in the mid-nineteenth century and then fell back to a mere 1 per cent today. But although these figures do tell us how few families had a grandparent in their own home, they can be misleading. The grandparent could have been living a few houses away. Indeed, an international survey of old people in Britain, Denmark, and the United States in the 1960s found over 40 per cent of them living within ten minutes' journey of their children in all three countries. This could well have been true in the past too: we do not know. Also, the figures depend on how many grandparents were alive in the population. Typically, because people elsewhere married much younger than in north-west Europe, they became grandparents younger—so there were simply more grandparents around. A large part of the contrast results from this. All the same, if we turn the figures about and look at them from the point of view of the older generation themselves, we still find that in early modern England only 10 per cent of sixty-year-olds were living with their married children or grandchildren. This is startlingly lower than the figures of over half reported from eastern Europe and the Far East; and it also looks as if co-residence was much more common in southern France, and also in post-colonial America. This contrast has continued. In Britain today only 9 per cent of those over sixty live with another relative apart from their own spouse, in contrast to 12 per cent in the United States, 14 per cent in France, and 29 per cent in Japan and China.[16]

The consequence of these household arrangements today are that a very high proportion of older people live alone. The longer they live, the higher the figure climbs. In early modern England the proportion of solitary 65-year-olds was only 10 per cent, while in the mid-nineteenth century it came as low as 7.5. In the East there were almost none. Today it has risen to over 40 per cent in Britain, Scandinavia, and North America, and 30 per cent in France, in contrast to less than 7 per cent in China and Japan. To put it another way, the English have always been prepared to let some of their old live alone. But one of the great changes from the past is that this possibility of living alone is swiftly becoming a probability.[17]

Yet a closer look behind these stark figures suggests that the

English have not been so peculiarly heartless. Their housing was very early on more ample. They were also early in being especially mobile, no longer tied to land which could easily be sold. So with each generation there was a 'scattering of children at marriage,' which left scarcely one couple in ten with married children in the same parish. On the other hand, there were much more likely to be single children still living at home. Women bore children late; widowed men commonly remarried quickly to a younger woman so that there was another batch of younger children in the family; and most children married late. There must have been many daughters like Margaret White, who described in the 1590s how she stayed on living with her widowed father, 'guided him and his household, and was continually with him in his sickness until his death.'[18]

In practice the widowed of any age were much more likely to stay in their own homes than to move to find support. The early modern English household listings show that over half (55 per cent) of all over-sixty-year-olds lived with relatives apart from their spouse, and by far the most common of these were unmarried children still living in the parental home. But the pattern varied distinctly between the married and widowed. Nearly all the married couples kept their own homes, half still with children, a quarter with other kin or lodgers, and a quarter on their own. Of the widowed and single, by contrast, only two-thirds now lived on in their own homes, usually with their children or lodgers, or very rarely grandchildren, but 12 per cent on their own. Over a third had moved, roughly half into their children's or grandchildren's homes, and half to live as 'lodgers'—sometimes with other kin—or go into institutions. Thus overall only one in eight sixty-year-olds were solitaries or institutionalized. In England, as elsewhere, 'even though their help could not be counted upon,' children and kin were providing the greatest share of support for the older generation of their families.[19]

Nevertheless, what remains especially striking and distinctive is the English reluctance to take back the elderly within the home as *dependents*. When, during the nineteenth century, there was briefly a sharply rising proportion of widowed older people living with relatives, this was above all in the cotton and pottery towns, where married women factory workers were exceptionally common. Grandmothers could therefore join their children's households to fulfil a direct need as child-minders.[20] Elsewhere the great majority of the older generation continued to run their own homes. And when they could no longer do so, they were more likely to become independent lodgers than to move in under their own children's roof. The other side to English hesitation in offering houseroom was a belief in the independence of the old.

Independence of course demands economic means: and this brings us to a last and equally basic issue. What resources were open to older men and women in the past?

There were a small minority of property-holders who could retire on their revenues, at a time of their choosing. Although at first mainly farmers, by the nineteenth century many more were substantial tradesmen, manufacturers, or professional men, suffering, like the Birmingham banker Samuel Tertius Galton, from 'commercial weariness.' It had become quite acceptable for such a man, in his early sixties, to shift his money to safer investments, hand over the family home next to the workplace to his son, and move into a house in the suburbs from which he could maintain a benevolent but less taxing interest in family concerns. As the Birmingham hardware manufacturer John Kenrick put it:

> The prospect of such a season of leisure towards the decline of life, is one of the strongest motives to a man to go steadily on year after year with the drudgery of business; indeed without it, the complete absorption of many men's minds in the affairs of the world in the early and middle part of life would be hardly justifiable.[21]

The great majority, however, carried on working as long as they possibly could. At any age, most men were still at work. There are instances of ninety-year-olds still at work in seventeenth-century England. Even in the 1900s the national census returns show over 60 per cent of men over 65 employed, in England, the United States, and France. Of American men in their late sixties and early seventies, 85 per cent and 70 per cent respectively were still recorded as employed, together with half of eighty-year-olds. The proportion in work had begun to fall, however, and from the 1930s dropped rapidly: according to official figures, today in England a mere 7 per cent of men over 65 remain employed. The earlier situation lingered longest in the countryside. In England older men could get contract work for hedging and ditching, maintaining public spaces, or minor building repairs, which allowed them to work at their own pace. Among the French peasants of *Village in the Vaucluse*, Laurence Wylie still found in the 1950s that nearly all the older people were still at work. Many had shifted to lighter tasks, such as delivery rounds, mending bikes, minding children or animals, keeping chickens, gathering firewood, or growing vegetables for sale. But the working old men also included a miner, two blacksmiths, and the three hardest-working farmers in the village.[22]

The lighter work to which men tended to shift as they got older was generally worse paid. Work for older women was as badly paid, but for many it was more of a gain because they had not earned at all while their children were young. For them new chances opened up in late middle age as their children left home. In York in the 1930s, Seebohm Rowntree found many older women would be earning a few pence, or gifts in kind 'for rendering small services. To "mind the baby" for a neighbour when the mother is out, or to wheel one in a pram on washing-day and do any necessary errand, will probably mean a square meal or "a mash of tea" and some coppers, as well as discarded garments, if the neighbour's husband is in good work.' More significantly, if they had a reasonable house they could take paid lodgers in their children's former rooms. These lodgers were quite often from among their own more distant relatives. The listings from early modern England show that up to 8 per cent of households of over-sixty-year-olds might have been receiving some economic support through lodgers. During the nineteenth century, as more people survived their last child leaving home, it became a particularly important form of support, with perhaps a quarter of working-class older people in some towns taking in boarders: a pattern which persisted until young people began to marry much earlier in the 1950s, setting up on their own instead—and leaving more of the old on their own.[23]

A third possibility, at first unusual but slowly growing with time, was retirement in the modern sense, on a pension. Retirement for men of property was, as we have seen, an accepted practice in early modern England. The merits of pensions, extending this practice to those on salaries, were debated from the late seventeenth century onwards, with leading advocates including Daniel Defoe, and later the radical Thomas Paine of the French Revolution years. The first small groups to be provided with pensions

were the lower-paid naval warrant officers in 1672, and soon afterwards customs officers; while an Act of 1749 set up a scheme for
master merchant mariners. The pioneering general pension
scheme was, however, for the Civil Service: first established in
1810, by 1859 a full pension scheme allowed retirement at sixty.
The first commercial companies to follow suit were public utilities
such as some railway and gas companies, which started pension
schemes for their clerical staff from the 1840s onwards. These early
pension schemes were all rewards for loyalty to a narrow group of
white collar staff, whose salaries were insufficient to allow them to
retire like more prosperous middle-class professionals.

It was only in the late nineteenth century that a sustained
campaign for pensions for manual workers began. Among the
pioneers, the Great Western Railway scheme of 1865 was notably
early. It was followed by some other railway and gas companies,
and from the 1900s a range of well-known paternalistic companies:
Cadbury, Colmans, Coats, Cunard, Wills, Marconi, and many
others. Their paternalism was sometimes explicitly mixed with the
desire 'to take the fire out of the socialist cause.' Strikers could find
their pension rights withdrawn. In this period, however, by far the
largest occupational scheme was the independently organized
Durham Miners Permanent Relief Society, originating in the
1860s, which by the 1890s had 140,000 contributing members and
4,000 pensions being paid out.

All these advances were dwarfed by the step forward made with
the introduction of a national state Old Age Pensions scheme in
1909 for *all* those over seventy on incomes of less than ten shillings
weekly—roughly a charwoman's wage. It could not be taken along
with poor relief, and those with criminal records were excluded; it
was only available at seventy, not sixty; and it was set at a very
mean level, a mere five shillings, below the bare minimum which
Seebohm Rowntree calculated was then needed for subsistence.
It was a supplement for the 'deserving poor,' rather than a true
pension. Yet its impact in allowing ordinary retired workers some
self-respect was enormous.

Paradoxically the introduction of the state pension seems to have
ended independent activity by workers' organizations, with even
the Durham miners' scheme fading out between the wars. From
the 1930s, on the other hand, the big insurance companies moved
in strongly to fill the gap between the state pension and the

standard of living for which most workers hoped, setting up occupational pension schemes for firms on a contract basis. The 1930s
also saw a vigorous campaign for better pensions for women, which
led to the introduction of a state pension for women at the age of
sixty in 1940. Men remained eligible only at 65. Public and private
sector schemes together covered one in eight workers in 1936, and
one in three by 1956.[24]

By this time retirement schemes were not merely rewards for
work and service. They also reflected a growing belief that it was
in the general interest for the old to stop working: a fundamental
change in attitude. This in part reflected the conviction of nineteenth-century experts that the later years of life were a stage of
general physical and mental deterioration. Was it not uneconomic
to employ older workers whose apparent competence simply
masked inevitably growing incapacity? By the 1890s civil servants
had become obliged to retire on reaching pensionable age. And
the message was soon to be taken up by American-influenced
scientific management in industry. The first major American pension scheme, by the Baltimore and Ohio Railroad in 1884, was
comparatively late; yet by 1926 three-quarters of American companies with over 1,000 workers had them. Pensions were now
'wise business practice,' ridding firms of 'dead weight.' Similar
efficiency programmes were soon seeking to remove 'dead wood'
from the public services; and by 1935 an American national pension scheme had been enacted by Congress. Already in 1913, as
the *Independent* observed, 'gray hair has come to be recognized as
the unforgivable witness of industrial imbecility.' In England too,
grey-haired workers were fearfully staining their hair with soot to
try to protect their jobs.[25]

What of those who could not work, and were ineligible for
pensions; or, as more often recently, whose pensions were insufficient? We have already seen through looking at where the
widowed lived that in England, as throughout the world, the
family was the biggest single resource for older people in trouble.
Through the centuries moralists, like Sir William Blackstone in the
1760s, urged that 'they who protected the weakness of our infancy
are entitled to our protection in the infirmity of their age.' As
Thomas Becon put it in the sixteenth century, it was a 'duty of
children' whose parents were 'aged and fallen into poverty, so that
they are not able to live of themselves, or to get their living by

their own industry and labour,' to work and care for them and 'provide necessaries for them,' just as in their own childhoods 'their parents cared and provided for them.' In early modern England, however, families were expected to provide care and company, but not cash: for the poor had scarcely any. Support was given in kind, mutually. One Edwardian farm labourer's family from Oxfordshire, described by Rowntree, may typify the best-spirited mutual help in earlier times too:

> The Allens are a cheery, plucky family ... Her father, a hale old man over seventy, with a fresh colour and benignant expression, was sitting at the table finishing his meal. Her husband had taken lunch with him, and would not be back till teatime. The old man generally comes to dinner two or three times a week, as he has no one at home to look after him, and on these occasions he generally brings a 'bit of bacon' with him to replenish the Allen larder.[26]

Inevitably there were always ways in which these 'family obligations' could be evaded. Alan Macfarlane has recently argued that the social pressure to enforce them was less strong in England than elsewhere. Certainly the fear of abandonment in old age has never been more powerfully put than in *King Lear*. On the other hand— and the two aspects of English attitudes could indeed be different sides of the same coin—there was an especially clear and early assumption of community obligation to support the aged poor. In the middle ages the lord of the manor was regarded as legally responsible for the relief of the poor and one-quarter of the church tithes were also customarily set aside for this purpose. After the Reformation these traditions were regularized in a unique Poor Law which made each parish responsible for its own poor, and obliged it to finance its aid by levying a poor rate on its inhabitants.[27]

This communal support for older people in early modern England could be on a remarkably generous scale. For the elderly, the history of welfare provision seems to have been less a story of steady progress over the centuries than an oscillation between phases of relative generosity and meanness. From the seventeenth until the early nineteenth century, parish records suggest that over one-half of widows would normally have been provided with regular pensions on the rates; and still more remarkable, when com-

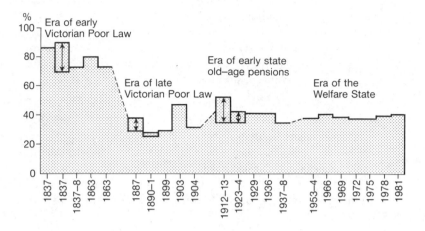

FIG. 1. Pensions and working-class incomes, 1837–1981, showing standard old-age pension as a percentage of gross income of a working-class adult. Boxed shaded areas represent extreme limits, where assumptions had to be made about family size. Source: Thomson 1984:453

pared with working-class incomes, these pensions were *twice* as good as those offered by state pensions today (see Fig. 1). The mid- and late nineteenth century saw a savage counter-attack on this system, with a reduction of pensions to a mere third of the value of the average working man's wage, and a concerted attempt to shift more of the burden back onto the family.[28]

Some Poor Law Guardians made attempts to enforce the new legal obligations which the 1834 Poor Law imposed on children to support their parents with money. In one case, for example, Reepham magistrates in Norfolk sent two brothers to prison for two months as a penalty for not supporting their mother, although both men were close on sixty and had wives and children themselves. But the new law failed to change normal practice, and such cases remained rare. It seems that these obligations were found more likely to stir up serious friction within families than to rally family help. Charles Booth noted in the 1890s that many sons would prefer to move rather than accept legal compulsion, and that their own old parents would often see relief as a right: 'the aged prefer a pittance from the parish (regarded as their due) to compulsory maintenance by children; compulsion makes such aid very bitter.' The simple truth was that in any case, few such poor families would have had cash that they could have regularly given away. On the other hand, among more prosperous working-class families customs were changing as real wages continued to rise. One Suffolk farm servant paid five shillings every week in the 1900s to help a sister keep their eighty-year-old mother. A skilled Nottingham engineer's daughter of the 1920s remembers her father 'would never go to see his parents unless he could take them some money . . . Three pound notes were usually left discreetly on the table after tea. It was never mentioned.' And a study in the 1940s reported that one person in every five over sixty was receiving some form of financial support from a son or a daughter.[29]

More immediately, however, the new policy was imposed through suspending pensions to the elderly themselves, and insisting that those on relief should move into the prison-like workhouses built in each Poor Law district after 1834. As a result, in the sixty years from 1851 the proportion of old people living in institutions almost doubled, rising to over 7 per cent of men over 65 and nearly 10 per cent of those over 75, and slightly over half this figure for women. Since the 1900s, despite the increasing numbers of the elderly, the proportion has again fallen back by more than a third. The regime of the workhouse was deliberately deterrent, and at least up to the 1890s married couples would be forced to live apart within it. Little beyond food was provided: not even false teeth to eat with. Middle-class visitors entering a workhouse for the first time could be deeply shaken by the harsh indignity of the prison-like routine, the grotesque, despairing toothless faces, 'the forlorn, half-dazed aspect of these battered human hulks who once were young.' There was no need 'to write up the words "Abandon hope all ye who enter here,"' George Lansbury wrote of the Poplar workhouse. 'The place was clean: brass knobs and floors were polished, but of goodwill, kindliness there was none.'[30]

Not surprisingly, only families in real difficulty were prepared to see their own older generation end their lives in such a place. One survey of aged inmates of the Newington workhouse in south London showed that a mere sixteen out of 725 had any relatives with even the space to take them in. Even in 1930, when the most draconian workhouse rules had been eased, another London survey of aged applicants for relief found that half had no family at all. Albert Funnel, a child in Brighton in the 1900s, evokes the long shadow of the workhouse over the lives of the elderly in the decades before Old Age Pensions:

> The people I knew had a terrific dread of it, and they very rightly dreaded it. Because it was diabolical, the workhouse. It was 'the spike,' we used to call it. And in those days if you were old and if you were poor, ... that was the end of the road. Because in the poorer streets, if you saw—the neighbours in the street knew an old couple, they were too old to work ... and if you saw an old blue van with a coat of arms on it with an old horse, old grey horse driven by an old grey man, drive up the street, stop outside the door, you knew that the old couple were on the way to the workhouse. The old man's come out— probably the old lady first with a bundle, and the old man'd come out with his few possessions in a red handkerchief tied up. They were gone. Never come out any more. The old man went into one wing of the workhouse and the old girl went to the other.
>
> I can't say whether this is true or not but I have been told, it was spoke about when I was a kid, that they never saw each other except if they were both of the same religion. On a Sunday, they could go down to chapel, the old girls'd to go down one side of the aisle, they'd go down the other, the old men, tried to put his hand out, touch the old lady ... If the old man was dying they'd maybe let the old lady come and see him or vice versa. And at the end they used to have a jingle:
>
>> Rattle his bones over the stones:
>> He's only a pauper that nobody owns.
>
> And that's what it was. That's why they built the cemetery up close to the workhouse, so they could take them over on a barrow.[31]

It took the rise of the socialist movement to turn the tide. George Lansbury himself became one of the first reforming Poor

Law Guardians in East London in the 1890s, and the social leg-
islation of the Liberals, including the state Old Age Pension
introduced in 1908, was a direct response to the rising political
influence of the labour movement. Nevertheless, the move back
towards a more generous welfare policy for older people was
hesitatingly slow. The pension was fixed well below subsistence
level. Walter Greenwood portrayed an old age pensioner in the
1930s who had to live on sixpence a day after he had paid his rent.
He could afford nothing for tobacco:

> I don't eat breakfast, just a cup of tea and a bit of toast if I can
> spare it. The butcher lets me have a pound of dripping now and
> then and I can make it last. Dinner I boil myself just a few
> potatoes, and I eat them with a piece of bread . . .
>
> There's a pal of mine who works at the wood yard and he
> brings me a bag of bits of wood that's been left over. He comes
> once a week with it and I've got to be careful to make them last.
> That's my biggest worry, keeping warm. Sometimes I can't sleep
> I get that cold.
>
> They give me the newspaper from next door when they've
> finished with it. And I go to bed as soon as it gets dark. It saves
> burning light and fire, and I can listen to next door's wireless if
> they've got it turned on loud. You can hear it plain through the
> wall.

Poverty surveys support Greenwood's account. In London, for
example, Llewellyn Smith reported in 1932 that 'lack of warmth
seems to be a greater hardship than lack of food.' Rowntree's three
surveys of York show that as working-class living standards gradually rose because of wage gains, smaller families, and from the
1940s full employment, poverty became increasingly concentrated
among older people. In 1900 they were no more often in poverty
than the working class of any age, but by 1935 they had become
significantly more vulnerable, and in 1950 the elderly comprised
over two-thirds of all the poor.[32]

The surveys also show that older people continued to be found
in some of the very worst housing. In Rowntree's examples of
typical streets in 1900, in the poorest streets up to a third of the
householders were widows, in contrast to less than 5 per cent in
the best working-class districts. Roberts has recalled the houses in
his own slum district of Salford where two or more 'old maids,'
or 'old faggots' as the teenagers mockingly called them, lived

together. Just the same refuges of the elderly also appear in the
Social Survey of Merseyside of 1934, where they made up a third
of the tenants of the largest multiple households. In one, for
example, a casual labourer and his wife in their sixties lived with a
woman of 79, her son of 57 who was a street matchseller, and six
younger tenants; in another a woman of 68 was subletting to
another woman of 65, a crippled woman of sixty, and two others;
while in a third household a 71-year-old sandwich-man lived with
an unrelated widow and widower of the same age and two younger
tenants.[33] Deprived, and often also dirty, these ageing social out-
casts, rather than ask help of the community, chose to huddle
together.

The poverty surveys are also remarkable in another way. They
are the first published documents from which we can glean personal details about ordinary older people in significant numbers.
Rowntree's investigators sketched in details of each household.
These show that half the older men were still at work. Still more of
the widows went out as chars or washerwomen, and a few minded
children. The atmosphere of the homes varied. At one extreme, an
invalid widow was described as a 'disreputable' hawker who 'ought
to be in workhouse. Hawks when able . . . House very dirty, probably used as a house of ill-fame.' At the other, in a respectable
working-class street, were the old couple living 'on his means . . .
"Resting after a life's hard work."'[34]

Llewellyn Smith's London survey of the 1930s similarly provided nutshell portraits of many old people, combining what the
interviewers noticed with comments from the older people themselves. Again, the contrasts are striking. Thus one couple living in
a basement were 'respectable,' 'very superior and very particular
about cleanliness;' the wife spent most of her day on housework
and mending clothes, while the husband 'does such things as
chopping the wood and mends anything that is broken. In the
evening they both listen-in [to the radio] and enjoy it very much,
especially the Sunday evening sermons.' By contrast, a single old
woman who lived in 'some very nasty flats in a very poor street'
seemed to be 'rather a grubby woman. Her clothes were very,
very untidy, not very clean and not too well cared for . . . I rather
wondered whether she drinks, as when I went in in the morning
there was a large bottle of beer on the table. She seemed to be
quite a cheerful old woman.' However, 'she said that she now has

really no friends or relations in the world and there are times when she feels very lonely. She is very frightened of falling ill in that flat as she has no one to look after her.' Another widow of 84 'had outlived all her old friends' and did not get much support from her children. She seemed 'rather frightened of her daughters and they seem to treat her very badly . . . One cuts her dead in the street if she ever sees her.' Several others, on the other hand, were 'on the best of terms' with their children, including two in shared households and another couple who said 'their children are very good to them; one daughter does their washing for them and their daughter-in-law goes up nearly every day to do their shopping for them.'

Of particular interest here are the minority of notably active older people, like the man whose 'great hobby is making toys for his grandchildren and great-grandchildren;' or the amateur painter always at his easel 'if the light is good enough;' or the old sailor, disabled for fifty years, yet 'a very contented old man,' who spent his time cooking, cleaning, and reading 'either novels or the newspaper.' He had sublet part of his house to a married daughter, and would also play with his grandchildren, 'amusing them when they come back from school.' He was also clearly fond of his daughter and 'likes her company.' Significantly, he said he was 'on the best of terms with her as they are quite independent of each other. He says that he would not get on so well with her if he had his meals with her, but as he lives quite separately they are very friendly and he likes to know that they are near if he wants company.'[35]

Perhaps the fullest set of early portraits of ordinary older people as individuals is provided by a Sheffield survey of 1919. This was concerned not only with poverty but with working-class culture more generally. Four women suggest something of the variety revealed by the 'intensive studies' which were included here.

Mrs Lowrieson was a widow of 69, an active Baptist, becoming infirm, but still keeping her shop going, mainly through the help of two 'devoted' grown-up daughters. 'One could scarcely find a more motherly kindly woman . . . good natured and the opposite of worrying . . . She is absolutely wrapped up in her children; she is a good and devoted mother; and others besides her children call her "mother" because of her kind care for them.'

Mrs Stappell, a widow of 72, was another 'exemplary' mother, but more striking in other ways. Sheffield-born and daughter of a

cutlery master, she was herself notably active, running an allotment and still a working cutler: a woman with 'plenty of initiative
and business capacity. She likes a glass of beer, but can control all
her appetites.' She was particularly unlucky to be alone, for she
had first married at 18, but after losing a child had been left a
childless widow at 25. She remarried to a railway worker three
years later and had 'several children' by him before becoming
widowed again. Her third marriage at the age of 47, to a widower
with a grown-up family, had again ended, after five years, with her
husband's death. This last marriage, although he had been a 'good
man,' was uneasy, and she now had 'no connection with the
stepsons and daughter.'

Mrs Roggson, by contrast, although a widow of only sixty,
seemed to have lost her energy for life. She had been a widow for
25 years and now lived in one room, earning a living as a charwoman. 'She says she is willing to work all her days just to keep a
little home of her own,' yet she also felt 'too old for the work.' 'She
is so tired when her work is finished that she just sits still and
rests.' But the most pathetic of all was the fourth widow, Mrs
Shepman, aged eighty and in poor health, who lived as a lodger.
She was a high-class cook who had worked in many parts of the
country including London. But after losing her only child, 'both
she and her husband took to drink and dishonest dealing, and
finally went back to South Africa under a cloud.' She had returned
since his death and was now drifting, 'sinking lower, cadging,
getting drink where possible—a pitiable object. Absolutely refuses
to go into workhouse.'[36]

These rare but vivid glimpses of the extraordinary variety of life
experience among the older generation in the early twentieth
century are not only precious in themselves, but suggest the
dangers of generalizing about the earlier past to make up for the
lost history of ageing. Certainly the historical evidence as a whole
gives little support for the quite widespread belief that older
people in the past enjoyed a much more secure and respected
position than they do in the present. The one undoubted gain has
been improved health, and with it longer life itself. But the continuities are equally striking. There have always been a minority
of wealthy older people and a majority struggling to survive in
poverty. The rise of the welfare state has brought much earlier
retirement from work, but has had little impact on the low in-

comes typical of later life both past and present. Nor has there been much change in the pattern of support from the family. Throughout this period older men and women in this country have preferred to live in their own homes and have maintained a strong belief in independence.

Within these continuities, the individual variety is also significant. There have always been some old people who were influential and highly regarded, in contrast to the many others who were treated with ridicule, antagonism, or at best patronized as dependents. And as we have seen, the life-styles of older men and women have been equally varied. So far, however, we have been constructing a picture only indirectly. Most of even the best material is second-hand, typically refracted through the rewording and prejudice of interviewers with strong points of view of their own. Although occasional direct personal documentation does exist for earlier periods, and more could no doubt be found, for the moment we have no choice but to sketch the history of later life in the past without the intimate testimony of older people and their families. It is only for the last century and a half that a direct picture becomes a convincing possibility.

3

The Autobiographer's Eye

IF we want to understand how later life was in the past through direct experience, we have three possible sources. Firstly there are contemporary diaries and correspondence. Diaries have proved by far the most vivid source for intimate family life in early modern England. When Thomas Turner, Sussex village shopkeeper turned thirty, confides his deep hurt at 'the seeming distant behaviour with which my mother treated me today, seeming so mistrustful that I should cheat her,' he takes us right to the heart of the complex mixture of love and pain which then as now underlies the relationship between adult children and the older generation:

> Oh, what pleasure would it be to me were there a good understanding between my mother and myself, when I am assured if I know my own heart, that I am so far from having any ill against her that I have almost undone myself to serve her . . . [But I will] only conclude with saying and thinking—she is my mother.[1]

How familiar does that cry sound? But unfortunately references to later life in diaries are infrequent. Our own search of 26 mid-nineteenth-century diaries for this book produced little worth noting. Elderly diarists were rare, and younger diarists not much concerned with observing the old. Both tended to step back and reflect on ageing only after a death. It was only then, for example, that John Bright, busy Member of Parliament, revealed that his stepmother, who had lived alone as a widow for nearly thirty years to the age of 95, the last ten years blind, was visited daily by his own wife 'to chat with her and to cheer with her in her solitude and blindness, or to render her any help in her power.'[2] It is significant, but for our purposes frustrating, that older people seem to feature so little in the consciousness of these diarists, preoccupied with the meaning and the daily bustle of their own lives.

Our other two forms of personal document are both retrospective: the written autobiography, which we consider here, and the recorded oral interview, which is the subject of our next chapter. British historians are especially fortunate in being able to draw on the oldest tradition of popular autobiography in the world. By the mid-nineteenth century it had already extended across the whole social spectrum. For our present purpose we have examined 145 autobiographies written by men and women born from the 1830s to the 1870s. A third of the authors were women, while in terms of their childhood backgrounds, 25 of them were upper class, 21 upper-middle class, 15 lower-middle class, and 84 working class.[3] What do they have to tell us?

Because we cannot question their authors, autobiographies can be tantalizingly elusive: but in compensation, what they omit or include is in itself evidence of the attitudes of the writers and of the readers they had in mind. In principle, autobiographies can refer to the experience of later life at three main points: through distant childhood memories of grandparents, through accounts of a parent's last years, or most directly, through reflections on the writer's own ageing. It is immediately noticeable that the great majority of comments come from the childhood memories. Old age rarely seems to be regarded by a writer as interesting in itself: it is relevant above all as an influence on a young, new life, and never as the culmination of a lifetime. Ninety autobiographies refer to grandparents, sometimes at considerable length. Only ten refer— usually more briefly—to their elderly parents, and only eight to their own ageing. We shall come back to two of these references to ageing; of the others, one is an oddity—a condemned criminal inspired by dreams of his mother and the hope that if reprieved he could 'comfort the autumn of her life'—and the remainder are mere passing notes. They tell us that a stonemason's third marriage at 57 was his happiest; or that a retired doctor found 'life was for a time difficult' for lack of 'any special hobbies.' A Yorkshire mill-owner's seventieth birthday is recorded as bringing 'callers all day, bringing little remembrances of flowers, fruit, etc;' while a Kent farm labourer, on reaching the same age after 51 years on the same farm, was given a pension from a local charity and gave up work. He had been moved to lighter work three years earlier: 'my Master took me from the farm work to do the House Boys work—

cleaning the Boots seeing to the wood and coals and sweeping up the back yard and the paths and looking after the poultry.'[4]

A much more consistent theme, highly significant for this generation which bore the brunt of the late nineteenth-century attack on community provision for older people, emerges when a parent's later years are mentioned: how their need for support was met. Most often it is described as care returned more or less explicitly in gratitude for what the author had been given in childhood. Thus a migrant son from a Scottish island croft answers his parents' call: 'when I grew old, I had to come home to be with them.' A Norfolk farmworker turned trade unionist writes proudly of how he took in his own mother and his mother-in-law in turn 'without receiving a penny from anyone . . . For 22 years of my married life I maintained these two old people.' Two men from poor northern city backgrounds, who later became very wealthy, tried to set up their elderly parents in comfort: Andrew Carnegie, American millionaire bachelor, gave his Scots mother, 'my best friend and trustiest counsellor,' a house and a carriage and pair as he had promised her when young, while a Manchester mill-owner failed to persuade his old mother to spend more than £1 a week, but 'would pet her like the sweetheart she was.'[5]

Not all were so positive, however. The harshest comment comes from an illiterate Yorkshire collier who had suffered a bitter, loveless childhood, tormented by a cruel brother. At 78 he still refused to stop work: 'My advice to parents is not to give up to the rising generation the place you have occupied in the world so long, because there are some who are very near to you who would turn round and put you out homeless and penniless.' Lack of trust or love framed his view of the world to the end. Equally revealing is a rare autobiography by an impoverished Norfolk farm labourer's son, who had turned professional poacher and been disowned by his harsh father. When the father turned 65 he gave up work, and 'at last he found he had a son, as later on in his old age I helped him and Mother all I could. But he never seemed to appreciate my help like poor old Mother did.' He felt more duty to his mother too, because she had brought up his own first son after his wife's death in childbirth. Symbolically, he allowed his father to have a pauper burial, but when his mother finally died at 97, 'I buried her.'[6]

The ambiguities of the parent–child relationship in these last years are also evident from two Lancashire accounts, both by writers who had become trade unionists. One says simply that her parents kept their 'strong, independent spirit; they would be no burden on their children.' James Sexton explains more fully. For twenty years his widowed mother had kept a small shop in a St Helens slum, only accepting an occasional small amount of money and putting off other help with 'the same naïve reply: "It's very good of you, dear lad, and I appreciate it, but as long as I can manage it, I shall prefer to have my feet under my own fender."' In the end Sexton took her literally. As her health began to fail, he and his wife invited her

> to come to my home for a holiday and a rest . . . After she had been with us a fortnight we told her, as gently as we could, that she was never going back . . . She *could* not go back, because we had disposed of the business, along with her tools and much of her furniture, but not her fender, which would arrive at Hale-wood in due course.[7]

No English autobiography of this period tells of that experience of powerlessness from the other side. The American Mary Vorse published her remarkable *Autobiography of an Elderly Woman* in 1911, which reflects at length on the reversal of roles that left her 'contriving to get my own way, for all the world like a naughty, elderly child, while my daughter was worrying about my head-strong ways as if she was my mother instead of my being hers.' She complained of being prevented from helping in the house—'You'll tire yourself out'—or from going out in cold weather, and above all, of not being taken seriously. She could not offer advice as a grandmother, despite her long experience of children; and now her own children had ceased to confide in her 'because they felt that the time had come when I ought to be "spared" every possible worry. So there is a conspiracy of silence against me in my household. "We mustn't worry mother" is the watchword . . . I move in a little artificial, smiling world away from all the big interests of life.' Mary Vorse pinpointed 'the time when old age finally claimed me' as the 'moment when my two boys were more thoughtful of me, when they didn't come to me any more with their perplexities.' That was the psychological moment: but she also remembered another, a turning-point in physical ageing, 'when I began to hate to look at myself in the glass.' And she could balance both the gains and the losses of becoming an elderly woman. There were some new freedoms: good reasons for escaping boring social duties, such as calls, or church sermons, or committee meetings. But on the other hand increasing age brought new social restrictions. It was thought improper for elderly women to wear bright clothes. And gradually, lack of energy cut into the hopes of fulfilling the dreams of special pleasures such as travel in these last years. It seemed for her that space itself was now slowly constricting. 'The size of the earth over which one may roam shrinks day by day, until it decreases to the house,—to one's room,—to one's bed; and finally to the narrowest space of all.'[8]

We can set that unique inside view of later life in America against only two comparable glimpses—brief but direct—from our own set of British autobiographers. An eighty-year-old aristocrat recorded his devastation when, on his wife's death, his town house was sold and his Norfolk home passed on to his son. 'I felt a homeless wanderer on the earth.... My daughters, as well as many of my friends, wished me to visit them, but I had no heart for any society.... I was ill as well as desolate, and all I wanted was to hide my wretchedness from everyone.' Before long he 'could not stand the horrid hotels all by myself... The loneliness of life had become unbearable.' So within six months the wealthy widower plunged into remarriage. 'Of course the world was affronted,' but, now again surrounded by 'devoted thought and care,' he could afford to ignore it. 'As to the outside world, I now take just sufficient interest in what goes on to be thankful that, though I am deaf, I can vote.' A working-class London woman, by contrast, though far less well-off, conveys a more positive experience of later life. Now she had become a pensioner she had been able to give up work as a midwife, and she spent much of her time on her allotment:

> I have a very nice little hut and can rest and read and do a bit of sewing between planting, hoeing, weeding, etc. I lined the hut with paper and put up pictures. I have a stove on which I can cook a dinner, and a paraffin stove for heating. Very often I spend long days on my allotment, and cook quite nice dinners of, say, breast of mutton and peas and fruit off the allotment for

myself and a [woman] friend who has been ill for a long time.... I love to watch the things grow. Just at the present time everything looks so fresh. The seeds I put in are just beginning to peep through. There is a railway bank covered with grass and beautiful dandelions. I can sit outside the little shed and see the church tower of old Hampstead Church. It is a nice change from my one little room where I live by myself, and do all there is to do, washing included.[9]

Sustained by her own independent sense of purpose, she still felt growth and life within herself.

Autobiographical recollections of grandparents, although indirect, allow us to push back considerably further in time than through direct memories: from the early twentieth back to the mid-nineteenth century. This in itself alters the picture. Over half the British population was then still living in the countryside, and among the older generation even more—fully twice the proportion today. And as we have seen, retirement was then much less common, and confined to a restricted social minority. Through the autobiographies we can identify the economic position of 72 grandparents. Today we could expect to find perhaps a dozen employed; but then, only 14 were retired in the broadest sense. The other 44—over 95 per cent in the working-class families—were still at work.

The 'retired' include nine middle-class and two working-class widows. Eight of them lived their last years in their children's homes. One grandmother, remembered as 'dressed all day in black silk,' had an annual income of £700 from the New River Company, which she 'spent in bringing us up' to make up for the incompetence of her solicitor son: she would sit all day 'upright in an armchair at the side of the fire,' opposite to her son's. Two North Welsh grandfathers also lived with their children, one above his son's butcher's shop and the other on the family farm which he had handed on to his son. In Robert Roberts's farming family this seems to have been the accepted practice on both sides: later on, as a young farm servant, he went to work for an uncle where his mother's parents still lived in the farmhouse. And as a child his own household included not only his father's father but his mother's grandmother, who spent most of her days hidden away 'in her own cabin,' but who would emerge on Sundays, always knitting a long stocking. Roberts's grandfather had made over the farm when his father married, yet remained the respected patriarch of the household:

He was now but a guest in his son's house, but I think my father lost none of his deference to him when he resigned the farm. The greatest respect was paid by all the family to his opinions on all subjects from farming to knotty points of theology. His large oak chair in the corner was sacred, and the words that he uttered from that privileged seat were truly spoken *ex cathedra*.[10]

For a man like this, still living in the midst of the work which had been his life, retirement had none of its typical contemporary implications: he retained his technical authority along with his social networks and his familiar surroundings. The same applied equally to elderly landowners. We come closer to contemporary retirement with the second Roberts grandfather, a man who had been much less successful at work, and after failing as a shopkeeper had nearly failed as a farmer until his son took over. He was 'a man of powerful intellect, though a little eccentric' to the point of sometimes appearing 'simple-minded.' After giving up the farm he 'amused himself with carpentering and the making of various fanciful machines. Among others he had a plan for discovering the perpetual motion.' Except for these older men who owned or tenanted land, however, only two were recalled as independently retired, and both were middle-class businessmen. In the Potteries a prosperous general dealer in china and earthenware had handed over his business to his sons, who subsequently let the business collapse: his grandson remembered him 'sitting in the sunshine . . . just below the house which was once his own.' More successful in his retirement was a London coal merchant who provides the single instance of the complete change of life and place which today is a widespread ideal for retirement. A keen rider of 'simple habits,' he was able to withdraw to an idyll of country life on the thousand-acre estate he had bought in Sussex.[11]

The other grandparents were still at work. They included three vicars, of whom one doubled up as an architect; a doctor who was also a horse-breeder; a barrister; a master builder; five shopkeepers; a smallholder and packman; and—by far the largest group—ten farmers. Among the manual workers there were two weavers, a mines steward, and a papermaker; a railway porter, a canal boatman, and a Thames waterman; a joiner and two brick-makers; a hawking couple; two midwives and three domestic ser-vants; a gamekeeper and a shepherd, and seven farmworkers. It is a strongly rural range of occupations, and it is especially striking how few were regular manual employees. Most were casual or self-employed workers who could not be made to retire, and many were also small property-holders—an important factor which also made their position stronger for continuing at work. One old couple who were village publicans used their house as a shelter for 'a very composite family' which included a daughter who did the pub cooking, a brother, and a son who used two rooms as his tailor's shop.[12] Even two of the farmhands rented a smallholding where they could grow vegetables and keep cows, pigs, and poul-try; while another was also a carter.

Because they continued to be economically independent, these working older people, both men and women, were often remem-bered as strong characters, like the Lancashire shopkeeping grand-mother, a 'powerful personality' who was without any doubt 'boss of the concern,' or the old North Welsh woman who 'was doing all the cobbling for the neighbours in Berthengam, and . . . they were done by her well.' But there is a harsh side to this independence. Those unfit to work were rarely remembered, principally because few survived for long. And there was pain as well as pride in working right to the end, as did the 99-year-old Suffolk widow who 'worked on the land all her life' or the Derbyshire midwife in her eighties who still 'would get up in the night and walk miles to attend a confinement.' Others were clearly no longer up to their profession. A Dorset village boy was sent 'to a very old man' to be taught to read, but learnt little: the old man stood 'facing the window, puffing away at his pipe, and when we would ask him to explain anything that we did not understand, he would tell us that he watched the chimneys to see when other people lit their fires. . . .'[13]

A sadder figure still was a once well-to-do, highly educated London grandfather who had quarrelled with his wife and retre-ated to live in a Battersea slum, running his home as a junk shop and seeking consolation in the local pub:

> He loved company and could be found at night in a dingy tavern a few alleys away; this was the resting place of riverside workers

and shady persons who obtained their living without work. This tavern was well-known to the police.... It seemed that he acted as a receiver of stolen goods.... More than once my grandpa's shop had been visited by the police officers, but, however well founded their suspicions, my relative usually managed to keep well within the law. He would play crib with zest with the lowest characters and would allow no argument. He could treat the loser and afterwards pay for drinks all round. Without doubt he was a peculiar man—a mixture of miser and philanthropist . . .

During the day he would cross the bridge to Chelsea to buy old clothes and other cast-offs, walking the streets with his cry of 'Old clothes and old hats I'll buy them,' or begging his keep in more fashionable parts from 'cooks thinking he was such a nice old man . . . He would get good food from the basement kitchens.' He would tramp back with his findings to his slum home, where the boys would shout 'Moses' at him and 'he would reply by shaking his stick at them.' His home was equally pathetic:

It was a dirty shop with small windows and cobwebs abounded everywhere.... Old clothes and china, any old things, an accumulation of valuables and rubbish crowded out ... bundles of dried herbs, ... sweets and apples ... books on shelves, clothes hanging from pegs and armour and swords in the corner, even the table was littered leaving just enough room to eat.... It was a puzzle to me to think that any customers wanted any of these things in the alley he lived, but he did have a few visitors, because he dealt in antiques, he knew a great deal about them . . .

He came to a macabre end. A typical miser, he hid his money in the house in various places. The largest cache was in his former kitchen basement, behind 'a carefully concealed trap door at the back of the counter.' But less discreetly, when haggling over prices in the house he could lose his temper and shout '"Don't think I am hard up," as he took from the cupboard a quarter pewter pot full of sovereigns' to flash at his antagonist. Rumours spread; and eventually the day came when 'he was found in his shop dead, sprawled amidst rubbish around him.'[14]

Any autobiographical evidence needs to be taken cautiously and read as an interpretation, a perspective, rather than as literal fact. It reaches us through not only the filtering processes of memory but also the demands of style: and this is particularly obvious in this instance. Although his autobiography was never published, the teller of this tale, James Mackenzie, was a professional show-man who ended up on the fairground stage. The Dickensian flavour in his memoir is strong, and also conscious, for he wrote that his grandfather's shop 'outvied the Old Curiosity Shop.' But it is also noticeable that Mackenzie wrote a much less dramatized description of his grandmother, 'a weird old lady' with 'penetrating eyes and a low voice,' who had only fallen a little less severely than her ex-husband, living as landlady in a poor alley with 'an old servant companion' in a house furnished with antiques. For it was she who brought up the young James after the perhaps fortunate death of his violent, drunken father in a railway accident. But his grandfather he only saw in brief glimpses, when James called in the hope of being given a shilling. The old man would often not recognize him, and at the most answered with a phrase or two or a grunt.[15]

We may indeed take the depth of the autobiographer's image of a grandparent as one measure of the quality of their mutual relationship—and an especially important one, for on such rela-tionships between earlier generations the insights which auto-biography offers are unique. To start with, over a third of the autobiographies have no mention of grandparents at all, or a bare reference. Occasionally it is explained that they had already died—and given the still short life-expectancy of the period this must have been so in many cases. But death was not the only reason for lack of memories. Two were out of contact because of physical distance: the fate of a Berwickshire couple who had emigrated to Australia was 'a mystery,' while even within the same county a Norfolk farm labourer's parents were too far away to visit on foot, so the family 'hardly ever saw them.' Others were psychologically out of touch: one grandmother is described as mad, another as losing her memory. Or the breach could be social. After Colonel Charles Maynard died, his widow remarried to the Earl of Rosslyn and found herself 'not on cordial terms' with her ex-father-in-law: so much so that he cut her out of his will, leaving all the family property to his granddaughter Frances, and so much embittering the family that Frances's mother 'feared the abduction of myself

and my baby sister.'[16] A bankrupt London draper's family had no
social contact with their landed grandparents: their social fall was
too severe.

Of those who are remembered, the more distant or briefly-
glimpsed a grandparent, the more likely the recollection is to be
no more than an external image. There are thus a considerable
number who appear in the autobiographies as simple vignettes.
Among them are a Duchess who inspired 'awe;' an engineer's
'stern looking' mother; and the 'tall and stately' wife of a farm
labourer sitting at the fire 'enjoying her "bit of bacca."' Most
formidable of all is the Scots joiner grandfather, 'dour, stern,
Calvinistic . . . a man of few words, just and honest in his dealings,
but feared by his family.' Complete silence was expected nightly
while he took stock of the world: 'after supper, the paper was
unfolded and the old man began reading the four pages; woe
betide if any noise or talking was indulged in by the family until
the task was completed.' There are other less forbidding images: a
shipping magnate with 'a kind face,' or a vicar's wife who 'used to
box dear Grandpapa' lovingly on the ears because 'he would sometimes slyly give the servant's elbow a tip when his daily table-
spoonful of brandy was being poured out.'[17]

The descriptions of two older people, each in their own setting,
bring out especially vividly the inequalities of later life. One was a
rheumatic Black Country labourer who would come threshing with
a flail, wearing a smock. 'A merry old soul,' he 'loved us kids,' even
though the children stole his cocoa and his stick, and he would
reply by singing them 'quaint ditties.' He lived in evident poverty,
lodging with a cobbler called Morgan, and when his grandchildren
came on Sundays to visit,

> We could hardly get inside for rubbish and couldn't see the
> floor, it was all dirt, and there used to be two or three benches
> on which we had to sit down; then old Morgan would read the
> Bible to us and pray, we had to kneel down—oh what a dry
> lesson.

A great aunt, who was also pious, but who lived in manorial
comfort, provides by contrast the most immaculate portrait of
respected ageing:

> Miss Froude matched her surroundings. During her later years
> she was never visible till mid-day, by which time she would, in

an upstairs drawing-room, be found occupying a cushionless chair at a large central table, with a glass of port at her right hand and a volume of sermons at her left. At either side of her stood a faithful attendant, one being a confidential maid, the other a Miss Drake—an old, mittened companion, hardly younger in appearance than herself—both of whom watched her with eyes of solicitous reverence, and seemed always ready to collapse into quasi-religious curtseys. Here she would receive such visitors as happened to be staying in the house, and subsequently reverential visitors, who appealed to her for aid or sympathy.[18]

Sometimes little more is said even of grandparents who were visited regularly. This is especially true of those remembered with ambivalence: grandparents who evoked 'admiration mixed with awe' or of whom 'we were afraid;' the swearing, free-thinking grandfather of a future preacher; or the high-minded but remote Wiltshire rector—'We were all a little afraid of him: he was so tall, venerable, so full of big words and bigger gestures. But he represented authority, parentage, religion.' One farming grandfather is remembered as 'open hearted, hospitable, a good sport,' in contrast to his 'stingy and penurious' second wife. Two other grandmothers who came on regular visits, one 'very generous' and the other an eloquent 'martinet,' died too soon to leave more than a 'dim recollection.'[19] Nevertheless, visiting could undoubtedly be important in enabling closer relationships to develop between grandparents and grandchildren. This was especially the case among the well-to-do, who had ample space for guests and the means to travel.

From working-class childhoods certainly there are memories of farm holidays, or travelling from Liverpool to Sheffield to see grandparents—but they are unusual. Such occasional visits could be important. One granddaughter of a carpenter's widow 'adored my grandmother, whom I seldom saw: my greatest reward was to be allowed to brush grandmother's long silken white hair.' A Buckinghamshire village boy 'liked best to go and stay' with a farming grandmother, finding a 'special quiet' and 'peace' about her; while a Yorkshire weaver's son who went to stay with his grandmother for several weeks 'during family sickness' always kept the bond they made then—'religious, yet loving, although seemingly cold, perhaps I had a special bit of her love, for she

corrected me with thrashing me.' But for him too, as for most
working-class children, the closest memories were of grandparents
who lived nearby and could be seen frequently. He describes his
other grandmother as 'a wee frail woman' in a mob cap, smoking a
long clay pipe and 'stroking my hair as I lay down at her feet with
my head in her lap,' while her railwayman husband also 'had a
great liking for me, and when he could spring to a halfpenny or an
apple or some nuts for "whiteheaded Benny," he did it. Once he
gave me a shining white metal watchguard,' a symbol of work
efficiency which he wore proudly to school, ' "swanking" with it
hung across my chest.'[20]

Similarly, a Norfolk farm boy 'used to spend a lot of time' with
his labouring grandparents: 'a dear old cupple, and I was very fond
of them and they of me, and would never hear anything wrong of
me,' although he was already in trouble with the authorities. His
grandfather, who taught him songs and ballads and regaled him
with tales of his own 'merry' youth when he fought with game-
keepers, clearly saw the young poacher as a chip off the old block.
Different lessons were passed on by other grandparents. A stonemason's daughter, later a writer, passed 'many happy hours' in
her nearby grandfather's cottage 'reading and dreaming.' A future
professor of philosophy was taught to read on overnight stays by a
keen chapel-going Welsh labouring grandfather. A Scots farmer
shared with his grandchildren a 'wealth of knowledge' on nature
and agriculture. A Thames waterman would take his grandson, on
his Sunday visits, out on his lighter, handing down his skills to the
fifth generation to work on the river: 'he was one of those metho-
dical old fellows who live quietly, and never get ruffled.' And
when the grandson left school, 'I worked in my grandfather's boat
just as he had worked in his grandfather's . . . It was a matter of
family routine.' A Northumberland collieryman 'of a most tender,
humane disposition' chose his grandson as 'a frequent companion'
on long walks, as well as racing, climbing trees, and teaching him
to swim: 'he had a great liking for children, and was full of little
plans and devices to interest and amuse them.' Above all, he took
the future trade union leader seriously, answering his incessant
questions, and calling him proudly the 'queerest bairn he had ever
known. One had need to be well-informed to travel with that
child. He is for ever asking questions. He won't be put off with a
surface answer, but he wants to know the far end of everything.'[21]

For the middle and upper classes, visiting often quite distant grandparents was a normal family pattern: so much so, that it is the commonest context of recollection. Most often these memories are positive. The 'charming and delightful' London lawyer grandfather who told stories, or the once stern parent who could find 'no limit to his indulgence for his grandchildren;' the weekly visit to a landowning grandfather 'to whom we were deeply attached;' the 'lengthened visits' from 'very kind' grandparents, or a grandson's 'happiest days,' being 'thoroughly spoiled' in the countryside, are all typical.[22]

Especially with upper-class families these visits were often directly linked with the handing down of their own distinctive family traditions. The family house itself assumes a special prominence which is unique to this class. Lord Ribblesdale thought of his grandparents' house as 'my second home.' For Louisa Coutts Trotter, whose hypochondriacal father was constantly on the move seeking new cures, her grandmother's Edinburgh house was a fixed point in their peregrinations; while Willoughby de Broke eccentrically opens his autobiography with a series of chapters on the family's houses, rather than on its people. In such families, pride in ancestry was quite consciously imbued. One grandmother is remembered as taking 'a deep interest in all her grandchildren,' reading and talking, walking and painting with them; and when her granddaughter became in turn a mother, it was her belief that

> parents should always arrange if possible for their children to see old people of marked interest in their lives, so as to carry on the links of tradition.... When two of my sons were little boys I took them to our old great-uncle Lord Albemarle's yearly reception on Waterloo Day, that they might hereafter be able to say in their old age that they had seen and spoken to someone who had been at the Battle of Waterloo himself.[23]

For the grandchildren of the Cornish Earl of St Germans, house and family memory combined to give an unforgettable magic to their long seaside summer and autumn visits to Port Eliot. 'We had our own large suite of nurseries in which to play,' wrote one of the earl's granddaughters, from which, when there were big evening dinners, the children would 'creep down the back staircase' to be fed with sausages, turkey, ice-cream, and nuts in the 'comfortable sanctum' of the housekeeper. The earl himself 'we children all loved,' remembering that their peculiar delight 'as a small child was to sit on his knee and inspect his watch, which could open and shut, and chief novelty of all in my eyes, could chime!' On these visits they would be joined by multiple cousins, and together 'we used to love to listen to stories about the past of the family:' stories which frame the opening of this granddaughter's own life.[24]

Their more ample resources also explain why it was least common for such upper-class grandparents to share a house with their grandchildren on a longer basis. The autobiographies show that homes could be shared for two reasons, with differing implications. Firstly, a widowed grandmother may be remembered as moving into the family home. While in such cases quite often the three generations 'got on together very comfortably,' there were also some significantly discordant memories. In one home a 'strong and masterful, buxom and choleric' grandmother took charge of the household. Another grandmother, while 'an unwearying entertainer' to her grandson, 'a familiar friend, ever kind—too indulgent,' was a less welcome guest to his parents, for whom her presence was 'not an altogether blessed arrangement,' and she was expected to retreat from the parlour to her own room upstairs well before the master of the house returned from work. A 'rather terrible' third old lady displayed such a regularly outrageous temper that she was constantly locking herself in her room, expecting her meals to be left outside the door for her. But even here, the conflict was not with her grandchild, who could benefit even when her parents did not. Two other living-in grandparents directly encouraged future autobiographers by teaching them to read, one at the age of three.[25]

It was quite different, however, when through parental death or disaster a grandchild went for a time to be brought up by grandparents. When this happened a much more detailed picture of them and their way of life is usually given; and in all but one case the memory is strikingly positive. The exception was a former aristocratic beauty who had led a bitter life, losing five children through death and almost leaving her soldier husband on account of his affairs. 'A frustrated and embittered woman,' 'melancholy' and 'puritanical,' she was an 'austere and repressing influence:' 'she had no affection for her grandchildren, but she was a conscientious woman.' But the typical memory is of 'generous care,' 'kind' treatment, a 'happy home' or 'happiest days:' 'she nursed me, fed

me, rocked me to sleep.' A great-aunt who performed a similar
caring role is remembered in much the same way, as the one who
'spoilt me . . . I loved her.' One upper-class motherless boy moved
to live with a great-uncle who 'treated me with the same affection
which he would have given to a son. He used to have me romp up
in his bedroom.'[26]

Grandparents were in a uniquely strong position as substitute
parents, for they were both progenitors and chosen friends. Their
influence could therefore be especially powerful. Many are portrayed as strong personalities: the Swansea shopkeeping grandmother, a 'wonderful old lady' who would tell historical stories of
the Rebecca Riots; the cultured, much-travelled Scots widow, a
'remarkable woman' who ran her late husband's estate; the toothless, pipe-smoking, 'mediumistic' Lancashire granny who believed
in ghosts and practised second sight; or the Scot ploughman's wife
who taught her grandson the Bible and catechism 'patiently, affec-
tionately, and prayerfully . . . and at night she would put me to
bed, wrap me snug and warm, and kindly teach me short prayers,
psalms, and hymns.' How deep such bonds could go is suggested
by a Sussex carter's grandson who had been 'very happy' as a child
brought up by his grandparents, 'much attached' to them, and who
writes of how he later found a house for his ageing grandmother
close to his own and nursed her through her last illness: 'no
mother could have been more kind.' Similarly a Yorkshire mill-
worker describes himself as brought up by a grandfather 'who
cared for me as perhaps few grandchildren are cared for;' when
the old man died during his teens, 'by this death I lost a friend.'[27]

Practical caring undoubtedly made the influence of these grandparents particularly likely to be strong. But lasting influence depended not only on some form of regular, close contact, but
equally crucially on a sense of affinity, of common inheritance and
character, which allowed a grandchild to see in a grandparent a
model for his or her own development. This model did not have to
be of the same sex. Willoughby de Broke saw something of himself
in his grandmother, 'a good whip and a good horsewoman,' who
taught him to ride and launched him on an obsessively pursued
career in hunting. George Lansbury saw 'a strain of my blood' as
coming from a 'favourite' fiery grandmother with a zest for political
talk. Marianne Farningham, religious journalist, learnt her faith
from a papermaker Baptist grandfather, 'a preacher of great force,'

who would sit 'in our kitchen, talking with some friend, each smoking a long clay pipe, and with a glass of home-brewed beer on the table,' debating 'on high themes, of Calvinistic doctrine and the heresies of Arminianism.' Andrew Carnegie, millionaire-to-be, believed his 'optimistic nature' and wit 'must have been inherited' from his 'delightful old masquerading grandfather;' while the future feminist Hannah Mitchell could see her own dogged persistence in the extraordinary working energy of the octogenarian grandmother who was 'the delight and terror of my young days.'[28]

This sense of inherited destiny could be especially powerful for those who were cut off from their real parents. A disobedient Norfolk farm boy was propelled into a lifetime of professional poaching by the combination of a harsh, flogging father, who for years 'never spoke to me nor owned me,' and an entertaining, caring grandfather who had poached himself: 'I'm not shure I did not inherit some of my sporting ways from him.' And for fatherless Havelock Wilson, sea captain's grandson, it was his storytelling grandmother who set him on his life path, despite a mother who banned him from the harbour at Sunderland. This grandmother had been herself 'a very efficient sailor and navigator' and acted 'for many years' as chief mate of her husband's ship. Now blind, she would recount to the boy 'strange stories' of her 'sea experiences. I used to love to sit and hear her talk.' He would come back entranced to his own home: 'from the window, right across the housetops, I could see the masts and sprays of tall stately ships ... The blood of my forefathers, all men of the sea ... tingled at the very thought.'[29]

Not all bereaved children could find such a grandparent in their moment of need. The importance of their support, in an age when poverty and early death threatened family life in childhood still more than divorce and deprivation today, is brought home by the story of a North Welsh orphan, baptised as John Rowlands. His father had died and his mother had married another man and completely rejected him. 'I was a disgrace to them in the eyes of their neighbours.' He did not meet his mother from infancy until the age of twelve, when they found themselves accidentally in the same workhouse: but instead of the 'gush of tenderness' between them of which he had dreamt, 'her expression was so chilling that the valves of my heart closed as with a snap ... She remained a stranger to me.' Fortunately he had been taken in by his mother's father up to the age of six, living in a cottage by Denbigh castle; but after this grandfather died he spent nine years as a child in St Asaph workhouse. At 14 he ran away, deciding to seek out help from his father's family.

John Rowlands's search ended with the discovery of his surviving grandfather, a 'severe and sour old man' who lived with two of Rowlands's aunts in an old Welsh farmhouse. He found him, stout and pink, in a brown suit, knee-breeches, and blue-grey stockings, sitting in the farm kitchen on the wooden settle by the fire, smoking a long clay pipe. The old man asked his story,

> who I was, and what I wanted, in a lazy, indifferent way, and . . . never ceased smoking while he heard me, and. . . , when I concluded, he took his pipe from his mouth, reversed it, and with the mouth-piece pointing to the door, he said, 'Very well, you can go back the same way you came. I can do nothing for you, and have nothing to give you.'[30]

When that grandfather, his last hope of a parent-figure among his own kin, turned his pipe, he pointed John Rowlands on the path which was to give him his place in history. Hopeless though it seemed, he did not abandon hope of finding a parent. Within three years he had emigrated to the United States. There he was to find an adopted father in his American employer, a New Orleans storekeeper. So it was under his adopted name, as Henry Morton Stanley, that he met Livingstone in Africa.

4

At the Edge of Living Memory

AUTOBIOGRAPHERS are unusual just because they are writers. However diverse their origins, this means that they cannot be presumed typical of their time; certainly many wrote their life stories just because they were exceptional. Recorded life stories, by contrast, offer a double advantage for those seeking to understand the ordinary experience of ageing in the past. Firstly, it is possible to choose who to record in order to collect a representative group of lives. And rather than being at the mercy of the autobiographer's choice of what to mention, we can ask questions and open up areas of significant memory which would otherwise have been lost.

We draw here on two sets of interviews, both based on representative samples. The first is much larger: 444 interviews carried out in the early 1970s. In these, however, no special attempt was made by the interviewers to evoke memories of grandparents or other old people. The second is the smaller group of interviews with 55 grandparents carried out specifically for this book, and intentionally focused on ageing through the generations. They differ too in time-span, for the first set of informants were mostly born between the 1880s and 1900s, and the second set from the 1900s to the 1920s. But the overlap in time and content makes it most convenient for the two groups to be discussed together.[1]

There is, however, one noticeable general contrast between the two sets. Because in the earlier interviews no attempt was made to stimulate recollections of grandparents, we have a clearer indication of how far such memories were important. In almost half the interviews, no grandparent is mentioned in any way. In many others there is simply a reference to a grandfather's occupation. Occasionally there is no more than an indication of the family's ancestry: of migration from Ireland, or of a strain of distinction. One great-grandfather had been an inventor, 'socially in a higher class,' while another family claimed 'a good background somewhere' through a great-grandmother who as a maid had eloped with a young aristocratic gambler. Five grandfathers are less favourably remembered as drunkards: at least two passed down their habits to their sons—'dad had a poor bringing up'—while a third son was provoked into signing the teetotal pledge.[2]

If we exclude these brief references, we can say that 290 of the 444 interviews contain no memories of any grandparent. It is also noticeable that slightly fewer men than women informants reveal any significant memory. In the second set of interviews, by contrast, when asked, five out of six informants recall at least one grandparent. Grandmothers are remembered twice as often as grandfathers—principally because they survived longer; but it would seem that physical survival coincides here with salience in the memory. Recollection of grandparents thus appears strongest between women: granddaughters remembering grandmothers.

In the later interviews it is only when grandparents were not known directly that there is no significant memory of them, and we can reasonably assume that this was also the commonest reason for lack of memory in the first set. Usually this was because the grandparents had died too soon, but in a few cases it was because of distance. Occasionally they were cut off for other reasons. The father of one family had no contact with their Irish Catholic grandparents because he had married a Protestant—although he did later inherit one of the grandfather's pawnshops. One grandmother had been the orphan daughter of a silk merchant, 'taken into care' and sent as a young woman into service. When she married a Kent farm labourer her own relatives disowned her: 'it wasn't a very happy thing, you see, that she married into this family . . . I don't think they had anything to do with her after she married him.' Such rejections could easily harden and become two-sided, obliterating family memory itself. A Lancashire insurance agent 'would never talk about his family cos they rejected him.' Similarly the wife of a Yorkshire brassworker could never forgive her parents for handing her over to be brought up by her retired grandparents, who had come to live nearby after their glassworks business had failed. 'They took two of the children and my mother was one of them. Because of this she never had any time for her own parents: my mother couldn't think it was right that they'd parted with two of their children.' They were considered unmentionable: 'we never talked about them.'[3]

These family stories of rejection are unusual. But more surprisingly, there is little sign of the positive family traditions which were so striking in some of the autobiographies of the wealthy. It does not look as if such story-telling was a typical element in ordinary family culture. Where grandparents were never directly known their occupations may be remembered, but rarely more than that. There are only two notable exceptions. Both come from workers' families with traditions of earlier independence and generosity. In one the grandmother was a country publican with her own farm, and 'on a Sunday she used to make broth and put plenty of salt in it, and then the children had to stop outside and we'd say, "Are you my granny?" And she'd say, "I'm everybody's granny."' In the other, the mother, a railwayman's wife, 'used to talk about when she was a girl,' and of her memories of visiting the great-grandfather, a Lancashire clogger with his own shop:

> They used to go down to the clogger's shop, which was at the bottom of the road where they lived, and he used to make toast, make a drink, and they used to sit round by the light of a candle, eating toast and drinking. And they used to make coltsfoot wine. It used to be in all the fields then, and he used to take all the kids gathering coltsfoot. You had to get the head in between young fingers and just pluck the head . . . And the lads used to go and pinch out of the girls' bags. So then he used to segregate them: they go over there, and they go over there. Make sure they didn't get in touch.[4]

For the most part, however, the interviews simply offer direct memories from childhood. What can we learn from them?

Let us begin with the economic aspects of later life. Unlike the autobiographies, the interviews rarely describe older men at work. In part this may have been because the trend towards larger-scale workplaces meant children were less likely to see them working; but there is also evidence of the now growing pressure to retire. A Glasgow publican was forced to give up his position and become a lamplighter 'because they said he was too old.' An Essex countryman who could no longer find any work 'drowned himself in a lake . . . He'd got just tuppence ha'penny in his pocket for his beer, when they found him.' By the time we reach the second set of interviews, where the question of retirement was clarified, only a quarter of the grandfathers are remembered as still at work in old age. One was an Abergavenny horse-cab proprietor who 'drove a lot of nobility around' although 'he was very aged;' he had married his housekeeper after becoming a widower, and lived in a mill where his grandson 'used to learn all about his horses.' Another was a Scots upholsterer who kept on his business because 'that was his life;' a third, a retired London stevedore who 'had a pub in Rotherhithe.' An Aberdeenshire small farmer had retired, but onto a seven-acre croft where 'they used to always have fences to mend and trees to cut down;' 'he used to take me round on the barrow, when he was cuttin' down trees.'

A more remarkable exception since he was not self-employed, was a Scots miner who worked in the pit until he was 75, 'six days a week . . . He was working on the Saturday and took a stroke on the Sunday.' For a miner who remained fit no standard age of retirement was enforced before nationalization in 1947. Another Scots miner, a great-uncle, is also remembered at work until he was 74, 'lookin' after the ropes and that in the shafts! . . . And he kicked up hell when he was told he had t'retire. It was after the NCB took over and he was told straight that he was t'pack in. He says, "Oh no wait, I'm no packin' in." They said, "Aye, ye are."'

Nevertheless, most of the grandfathers were retired, and so was one elderly father, a Kilmarnock tinsmith. He still worked a little for pleasure, mending urns and clocks: 'he was good with his fingers . . . So he did a lot of that, for nothing. Just bring it and he did it.' But he had married a greengrocer—a much younger woman—and 'retired early' partly to help her: 'he worked a lot in the house. You know he used to see to a lot of our meals, and see that we were away to school and such-like.' Their marriage was certainly not typical, yet it is possible that even in the early twentieth century it was not uncommon for retired men to take on more responsibility at home, as many do today: for lack of other evidence, we can only speculate.[5]

In the first set of interviews there is another interesting aspect of references to work. In more than half the cases where the occupations of grandparents are mentioned, this is partly because the father followed a grandfather in his own work. A small number were textile millworkers, others were miners, fishermen, or seamen, skilled craftsmen, or farmworkers. An even smaller group were professionals, most commonly clergymen. The greatest number, however, were self-employed men who often had some small property to hand down along with the know-how of their trade. The variety of their occupations gives a sense of the remarkably diverse bases for economic independence still open at the beginning of this century. They range from a cotton mill-owner to outwork stockingers and frameknitters, through cornfactors and wholesalers, master builders, shopkeepers and market stallholders, hatmakers, shoemakers, and wheelwrights. There was often a special pride that the family were 'all in the trade;' 'all my people have been in the dealing world;' 'we've been blacksmiths for generations;' or they had been self-employed Portland quarrymen 'right back a hundred year back.'[6]

It is this same group who most often remember grandparents as providing significant direct financial aid either in their lifetimes or in their wills. Out of sixteen instances, four were shopkeepers, one a hotel proprietor, one in insurance, and four were farmers; and nearly all provided either houses—in one case paying for the maids, coal, and gas as well—or land. 'My father passed the farm on to me and I shall do the same for the two boys.' Inheritance within working-class families was rarely significant, their struggles against the poverty of old age itself exhausting their scant savings. By the time a Scots undertaker's horseman and his widow were dead, 'the little they had was all gone;' and this would have been typical enough. Even the goods manager at King's Cross station, a salaried employee, left his children no more than some bedroom furniture.[7]

With rare exceptions, in working-class families aid from grandparents to their adult children was at best symbolic: a parcel of rabbits from the country, or a turkey sent for Christmas. Even small gifts could strain resources. A London postman's daughter whose grandmother lived next door remembers how the old lady 'used to pass one or two little bits and pieces over to us, but she used to say to mother, "I can't do much for the grandchildren because we have no pension at the end."' Family help could not be relied on, even in a crisis. Some grandparents are remembered as explicitly refusing to give any help, as for an illegitimate, fatherless grandchild, or for a parent who drank. A pottery fireman lived opposite his wife's parents, but because of her drinking 'they wouldn't have nothing to do with her . . . They said it was up to me father to try to alter her.' Only middle-class grandparents could afford the exceptional indulgence shown to a Yorkshire coalman who regularly gambled away in the pub his weekly takings from customers. 'They helped him many a time to keep his head above water or else we should have been in a poor way.' When he was sunk by the 1926 miner's strike and had to 'sell everything he had', they came to the rescue again. 'I don't think he were ever in't position to pay them back. They never came and bawled him or nattered for it. It was just off and forgotten.'[8]

The still greater rarity of references to the economic activities of grandmothers than of grandfathers reflects the shrinking participation of married women in paid work at this time. But a number of older women did find ways of earning, especially after they were widowed: as a midwife, nursing, or doing 'a little bit of needlework to keep herself going,' or baking cakes for sale. One ran a cooked-meat shop and dining-room; another specialized in funeral teas. Others used their empty houses to run a corner shop or to take in lodgers, sometimes both together. Two old sisters in Portsmouth kept shops side by side: the great-aunt running a coal shop where 'you had to go in there with your pail, and they weighed the coal,' with vegetables as a sideline, while 'my gran she had a wee shop and she used to sell toffee apples.'

We have seen earlier how lodgers provided another means of support for older householders: and there were lodgers in some childhood homes too. They are recalled as somewhat sad, dependent figures: a 'poor old fellow' who went out to his sister for his meals; 'a right cripple' who had been unable to work for over ten years; 'a very old gentleman' who scraped together a living by selling vegetables and tomatoes which he grew in his greenhouse, but was 'very unhappy' because he had quarrelled with his drunken son. He lived for twenty years with the family as a lodger with meals included: 'he had a home with us, all those years.' Another working-class London mother took pity on an old couple who could not work and had no pension, and lodged them rent-free. The old man had been a seaman, and they had come from Chatham seeking a relative who had once lived next door, but who they found had moved. 'They said they had nowhere to go, so mum took them in.' Auntie Kate, as they called the old wife, proved 'a dear old soul, and of course the old boy, he used to tell us all stories about over the sea.' But such charity was rare, for it meant real sacrifice. 'I know my mum was very very worried. Because things were very hard for us.'[9]

One has a brief glimpse here of the fate of the elderly who were childless or out of touch with their children. Their poverty and loneliness were part of an isolation from ordinary family life which left them at the margins even of childhood memory.

Very occasionally there are recollections of helping other older people in the neighbourhood. In a Welsh mining village the boys 'were told to go and carry water for the old people . . . and see about firewood for them for the week. When we'd see these old people, we had to help them in every way, we were taught to do that.' Similarly a London fireman's widow sent her daughters round to an old lady after school. 'I'd only be about 6 or 7, and she'd always have the door open, she was always in bed, very old lady . . . And no light, only a candle. And we'd light the fire and go run any errands, and wait till her son used to come home.' In some cases the benefit was mutual. In a Devon village the teenage boys used to keep company with a lonely old woman 'called Granny Vasey. Her used to be working on the roads, see, quarrying, work on the roads, crack stones.' Joe Orr, the publican's son, would surreptitiously take a beer bottle, 'fill it up when his father wasn't about, see, and put it in his pocket, then take it up to granny. And us used to go up there . . . There was five of us, five boys.' By her fireside there was a settee and a table, 'and old granny was in the corner. Well us used to sit around the table, give granny her bottle and a glass, then us'd play a game of cards, see. That's where us used to go up night times when it was raining and that cold.' But while some neighbours could be generous, others were callously exploitative. A Lancashire railwayman's son remembers how in his street the men and women insured older neighbours as a speculation:

> Supposing you knew of somebody you thought, 'So and so'll not be here long,' you'd get a policy on 'em. They did. In them days they used to get policies on people as weren't relations. I know one fellow called Ashworth, he were bit of a coal merchant, I remember him shouting one day across to somebody, 'I backed a winner.' He'd backed a winner—he hadn't paid as much in contributions as money they could draw from dying. They did that, they could insure anybody.[10]

Childhood memory is however typically family-centred, touching only haphazardly on the unattached. For our purposes the special strength of the evidence from the interviews, as from the autobiographies, is for relationships within the family, and those must be our main concern here. But it is important to notice how the idea of the family at this time often stretched beyond the normal three generations of direct descent. There were in fact a variety of entrances to the grandparental role. By no means all required a blood relationship. A Shetland crofting family, for instance, had moved in with a childless older woman, who became 'one of the family . . . We used to play and the noise was terrible . . . climbing on her back and shouting . . . We used to call her granny, she was really no relation. But she owned the croft, you see.' And in gratitude, 'the old lady gave it to my father.' In the cities it might be a neighbour up the street who took the part of grandparent, as for the Stoke pottery fireman's son whose mother was always seeking advice from 'your Grandma Coates'—'I could never find out what relative she was to me mother. But she always used to say, "Well I'm a bit doubtful on the question. Wait until I've been up and seen your Grandma Coates." Cos she was the one with the knowledge.'[11]

In families without a surviving grandparent there might be other relatives to take the part. A Welsh farming family called an aunt by marriage 'granny;' a Grantham print manager's family took in a grandfather's cousin 'too old to live alone' who just 'spent her time knitting' and 'seemed something like a granny but she wasn't.' Great-aunts were sometimes significant: a Scots farmer's old sister, 'very straightlaced . . . you sat like a mouse;' or the great-aunt of a Portsmouth docker's daughter, 'an old, old lady,' who liked to celebrate receiving her weekly pension—'Every weekend, pension day, she had a wee brown jug and she used to send me up the beer shop to get half pint o'stout. And when I come back, she had the poker in the fire: they used to put it into the stout.' There are also hints of the four-generation families which longer life has now made so much more common, when— though still very rarely indeed—a great-grandparent is recalled. An Enfield clerical family took in a great-grandmother in her nineties for her last two years: 'she didn't want to go in a home and she wrote to my mother and asked if she could possibly look after her. Of course, my mother gave in. Shouldn't have really, because she hadn't got the room . . . She was no bother. No, she would just sit and look at us.' A Nottinghamshire miner's daughter remembers being taken to the fair by a ninety-year-old great-grandfather, 'a very big man, bonny man.'[12]

Some grandparents were acquired through adoption, or through remarriage following family break-up. An Essex girl was expected to call her foster-mother's mother 'granny,' and to shop for her. 'Poor old lady, she used to say, "There'll be a penny change and you'll get home some nice rock.". . . . The foster-mother said, "you light Granny's fire before you come." And I was only a wee mite.' She was also sent to the old lady's house to sleep, 'because she was alone. And it was very dark, but I had to go up every night, and I didn't like going up in the dark.'[13]

Much more common were step-grandparents. Of these, some left openly hostile memories. A Moray Firth fisherman grandfather, for example, had remarried, and his new wife 'was very hard on her family . . . I remember the stepmother, yes—didn't like when I saw her comin' t'the door. But eh oh no, she was a hard woman, very hard woman.' Some strongly objected to the possibility of taking on a full grandparental role. An Edinburgh postman's second wife protested when a cousin congratulated her on the birth of her first step-grandchild, ' "You'll be a granny now." "Oh," she says, "I'm not going to be called a granny." ' So they called her 'Auntie Granny' instead. A Potteries child who was brought up by her grandmother and 'treated her as me mother' remembers how 'grandad always used to turn and say, "I'm not your daddy you know." If you said "daddy" to him, were putting your arms round him—"Well, no—you know I'm not your daddy." He used to drill it in us that he wasn't, he was only my father's stepfather.' But others, more spontaneously affectionate, are remembered very positively. A Dumfries horseman step-grandfather used to look after horses at the county balls: 'look after the horses while they were there. All the aristocrats. Well they used to get tips, it'd be sixpences and threepenny pieces. And when my grandfather came in he always had a pocketful of these tips, and he would give us all some sixpences and some threepennies.' When the sales were on, 'he'd put his hand in his pocket and gave my mother sovereigns—"Go and get them all something." And he used always to buy us shoes and boots. . . . We always seemed to be lucky in that way.'[14]

Step-grandparents, like step-parents, need to win a child's approval. But to a lesser extent this is true of natural grandparents, too; they cannot, like parents, assume their significance to a child. As we look at these memories, it is clear that the relationship depends both on the opportunity to know each other and also on the degree of compatibility between grandparent and child. Too early death, or severe infirmity, or excessive distance could eliminate any possibility of a significant relationship. Villages now a mere half-hour apart by car could then be prohibitively far away: the daughter of an Essex farm horseman was taken to see his parents across the county boundary in Suffolk for the first time only at the age of 14. But with regular visiting, or through living together, grandparents could become important and sometimes crucial figures in childhood.

With grandparents who were visited, quite often the memory is mainly of the occasions when visits took place, or of the setting: of 'lovely times' staying with grandparents at Christmas, or of playing games—'beggar my neighbour' and 'old maid' with a grandmother, dominoes and stories with a grandfather. One Lancashire grandfather's warm hospitality was more dubiously remembered:

he was a very jovial man. And he always had a pot of linseed and black Spanish, and we always had to have a drink of this, cos he thought it was fantastic. It was horrible. They had old-fashioned grates and it was always there on the side keeping warm. So you was always greeted with a drink out of this pint pot.

There are idyllic memories, especially in the more recent interviews, of holidays in the countryside, learning to grow vegetables or brew beer, and bringing home fruit from the farm. One Midland industrial city child could vividly recall the country cottage of his gardener grandfather:

a lovely cottage, thatched roof cottage they lived in and it had an apple tree in the front, and a pear tree down the back, and all fruit trees. You had to go right down to the bottom to the lavatory: that was a game, that was. It was all beams, ever so nice.

And inside the cottage were his grandmother, 'a very buxom lady' who was 'the spittin' image' of his mother, and the grandfather, who 'looked like a little bird' with his wavy hair and pointed beard and bird-eyes.[15]

Some families congregated weekly at their grandparents' home

for music. One family would gather on Sunday evening round the
harmonium; another would go to their grandfather's village shop,
boys and uncles each with a fiddle or cello, to sing or dance to
their own tunes—'we really enjoyed that;' while a Yorkshire mill-
owner's family used to ask all their kin for weekly musical parties,
taking turns to host these 'dreadful performances.' One Manchester grandmother had seven daughters, of whom two were amateur
opera singers,

> and they all had their own songs . . . Oh yes, it used to be
> wonderful to go there. . . . And she was crippled with rheu-
> matism—she used to go with a stick, and she was the boss. I
> remember one time when Auntie Margaret back-answered to
> me grandma and me grandma couldn't get to her so she tipped
> the table upon her. And walloped her with her stick. But they—
> oh, they daren't give any cheek.[16]

Other memories are no more than a nutshell description, a
fleeting image, perhaps of an eccentricity. 'Me grandfather, aye, I
can remember me grandad,' a Durham railwayman's son recalled,
'A very old man he looked to be with long white whiskers. And
the last time I saw him, he was in the yard. He was sitting on a
three-legged stool chopping sticks. Aye, chopping firesticks. And
that's a long long time ago.' A former Clydeside shipyard worker
and a keen Mason had 'got a bit chesty:' 'I remember him sitting
by the fire all wrapped up an' coughing.' But the other grandfather
in the same family, an old Ulsterman, who lived with an aunt, still
spent much of his day with his former workmates. He 'used to go
round by the harbour. There was an old deckhouse off a ship and
these old chaps used to meet there and I suppose they'd be talking
of old times—shipbuilding. They would go for a drink and then
toddle off home.'

With a grandmother, it might be an odd domestic habit that
is remembered—'you know she used to polish her table legs and
brass—and she used to cover 'em up after'—or simply her appearance: 'I can just see her with her white apron on, and cap;' or 'she
had a beautiful sequin coat, cape and a little sequin bonnet;' or
again, of a duchess, 'I can remember a tall gaunt woman in black—
rather frightened of her.'[17]

Occasionally a grandmother and grandfather are remembered as
a discordant couple. One old sailor kept a custom from his nautical

days. 'Last thing at night he always had his tot of rum, and it used to smell the room out. I can smell that rum now.' He and his wife were a 'very, very thrifty,' simple-living couple, and right at the end of their long lives quite close. But before that, 'unfortunately, their domestic life wasn't very happy and there was a period in their lives when they both lived in the same house but didn't speak to one another. And if I visited my grandfather I went upstairs to see him in his rooms and I came downstairs to visit my grandmother.' Another old London couple were dominated by a 'matriarch' of a grandmother. It was rash to complain of anything there: 'the slightest—you know, when my throat's dry, you'd get dosed with blackberry syrup, or if you felt a bit hot then you'd get dosed with ground ivy tea. Some most awful concoctions, the whole cupboard was full of. She had a remedy for everything.' And as for her husband, 'poor old grandad liked his pipe, but he was never allowed to smoke a pipe in the house. He had to go and sit in the woodshed and smoke it. And he was never allowed to keep his tobacco in the house. He always used to tuck it underneath the water butt. Oh yes, she was a very very strict old dear.'[18]

Sometimes it is all held in a single incident. A London chemist, a sturdy, blue-eyed man with a long white beard, would take his grandson for walks. Once, going through a churchyard, 'he held my hand . . . He said, "Don't fear," he said, "the dead don't hurt you, it's the living that hurt." I've remembered that all my life.' Part of the fascination of the old for the very young could be the sense of contact with a long-past world, half haunted. A Durham boy had an old aunt, a frequent visitor, a 'very fine woman,' still an agricultural worker.

> She was grand, she would sit and play concertina . . . She used to smoke a clay pipe and shag tobacco. Me father used to sit at one side of the fireplace and me aunt at the other one, and they would sit and talk about the Bible. And every night before we went to rest. Every night . . . If there was a moon she used to go out into the yard, and look at the moon, and prophesy what the world was going to be like tomorrow. And this particular night, it was a full moon. She used to wear very thick-lensed spectacles, and they were thick, very thick. And a very broad-knitted hairnet, about half inch square net. And this particular night she went into the yard, the yard door was shut, she went into the

yard and was standing, looking at the moon—when the ticket lad
came up with a ticket for me father. He took one look at
her—and he off. He didn't leave no ticket. He off. He went up
to the office, he said, 'I've——,' he said, 'I've seen the devil in
Turnbull's yard.' Aye. She frightened him.[19]

Most grandparents known only through visiting did not leave
a strong emotional mark. But almost a quarter of the childhood
memories do express distinct feelings. Some were of definite dislike. One younger Welsh hill farmer used to go up 'to help his
father in evenings with the few cattle they had,' but afterwards at
supper the older man expected the grandchildren to keep silent,
and if they spoke 'he'd look at us fiercely.' A London postman's
daughter whose grandparents lived next door contrasted the
couple: 'oh she was a pet, but not him, he never gave us any love.'
He was 'a very very severe Edwardian,' looking a bit like the
king, with

> his beard and everything to a T. He'd sit at the top of the table,
> have his stiff white serviette tucked into his waistcoat, and he's
> lifted that carving knife and fork until—you sat there and you
> never said a word. And then he'd carve and he'd pass round all
> the plates. You dare not lift your knife and fork to start your
> meal until he started his. You daren't say a word. And if the
> meat was not quite to perfection he used to grumble at my
> grandmother . . . Oh he was severe.

Grandmothers could be equally daunting. An Oxfordshire
carpenter's daughter 'lived in fear' of a 'very puritanical, very
strict' grandmother who 'bossed the village, and kept everybody in
order.' A Liverpool naval engineer's daughter was sent on her own
each week to her grandmother to collect her weekly sum for the
thrift club run by her mother. The grandmother was a Manx
seaman's widow, 'always smart,' in long skirts and an apron, 'always cooking, baking, and sewing: always clean . . . immaculate;'
yet somehow without warmth. She lived in a top flat 'up a hell of a
lot of stairs, and she used to have a parrot on top of the stairs.' The
girl would 'just sit and talk to her. Hating every minute of it. Cos
we had to go you see, and you had to put your Sunday clothes on,
your best coat and everything; and then when you came back you
had to take them all off again.' Still worse, however, were visits to

a Kilmarnock grandmother, a tough 'old tartar' of a truly 'grim disposition,' who 'just lived and lived and lived' in her spotless 'scrubbed white' house. When her granddaughters came they were expected to scrub too: 'I've seen my eldest sister, the minute she went in she was made to scrub the table—and it was white—scrub the floorboards—which were white.' But the younger children, being less useful, 'weren't even allowed in. We had to sit outside on the front steps, which were also white. And you couldn't move . . . Couldna look at her. We had to sit outside, we couldn't speak. Oh no, we didna like her at all . . . We hated her.'[20]

Against these negative memories may be set more frequent instances of closeness and admiration. One Manchester grandfather, a market fishmonger and former wrestler, died when his granddaughter was only six. But she did not forget 'sitting on me grandad's rocking chair combing his hair and I can always remember him sat there and me stood up behind him: I'd comb his hair for hours and he just sat there and let me.' Another influential grandfather was a Scots miner who had retired from the pit to become the gardener of a big house at Broomie Knowe. He was 'a great Labour man,' a non-smoker and non-drinker, an elder of the kirk until the minister mistakenly suggested he had a hangover—'and it was the last time my grandfather was ever inside a church. And he was buried without a minister: he specified it.' Again on principle, he and his wife 'refused point blank t'draw their pensions: "We're no wantin' charity."' They were both 'rant Labour' and at elections the campaign office was 'my granny's front room.'

> I used to go more or less t'my grandparents, almost every day . . . You always went to them. They had a house in Broomie Knowe at the bottom: it faces onto what is the public park now, the big hill. And he had a grand garden, he had everything in his garden. Fruit trees: apples, pears, plums, cherries, rasps, gooseberries and redcurrant and blackcurrants . . . He had more or less green fingers, my grandfather. He could grow anything. And anything that was eaten in my mother's house was either home grown or home baked.'

He kept hens too, and was also a pigeon enthusiast. 'My grandfather was . . . always an active man, right t'more or less about the last year that he died. He was always active, yes. Oh aye.'[21]

More often it is a grandmother who is remembered as a 'guiding influence.' A Yorkshire pay clerk's widow was able to play a 'big part' in her granddaughters' upbringing because she lived next door across a common yard and could be 'always there,' in and out of the house. She would watch her granddaughter wash the door-step and come out to comment:

> 'Now Kathleen,' she says, 'there's a right way and a wrong way to do everything,' and she showed me how to wring out a cloth . . . I never saw her with a hair out of place. She always looked absolutely immaculate. When she got up in the morning, always had amethyst earrings—and she left to me actually—and she always looked absolutely immaculate. And whenever she bought it always had to be the best.

This grandmother was a lasting influence, 'because she always insisted that you had to have the best of everything. Nothing else was right, you had to go for the best in life, and I suppose we've always felt that.'

There were several families where extra closeness to a grand-mother was encouraged by a strained relationship with the mother. Thus the daughter of one mother who drank asked to go to live with her grandmother, in her well-ordered 'nice' home: 'but they wouldn't let me go. I was the eldest daughter and they really wanted to keep me.' In another instance, a Portsmouth docker's daughter had grown close to her grandmother through helping her go out to shop or visit, or just sitting with her—'her and I were never separated.' The old lady 'was in our house more often than she was in her own.' As the granddaughter grew into a young woman, they still 'always got on, and she always stuck by me;' when she was told off by her parents for coming home late at night, the old lady would ask them, 'Were you never young once?'

In a London wheelwright's family the grandmother had a crucial influence, in particular because the mother was 'very prudish' on sexual matters. 'One day I asked her a question as I was getting on, and she just smacked my face. . . . You had to learn all about anything from other girls.' But unusually the daughter was able to confide in her grandmother:

> Thank God I had a very wonderful grandma. Perhaps it's not right to say it, but I loved my grandma much more than I loved my mother. . . . She was sweet, she was really lovely. Not only her own people but other people used to come to her for

advice. . . . And when I was beginning to grow up and I used to visit her. She'd say to me, 'Come and sit down, ducky.' Used to go and sit down. 'Getting a big girl now,' she'd say. 'Well, you know what you've got to do, you've got to be careful.' And I used to look at her. 'You've been talking to the girls?' 'Yes.' 'Well,' she said, 'listen. If there's anything you don't understand, I know your mother won't tell you, you come and tell gran.' And I used to.

Later, as a 16-year-old, she went into a wartime gas mask factory working beside 'real cockney women': 'I was shocked . . . I couldn't believe what they said.' So she went back to her grandmother.

She says, 'Come here, sit down,' put her arm round me. 'Now,' she said, 'they've told you in a very bald way. That's wicked. Yes, the baby is born like that.' So I said, 'Well how does it get there?' You see? So there's my grandma telling me the difference between a girl and a boy. And the way she put it, she ought to have been alive today, she could have taught them how to tell people about sex. You know I thought when she explained it to me, not like some people think it's dirty, I thought it was wonderful. I did really . . . I think that's why I got through life as well as I did. Because I'd had the grand advice from my grandma.[22]

Another basis on which close relationships commonly developed was a pattern of visiting which included the exchange of help and caring between the generations. But again, this did not necessarily follow: the spirit of the exchange mattered too. While grandmothers who brought cakes or made clothes for their grandchildren did so from their own choice, childcare stemmed principally from the request of mothers. These were mostly working wives: mill or munition factory workers, cleaners or outworkers. Grandmothers would help them by minding the children after school, cooking their dinners, and sometimes having them overnight. Typically they lived very close by. A Durham miner's daughter 'could shout down the passage and me grandma would soon know if there was anything the matter with us.' The grandchildren always bathed in her kitchen rather than at home, and she 'looked after our heads' for lice, while after the bath the blind grandfather 'used to tickle our backs with stick in front of fire.' Some grand-

mothers were not enthusiastic for this role. A Lancashire mill child
assumed that although her grandmother fed her, 'mother must
have paid her of course,' a quite regular practice in the region. A
Tyneside girl disliked going for dinners to her grandmother because 'she used to threaten us with this monkey stick, hung behind
the door.' Some grandmothers took children only at times of crisis:
when the mother was ill, or when parents were locked in dispute.
Thus one mother was an East London waitress, first married to a
shrimp-seller and later living with a docker. Her daughter was
'pushed around' between various homes, never secure: 'it wasn't a
home life really.' She found consolation in her grandmother, 'a
mother or an angel . . . I loved her. Anything that went wrong I
always went there.' But her grandfather was 'a very strict man,'
and although she went to live with them 'just now and again when
things went wrong at home,' this never lasted: a respectable
mechanic and chapel man, the grandfather could never forgive his
daughter's errant ways. 'I was being punished for what my mother
did. . . . He seemed to have spite on me . . . So I got turned out of
there.'[23]

Against these, we may set happier examples. A London girl
whose father had died lived at times in the next street with her
grandmother, moving between the two homes. She remembers
how 'in the evenings we used to sit by the fire and grandma'd let
me comb her hair. She had lovely long hair and I'd roll it up all in
little merry widow curls. If you got tired and worried, she'd say,
"Come on, comb my hair for me."' A Plymouth dockyard labourer's daughter lived across the road 'as much with grandma as I did
with mother. Well I'd rather go with grandma, rather than my
mother.' She ate there often; and since her grandmother had been
a gentleman's cook, she ate well. The grandmother of a Cornish
smallholder's family would stay the first three days of each week 'to
help my mother to do the washing and buttermaking . . . and to
help to do the mending;' and when the children were not at school
they would walk the mile and a half back to granny's own 'little
thatched cottage.' She kept a cow, and although there was only
water from a well 'up top of the garden,' this was another spotless
house: 'she always kept a nice white cloth down over her stair
matting, washed and ironed each week. And her brasses shining,
slab scrubbed. The back kitchen had an earth floor, and that was
sanded.'

A Dumfries house factor's daughter would visit her grandmother each morning on her way to school,

> to see if she wanted any messages, corn or meal for the hens, she kept hens. There was a wee window you could look into before you came to the back door and she was always sitting reading the paper. She was very religious . . . had texts hanging on the wall, framed text. I can remember grandma's text: 'Cast all your care upon Him, for He cared for you.' And she was a good living woman.

If her parents needed her to be looked after, she would be off there again later; or she would go there in the evenings to read a book to her grandfather, or play games with him, or listen to one of the old pair storytelling. The grandfather was a favourite with the neighbouring children too, 'a great one for stories,' and in the summer would sit them on a seat outside his door, 'not only his own grandchildren but other children about, listening to the tales he used to tell, about old Dumfries': of the murderess Mary Timmony, for example, the last woman publicly hanged in Dumfries. Here again, it was easy for the grandchildren to call in frequently: the two houses were both in the same 'raw—this "raw" was a row of houses. As a child I remember I used to call my mother at home, "mammy up the raw," and grandma was "mammy down the raw" . . . So that I had two homes really, because as often as not I was down at her house, as in my own home.'[24]

There were some families in which domestic help from a widowed grandmother was really a disguised form of assistance in the other direction. An Oxford painter's wife paid her mother a half crown a week for coming to help on washday: 'a little bit of pin money . . . This was my mother's way of helping out a little tiny bit.' And although the flow of mutual aid was markedly more often from the grandparent so long as the two generations were living separately, there were several cases in which visiting was explicitly intended to enable the grandchild to convey help. A Bolton engineer sent his daughter each week 'up to me grandmother's, take her a shilling.' A London grandmother was particularly troublesome because of her drinking sprees, but her granddaughter was expected to clean her front doorsteps every Saturday: 'the old bugger used to sit at the window and watch me clean 'em. Hearthstone all the lot you know, from outside the door right the way

down to the steps.' Some children were sent to widowed grandmothers to live with them for company, or just sleep a few nights,
like the seaman's daughter on the Western Isles who, when all the
men were away at the fishing, 'used to sleep with granny:...
bringing the water from the well and bringing in the peat, tidy-
ing up the floor and singing songs, for granny she was a very
musical lady, yes she was.' Another widowed grandmother chose
her grown-up granddaughter, who had had dinner with her every
day as a schoolchild, to be her companion on seaside holidays. 'We
used to go and sit in the park, on the river bank, and she'd have a
book and I'd have a book...Yes, we got on exceptionally
well....I suppose it was a gentle hand really. She seemed just
happy to see us.'[25]

Less often, a widowed grandfather was helped. A Stepney dairy-
man's daughter had to call every Sunday morning on the way to
church, to read her grandfather a verse from the Bible. After
listening, he would say, '"Well now, you've got a good home. Go
to church." I said, "Yes grandad." And he always left a little bag of
sweets and a threepenny bit.' A Luton shoemaker's grandfather
would come every Friday night for a bath and a meal of pease
pudding and chitterlings in front of the fire. And in a four-
generation family of Dumfries master slaters, the 13-year-old
granddaughter was daily housekeeper to the eighty-year-old grandfather, cooking and cleaning for him: 'you just did what you were
told. I was sent—"Go up...."' In return, she was given a half-
crown a week.[26]

Although visiting grandparents was the basis of many significant
memories and relationships, it is surprising that in the first set of
interviews there are even more significant mentions of grandparents who at some point lived in the same house as their children.
Even in the second set, where memories were specifically pressed,
one third of the grandparents who were remembered had at some
time lived in the same household. But we know that three-
generational households were in fact as rare in the past as they are
today. What lies behind this apparent conflict between memory
and historical reality?

Statistical averages are often deceptive of social practices. There
can be no doubt that the normal British ideal was for adults of
different generations to live in separate houses. 'No, I never lived
with any of my parents. No damned fear. I got out of the way, on

my own.' Nevertheless, there were four situations in which an 'extended' multi-generational family was, at least transitionally, a regular practice.[27] The first was early in a young couple's marriage. It is a remarkable finding from these interviews that of those informants who married before 1918 almost half—and over half if we include those with soldier husbands—lived for an initial period, sometimes brief but often two or more years, with one of their parents before moving into a house of their own. These were years of housing shortage and this was frequently the reason. Much less commonly, in a small number of families these mutual arrangements continued for many years. This happened typically where both generations participated in the same family business: most often, but not always, a small farm or croft. Here housing and common work meant co-residence was to their mutual advantage.

A second, but also rare, situation in which an extended household could arise was when an elderly person was able to obtain the support of either an adult child or grandchild to continue living in his or her own home. Grandchildren could be used to help when small, and there were also a few instances of a grandchild moving in during adulthood. In a similar kind of way, one an Essex farm labourer's daughter was called back from service to live with her ageing parents again, the household supported partly from the wages of younger brothers, and partly from pigs and hens which the old couple kept themselves. Interestingly, it was not only daughters who could feel such a binding duty. A Devon labourer who promised his mother not to marry in her lifetime, finally married only at the age of 51: 'bugger, we was courting for seventeen year. Yes, her and I went together for seventeen year, before us got married.'[28]

The third situation, much more common, was when a grandparent abandoned living independently, either following widowhood, or through infirmity. This does not show up in the household statistics because many of these stays were for a brief few months right at the end of life. It was above all grandmothers who came to live with their children in this way: five times as many as grandfathers. This was partly because grandmothers lived longer and were more often widowed, but also because they were more helpful. As children sometimes realized, a wholly dependent old relative was a serious burden—'It half killed my mum looking after her.' Some families managed to postpone sharing house by well-organized support for a grandmother in her own home. A Lancashire miner's daughter, whose grandmother 'was very sprightly, very clean . . . very like prigmeat, you know, everything in its place,' remembers how one of her brothers moved into the next-door house when he married, and 'they helped with them when they were older.' When the grandmother was in her eighties and widowed, 'we went religiously one of us each day, one sister and another, each day. And then this brother lived next-door and his wife popped in and out. And they'd good neighbours as well. We kept it up. Cos she used to say, "I never had daughters but I've ended up with three." Cos we went religiously.' They also all helped with the cleaning in turn, 'like do the curtains and windows and give it a general do over.' Although in the event the old lady died first, towards the end it looked as if she would need to be taken in by one of her descendants and this caused distinct tension: 'we had least room and everything—and least money,' but 'there was a bit of squabbling in family. And we decided we'd have her.' Other families showed astonishing generosity, even for grandparents for whom they felt much less sympathy. One grandfather had earlier abandoned his own responsibilities: 'when his wife died he went off and left his family,' with his eldest daughter shouldering the task of an unsupported mother of the younger children. Nothing was heard of him.

And then me grandfather suddenly appeared, many years later, when they'd got children that were grown up then, all of them, he appeared to these girls, would you believe it? His two daughters who he'd never really done anything for—expecting them to look after him. Which they did. Much to their credit. And they had him there until he died.[29]

It was not uncommon, when it was unclear who should be responsible for an elderly relative, to take turns. A Lewis grandmother was moved between her daughters 'as the family arrive'— she had to move on to make room for infant children. A Stoke pottery manager's parents retired to the south-west, but returned when they could no longer live independently, moving 'to each of our houses in turn. Fortnight at each house, with each—all seven of us . . . with each of us a fortnight, each time, each of us in turn.' Similarly a Bolton great-aunt 'spent her time with various relatives.' Bachelor uncles were the worst difficulty. One Keighley mill warper's wife found herself with four to care for; and even one could stir up great resentment. A young Scots miner's wife found herself saddled with a great-uncle:

> he had six sisters an' a brither an' he wouldna stay wi' any o'them, cause he wanted to stay wi'me, so I took him in. Cause he had been used to me lookin' after him doon at my mother's hoose.... We didna have any option, we never got any option. They jist had a meetin' an' telt me, 'Bruce's stayin' wi' you.'

He was with them 13 years: 'We were never on oor own, we were never—didna seem t'have the hoose t'oorselves.'[30]

Grandparents who moved in only at the very end of their lives, just for a few last months, rarely left much of a mark unless earlier contact had been important. 'I don't remember her really, only as a figure sitting in a chair . . . She wasn't able to walk. She had two enormous lumps on her head . . . Lace caps with black velvet bows: she always wore those.' One country child born in the 1870s was an exception to this, for she had to share her grandmother's bed— until her parents removed her, having been superstitiously warned that 'she took my young breath.' Closeness to a grandmother's death seems never to have invoked the intense emotional experiences which those who nursed a parent or spouse sometimes recall with such striking physical intimacy. No grandparent is remembered in such a way. It was their activity over longer periods which mattered to their grandchildren, not their passing. Many grandmothers who lived with their grandchildren helped look after them, made their clothes, got them up for school, minded them while their mothers went out to work: 'I thought of my grandmother even more so than my mother cos she was always there, you see. We were never left alone. And very good she was too.' And whatever may have been socially expected of them, some grandfathers evidently helped in a similar way. In a Welsh farm family the grandmother was bedridden, and child-care fell to the grandfather: 'cause he was in the house, he was the one that looked after me and kept me in order.' In a Nottingham mining family the grandfather was named as a second father: 'I used to call him "father" and me dad, "dad".' Another grandfather, a retired Manchester newsagent, would light the fires, mend shoes, and peel the potatoes, while in a south London stableman's home the grandfather would clean the shoes and cook too—'We always said we had two mothers and two fathers, always.'[31]

Some inevitably left a much less favourable impression. One

grandfather 'was a very wicked man . . . whom we disliked.' A Jekyll and Hyde journalist, who 'never drank tea or coffee—he believed in water, "God's ale" as he called it, he was a natural vegetarian, he didn't believe in killing anything.' Despite these high principles he had driven his wife to drink by abandoning her, and a crippled daughter into prostitution by making her pregnant: 'You see, our history's really rather dreadful. And all that we daren't say anything about; I didn't even know until long afterwards.' Whether explained or not, the family's disapproval of this incestuous old man was clear enough.[32]

Nor was it easy to be thrust together with some grandmothers. Some were difficult because they seemed too controlled, or controlling. One grandmother was 'like a queen, unapproachable. I don't remember her kissing anybody. . . . She sat upright, always. You never spoke out of place. . . . She used to sit and knit, socks, she knitted all our socks . . . on four needles. She was always occupied, but you never went near her.' Another was 'a bit of a boss, and she moved about from one daughter to another. . . . When she found out that she couldn't boss the children, she moved on. Well, when Gran came to us, ooh—she was a tyrant.'[33]

Others are recalled as causing unease because of ways thought unsuitable for women of their age. One grandmother, who had been out to the Australian Gold Rush and back, was inseparable from her pet chaffinch and her nightly glass of porter. 'She used to take it in bed and that was her night cap. . . . She was a lad, she was.' Another, born in Ireland, whose son was a Yorkshire steelworks labourer, also liked a daily drink, but went out each night to the pub and was back regularly as it was 'just turned seven.' One night, when she was in her nineties, she failed to reappear and the labourer's wife went out to look for her:

So I look in this public, I can see it now, stood back at top of Hope Street, and there were two steps and a little snicket—and there were about four in there. Four old women. See I just went like that, looking up: 'Come on, its bed time. I've been worried to death over you,' I says, 'wondering where you was.' They were all having a packet of chips and fish—whoever fetched them I don't know, cos they were all up for a good age: tell you, she were a hundred just in St Patrick's Day. I said 'Come on.' She'd got her glass of beer. She come out, I gets hold of her arm . . . I said, 'Do you know, you frightened me to death?'

But the old lady's humiliation was not over.

> She got in trouble when I got home. He says, 'Where the hell have'—he were right snotty—'have you been?' She says, 'What do you want to know for?' She was right haughty with him. 'You frightened Alice to death,' he says; 'you never stop out like this.' So she said, 'If tha wants to know, I've had a gill of beer and me chips and fish.'[34]

No wonder, with such threats to independence a possible outcome, sharing house with the younger generation remained usually a last resort. Yet if living together could create problems, it also resulted in some notably strong relationships between grandparents and grandchildren. 'I liked him,' one daughter summed up a grandfather who had been orphaned in the Irish potato famine: 'he was an old man, and I was only nine when he died, but as our father was at the [First World] War, I suppose he was the only man in the house. And he was very nice to us. . . . He was a great one for singing because he'd sing sea shanties and Irish songs.' And a Kent farm labourer's daughter recalled with special intimacy her grandmother who lived into her nineties, only moving from her own cottage in her last five years. 'We went to her house a lot. We'd pop in any time, and I have been to stay with her. . . . She used to have me in a big feather bed with her. . . . She cooked all outside—the fire was outside the house. . . . She had every tooth in her head. . . . We didn't discriminate so about age. My grandmother was just one of the family.' Most remarkably, she used to talk to the girl about her grandfather's dying:

> You see, we'd got such confidence that she told me that when he died, she said, 'He died in his bed here,' that we were in, you see; and she said, 'I then closed his eyes and I laid down with him till the morning so that nobody should be disturbed.' So I said, 'Ooh gran, did you? . . . Were you frightened gran?' She said, 'No. Love casts out fear.' She was very, very fond of him. 'Love casts out fear,' she said: 'you'd better learn that as soon as possible.' I did. And it does. . . . Wonderful old lady.[35]

One last form of co-residence brought some of the closest relationships between grandparents and grandchildren, as well as some of the most sustained instances of tension. This was when the need to live together came not from the older generation, but from the child's own family. There are altogether thirty instances of this in the two sets of interviews, resulting from three different situations which occurred almost equally commonly: need for housing space, death, or desertion.[36] Sharing house space has the fewest implications. In typical instances, in the cities a widowed and formerly more prosperous grandmother might still be living in a larger, now empty house: thus a Liverpool labourer and salt-packer's family moved in with the grandmother, who kept a secondhand clothes shop. Or in poor farming areas, the farm-house might be divided with the grandparents 'living in the old room.' A Barra fisherman's son, one of eight born to a couple who lived as squatters in a foreshore hut, 'was brought up in my grandfather's' across the road: 'I had everything in their house. I had nothing to do with meals or anything at home.' Not all such arrangements were easy. A Welsh smallholder quarryman moved into the family farm so that his wife could go out to earn as a washerwoman, but the children did not get on well with their step-grandmother: 'there was a very hard side to her, she was a very stern woman, and we didn't like her.'[37]

It was quite a different situation when a grandchild came into the grandparents' home through the death or desertion of one or both parents. Sometimes an older child made a deliberate choice to do so, having already got to know them well, but others could find themselves suddenly in a new home with no say at all. Thus when a Lancashire miner died, his widowed wife went into service as a living-in maid with a doctor and 'put us in with me grandma.' Another girl was 'sent away' for two years because her mother was severely ill after childbirth. Brothers and sisters were quite often split from each other, as well as losing parents, in these moments of crisis. Thus a London ship's carpenter's daughters were sent to one grandfather, and the boys to their other grandmother. Old people who took in their grandchildren at such moments might have few resources and little space themselves. The son of a drunken soldier lived for six years with his grandmother in one room. A girl from another broken family 'used to sleep in the same bed as grandma—I was sleeping with her the night she was found dead the following morning.' The grandparent could feel resentful at such unexpected burdens, and sometimes grandchildren were aware of this: 'course there was—bits of squabbles at times with me father and me grandfather.'[38]

The typical tone of memory, however, is very different from

this: a special sense of love, even devotion, in the grandchild for a
'wonderful old lady:' 'I treated her as me mother,' as an abandoned
farm-child sent over from Ireland put it; or a motherless Bolton
spinner's son—'she were a love. . . . We've grown up as if she was
me mother.' The sense of rescue undoubtedly gives a special strain
of idealization to these comments, but this seems to go back to the
childhood experience rather than to be a retrospective gloss. A
Wiltshire cowman's son, for example, had lost his mother.

> They were going to put us in the workhouse. Only there was a
> lady lived at the manor, and she said—come up and see my
> grandmother and if she'd look after us, she'd keep us in clothes
> and food. So she did. So my grandmother brought us up . . . took
> care of us. . . . Always sewing, making things. Yes, she was very
> good at looking after us. We were never untidy, always clean
> and always well fed. . . . Oh wonderful, wonderful grandmother!

But he felt strikingly differently about his grandfather. 'He was
always grumbling at me,' and threatening him with a stick. 'Grandmother used to say, "Now grandfather, you begrudge the food that
boy eats" . . . I didn't like my grandfather. He didn't like me. He
liked my brother and sister.' The relationships described here are
much more complex than a simple retrospective stereotype.

It is equally notable that in four other instances, children who
later had a choice stayed on with grandparents, rather than return-
ing to their parental home. One grandmother, a London insurance
broker's wife, had originally taken her grandson because he was
seriously ill and the mother—who suffered from depression—had
another infant only a little younger. 'Granny came up one day and
saw her, and she said, "You can't go on like this: I'm taking the boy
back with me." And she grew so fond of him. . . . And every year it
was put off. So he finally stayed with her altogether. So he was
brought up with her.' And a Liverpool painter's son, who after his
father died 'was brought up with me grandmother,' calling her
'mother,' chose not to return to his real mother when she remarried and could offer him a home again: 'They'd brought me up, and
it wouldn't be fair for them to take me after from rearing me.'[39]

Similarly, a motherless Glasgow soldier's daughter was taken in
by her grandparents and brought up with the help of an aunt, who
married soon after but stayed in the same home. The grandmother
had 'a wee shop' and the aunt was 'a dressmaker, she made dresses

and sold them cheap, round about the doors.' The grandfather, a former soldier in India and retired horseman, had had a leg amputated: 'he ended up wi' a stump, so he used to sit in this . . . old chair in the corner . . . and nurse Aunt Lillie's children.' The girl does seem to have been closer to her aunt than to her grandmother who died relatively soon, in her sixties. Nevertheless the grandmother was a strong influence. She had been a teacher, and made sure the girl went to a good school: 'my granny had more influence on me education-wise. I mean she was the one that would push ye. She sent me to that convent, thinkin' she would make something o' me.' She also gave her a sense of family background. They would visit the cemetery together: 'she would take a tram car, see she'd one or two buried there, it was her own family, and we'd go to the cemetery nearly every Sunday if the weather was good. And she would take ye a wee walk round the cemetery, and I can remember pinchin' rhododendrons comin' out the gate.'[40]

Being mothered by a grandparent was certainly not always a happily remembered experience, and for one illegitimate Scots girl it generated a lifetime of mutual bitterness. The grandmother was always frightened that she would follow her mother's mistake: 'she always said I'd turn oot t'be like my mother . . . Cos my mother worked through in Glasgow as a maid, and—eh—she had me t'a dentist—well he was a university dentist—fae doon the myre. His father said if he married her he would be cut oot, cut off withoot a penny.' Her grandmother made the illegitimate girl into a Cinderella: 'I was made to work in the house . . . a house slave.' Every week she was expected to clean the house right through and make the dinners, while the grandmother had her outing to Edinburgh: 'she had jist t'come in and sit doon like a lady.' Then as soon as her grandfather had died, she was sent out to earn as a butcher's shop girl.

Yet when the girl grew into a young woman, she seemed unable to break free of her grandmother. She moved out for a while, but carried on cleaning for her; and then when she married, she moved back in again, and had her first child there. The old lady had scarcely mellowed. When her granddaughter quickly became pregnant, 'she thought it was disgustin' . . . pure disgusted shameless young woman. . . . I said, "Of course you had grandfather and you only kissed an' they were there." That shut her up.' The grandmother was also 'involved in interfering' with the upbringing of her great-grandson: 'I darn't speak t'Gordon rough. I remember one day she slapped me across the jaw. For hittin' him. Said I was cruel.' After six years she moved out again into her own house, but continued to visit daily. And when the old lady finally died suddenly in her eighties, she felt utterly bereft. 'I wis lost for a while, because I had went there every day. When she died, I just felt I had naewhere t'go. Cause I hadna made any friends. I just kept the bairns t'myself an' went doon an' did her work ... I suffered maist fae her dying, than her ain family did.'[41]

It is above all those children who were cared for actively by their grandparents who recall them in depth and with strong feeling. But the acute tension in this account is exceptional. It was in fact rare for a grandchild to be so entirely dependant on grandparents, even after death or desertion. Normally at least one parent remained in the home, or if not, close by; and in many cases aunts of the parents' generation were involved in caring. Larger family size alone usually made for a very different situation from that of a grandchild brought up alone by a grandparent today. We may conclude with a less unusual example, from a South London family.

Here the father was an Irishman, a stableman, drunken and violent, who eventually deserted, leaving the mother with her own parents. They were originally Wiltshire country people, the grandmother and mother being both illiterate, and the grandfather a blacksmith. The grandparents took on responsibility for the house and the children together: 'my mother went to work all the week, she never done no cooking.' It is the grandfather, however, who emerges most clearly in his granddaughter's recollection. He was evidently an ingenious man, and after retiring from the smithy would earn from carpentry:

> Man next door, he used to say he wanted—some chest of drawers. He went and got the wood, he done it all .... Christmastime, he used to go and get some wood, and he'd make engines, great big engines and ... tip-up cart with two wheels. He used to ask us for the pearl off our coats, collars, put on the horses, make 'em all. And I used to take 'em round the pubs and put 'em up for raffles for Christmas. And got him his beer money for Christmas.

He also made a creeper-covered trellis in front of the house door
and did all the garden, 'do all the flowers.' Inside, he 'used to
make all the mince pies for Christmas,' peel the potatoes for
Sunday lunch, and every morning make breakfast: 'you never had
to get up and make a cup of tea of a morning, he'd get up. He'd
fetch us all up a cup of tea in bed with a bit of toast.' He also lit the
fires; and 'we never knew what it was to clean boots or shoes. He
used to clean all our shoes and put them along the floor. Then as
we got older, about 16 or 17, we used to give a couple of bob at
the end of the week to keep all our shoes. That was his beer
money, his bacca money.' He was fun with the children when they
were younger, too, telling them stories about life in the countryside, taking them out—'go all over the place with him, yes'—and
seeing them to bed: 'he always give us a piggyback up the stairs to
bed.' And when they married, he gave each grandchild a wedding
present from his own handiwork. 'He used to make us a rolling
pin, a dough board and a rubbing board . . . They lasted donkey's
years. Donkey's years. Yes, he was a wonderful carpenter . . . Good
old man' our grandfather was. You know, really good old boy.'[42]

It would be unwise to suggest that any of these remembered
families can stand as typical. On the contrary, the most telling
message which these interviews have to convey is the great variety
not only in circumstance, but also in responses to later life of the
older generation in the earlier part of this century.

Autobiographies and interviews, each constrained both by what
children could see and also by what they would remember as
significant, offer inevitably partial glimpses of the experience of
ageing. They can only hint, for example, at the group activities of
older people which excluded a child, or the pain of bereavement,
or the loneliness of those without family, which then as now, must
have been widespread. But put together, they certainly can help
us to fill out the picture of the earlier experience of ageing. They
bring home the inequality of material conditions: at the one extreme old men in filthy lodgings choping a few sticks to keep
warm, and at the other the lady of the manor supported by
servants and a companion in her immaculate drawing-room. They
emphasize the importance, both for keeping independence and
for helping their descendants, of owning even a small amount of
property and passing down specialized occupational skills. They
show how retirement, earlier a privilege of the middle classes,

becomes a general and sometimes threatening expectation. Working grandfathers, originally the rule, become the exception, and working grandmothers rarer still. They suggest some of the typically simple pleasures of later life in the past, such as keeping parrots or pigeons, gardening or baking, playing dominoes, drinking a nightly glass of porter at home, or going out to gossip with old workmates.

Most of all, they give us a unique insight into the quality of family relationships in later life, and the variety of ways in which they could be constructed. We encounter the contrasts between at one extreme domesticated grandfathers, and at the other, elderly couples at war. We can see how family memory is socially shaped, and also the willingness to incorporate substitutes, not always related in any way, for absent grandparents. We are able to trace the patterns of practical aid and its mutuality between the generations, and in an especially full way, of house-sharing. Above all we can observe how closeness between grandparents and grandchildren can develop: the significance of visiting, and of practical caring, but equally of personality. It becomes abundantly clear from these accounts that then as now, family support was a two-way process, and that responding to a crisis could result in intense friction as well as in deep affection. Grandparents could not count on natural loyalty: rather, they had to positively create their roles by winning a child's affection. So some were hated as insensitive and disciplinarian, while others were remembered as models or guiding influences through relationships of striking tenderness and intimacy.

In short, in the past as in the present, both through fortune and also through choice, the experience of old age could differ sharply. At one extreme were those so inert, so withdrawn into themselves, that they gave out nothing to the young. At the other were old women and old men up and about, actively using old skills, adapting and developing new ones, able to play and to care and confide; still open to new love from the young.

Part Two
Now

5
Sources of Difference in Ways of Living

WE have reached the present. Let us begin at the simplest level. We asked all our interviewees to describe how they spent a typical day and a typical week. Nothing could bring home more forcibly the diversity of ways of living the later years. With some, the description was a few bare lines; with others, a meandering discussion as elaborate as the variety of their days.

A lonely bank manager's widow described her typical day as 'sitting here.' Louise Barrington has no regular routine at all. Her time of getting up 'varied; it depends whether I sleep well or whether I don't.' She shops 'when I feel like it . . . I just go out when I want, and if it's a nice day, I might walk to the shops . . . I like to get some fresh air.' Helen Burnsall, a collieryman's widow, had little more to say:

> Well, at the moment, I haven't had much of a day. I'm up by half past seven and I mean—there isn't the same work to do. Like, when you're cooking for two and then you come down to cooking for one, you don't bother, do you? And I go out in the morning, if I can. I can go into the town for five pence, with the elderly card—bus pass—and to Sheffield for the same, five pence. Just go round, have a coffee. Sometimes you pick something up that you really want and you meet people. And that passes a morning—well, into the afternoon. I go out somewhere in the morning because I think that if I didn't, I think I should never get out.
>
> And then in the afternoon, I have gone for a walk when it's been nice. And then I haven't gone out in the evening. Only when I've gone dancing, on a Thursday night, down in the next village.[1]

Both suffer the special loneliness of widowhood. Yet by no

means all widows live such apparently meagre lives. Contrast Sally Peel:

> I get up about nine o'clock. *Monday* I do my washing, and then at dinnertime I go and make somebody a dinner—one of the sick people I'm looking after.
> Then I come home. Sometimes I go and have a game of bowls. Or do me work, or do the garden—but that's killing me. Or I go to a Monday afternoon club [at the church].
> And then I go playing whist at night. I go to the Old Folk's Clubs.
> I go to the Conservative on the *Tuesday* nights . . .
> I go playing whist *Wednesday* afternoon, at the Old Age Pensioners at Timperleys, that's a lovely club.
> And then I go and sit with Mrs Simpson at night . . .
> *Thursday* night I go to Nine Elms, at Timperleys—that's a lovely club, an Old Age Pensioner's Club, and we play cards. That's Thursday.
> *Friday* I go out with Martha [a friend]. We go bowling Wednesday afternoon or Friday afternoon.
> And then I go and sit with Mrs Simpson Friday night.
> *Saturday* I go to the Old Age Pension at Lytham Court . . . to the Club. We have a cup of tea, and a vicar comes.
> And then Saturday night, I go to Timperleys, the Old Age Pensioners—I don't know what I'll do when I've got no car—and I take somebody with me . . .
> *Sundays* I go now to Woolton Parish Church.[2]

There are equally striking differences in the descriptions of routine from married couples. Meg Jacks, wife of a redundant factory worker, simply said, 'We haven't got a routine, because Tom doesn't have to go to work, and we can get up when we like.' She goes into the city to shop once a month. 'But normally we just get up when we feel like it and do the housework. And Tom does a bit of gardening . . . There's nothing really to tell you.' Norah Allen, a retired postman's wife, gave a barely longer account. Weekdays and weekends they get up at nine and have breakfast,

> Then he goes in and washes up and sorts the kitchen out and I do the lounge and bedroom, or he'll make the bed with me if he's finished. Get the housework done. Then if we've any shop-

ping to do then we'll go. If the weather's decent we'll walk to
the shops; if not we'll get the car and go.

Then come back and have a bit of lunch—a sandwich or
something, nothing much. Then we just . . . I'll sit and knit or
read; put the tellie on if there's anything on.[3]

A working wood-machinist's wife who still has a part-time chipshop job has a much more elaborate week:

> *Monday* I work. And this friend of mine comes down like I say
> for a couple of hours then in the afternoon . . . piece of cake
> and that. And then sometimes we might go shopping together
> . . . and then I don't really do anything much on a Monday.
> Perhaps put some washing in. Don't do a lot really—not
> every week. It just depends. Things crop up. You know, like they
> ring me and say, 'Would you fancy going here—there?' Every
> week's different in a way.
>
> Now *Tuesday*, I've always worked Tuesday but I've knocked it
> off now. Give me a bit more time to meself. Like I say I've been
> to market today and not done much really. Just tidied round a
> bit upstairs, bits, things in general; then I've been to market.
> Come back, had a tea, and that's that again . . .
>
> Now tomorrow (*Wednesday*) I may go somewhere with our
> Julie [daughter]. She'll ring me in the morning. Have a ride
> somewhere. It just depends what day's like.
>
> *Thursday* I work all day. Dinner and tea in chip-shop. . . . It's
> hard work there 'cos I cook . . .
>
> *Friday* I mind twins [her grandchildren].
>
> *Saturday* I mind twins.
>
> *Sunday* I go to baths. Then just depends what weather's like.[4]

All these answers have been chosen deliberately from old people
who in simple social terms seem to be very similar. They are all
women, and except for the very first widow, they have all married
manual workers. Their variety of approaches to daily life has more
to do with spirit than with material circumstance.

They do however share one good fortune. They are all in reasonable physical health. This gives them a choice in life. One last
account is worth adding at this point from a retired cleaner, married to an invalid ex-miner. Agnes Dunbar has a notable advantage
in three supportive children living close by. But she is now almost

confined to her home, doubly trapped: scarcely able to walk outside herself, or to get away from her deeply miserable husband:

So you get up in the mornin.' Then soon as Mr Dunbar
wakens, he complains about his arthritis. He complains all the
time. Some nights I don't get a good night's sleep. In fact I'd to
go into the other bed last night, he's so restless. And now when
he turns, he can't turn as you or I would turn. He's bumpin' on
the bed to get round and it's not very handy.

But—eh we get up, and I have a cup of tea first. We make a
nice pot o' tea. We have a wee pot o' tea. And then we sit an'
drink tea. I look at the headlines—I can see the black headlines,
after that I've had it. And Mr Dunbar reads the paper and
maybe picks his horses. He'll maybe go upstairs if he feels he
wants t'stretch his legs, and he'll have a wee walk up and down.
And while he's up I just tidy around and wash up the dishes. By
the time he's ready for coming back down, we'll have a bit o'
breakfast . . .

And then, well I have that home help two days . . . Then some
days, we'll sit and listen to the news: the one o'clock news. And
if she's not here, I go up and maybe spread the beds up and see
if there's any wee bits o' washin' to do . . .

I do the essentials. I've got to wash the dishes and make a
meal and maybe spread the bed up . . . I just don't feel the
energy to work now . . . [Her daughter shops for her and helps
cook.] The only thing I go out for—I go to the fruiterer's and I
get a bit o' fruit off Nessie, cause she stops at the door for
me . . . I get the eggs off Nessie, the fruit girl . . .

But sometimes I can go down to Irene's [daughter] if the
weather's good. If I ring the phone they watch for me comin'
and help me to get across the road. Go down there maybe on a
Saturday or a *Sunday* and have a wee cup o' coffee. Then they
bring me back . . .

Then he usually, if the racing's on he watches the racin' . . . In
the meantime, I just sometimes sit and have a wee rest, after
I've tidied up. Then we make the dinner. We have the dinner
about four o'clock.

When Peter [son: a teacher] comes in from school, he always
has a cup o' coffee and a wee blether. Then he goes home for his
dinner. And then—see sometimes people come out and in and

distract ye . . . And then at night, I'll maybe have Melvyn [son] for an hour. Then if he doesn't come the night, he'll come the morra night, cause he does a bit o' the booking wi' his dad. So he comes up pay the coupon . . .

Then we watch the news at 6 o'clock. Then if there's anything on tellie fair enough. If there's not, sometimes I go up and play my tape, my talking machine [book] . . . I really like them because they take you away for a wee while, ye get ye out yer environment . . .

Aye sometimes I feel them long [the days] . . . I haven't the initiative nor the energy . . . Ye're stuck in and ye lose interest . . . Ye're waitin' on somebody else maybe doin' something for ye, because ye're no fit t'do it.

Then of course Mr Dunbar does nothing . . . If I let go like Mr Dunbar—sometimes he just lies there and he only answers people—I would hate to be like that . . .[5]

Agnes Dunbar's daily struggle is one of the most difficult of those described to us. But she has *not* let go.

The most extraordinary accounts are all to come, extraordinary because they illustrate in a *positive* way the creativity with which some people use these later years. But by no means all of them. The men and women who told us their stories are each unique. There are many different ways in which we can and will divide them up: men and women, older and younger, married and widowed, comfortable and badly-off. But the way which seems to spring most immediately from the life stories themselves is as individual personalities.

There are the sad ones: the lonely widows, the mothers with empty nests, the househusband's depressed partner, the redundant workers, the proud, isolated ex-golfer. There are the useful nurses and their friends. There are the workaholics, the rags-to-riches businessman and the unstoppable worker. There are the comfortable couples retired to the country: the winemakers, the Devon villagers, the Metropolitans in the Cotswolds. There are the couples locked in bitterness: the captive housewife, the reluctant grandmother, the jealous, unforgiving wife. There are the companionable: the saloon-bar widower and the bored Irish club-widow. There are the spent carers. Some can only stand on their own: the domesticated fisherman, the rescued waitress, and the

sex-starved pitman. There are the astonishing creators: the venturing widow, the Green Belt seamstress, and the floral champion.
And there are the lovers: the post office couple in their garden,
and the two dancing couples. In one way or another, we shall meet
them all.

Before that, however, some general comments. First of all it is
worth making a rough division between those who seem depressed
or unhappy, and those who convey a strong sense of contentment
and purpose in their lives. This of course involves some rough
judgements, and the largest group end up somewhere in between.
But it is striking, and heartening, to find that a third fall into the
contented group, and they outnumber the quarter who are discontented (see Table 1).

When we look for obvious reasons why people may have fallen
one way or the other, it soon becomes clear that none of the
simpler explanations work. Men and women are equally often
positively happy, although there are proportionately somewhat
more overtly discontented women. More surprisingly, those who
are younger seem to be less happy than those who are older: we
shall return to the reasons for this shortly. Those who are still in
their first marriages present their joint lives less positively than the
widowed do in retrospect; only the few who are remarried appear
notably contented as couples. And while the middle-class men and
women are the least often unhappy, they are also distinctly less
often positively happy. The working class divide much more sharply between those who are contented and those who are not, with
fewer in between.

Is it just then a question of individual character? Certainly our
interviews support the view which has been put forward by Rex
Taylor and Graeme Ford, that in later years the usual class boxes
are of decreasing value in predicting how people live. They see
later life as a time when people have a special freedom of choice,
just because they are not tied down to jobs which impose a
relentless rhythm on their lives. Without this new freedom, the
variety of ways of living which we encountered would not be
possible.

But some are more free than others. And this is where earlier
experience, including social-class background and occupation, does
have a crucial influence. It works in a number of different ways.

First of all there are the unequal chances of continuing life itself.

This shows in the fact that those who had been in manual occupations were heavily concentrated among the under-seventy-year-olds. Equally striking, if we look at those who were the children of manual workers, as well as those who remained in the working class to the end of their lives, we can see the toll of death in their families. Although a younger group, they had already lost a third of their brothers and sisters. The older group born into the middle class, by contrast, had lost only a quarter of their siblings.

It is possible to see from some of these life stories how this difference came about. Several working-class husbands were chronically ill, or had already died, from accidents or illnesses directly resulting from their work: two had been miners, and four others had become clinically depressed following redundancy. Another factor could be diet. Two working-class wives were especially seriously overweight and both were unhappy about it. Yet one had even given up dancing after seeing a video of herself at a wedding-party—'I don't feel as though it's very dignified'—and they simply joke about their mutual dice with death: 'we have a laugh about whether he's going to kill himself first with smoking or me with overweight, don't we?'[6] A family who ran a fried-food café had a stunning mortality, with three out of four siblings dead by their sixties. More certainly, smoking and alcohol take a heavy toll. The regular pub-goers were nearly all working class, and nearly all in the younger group; and their lives stand out as inharmonious or discontented. As a whole the depressed group consisted overwhelmingly of younger working-class men and women. Depression in later life is associated with a more than doubling of death rates—both because illness brings depression, and because the depressed are more vulnerable to fatal illness. They lack the sense of meaning and the self-esteem which are essential for life itself—and which are indeed manifest in the older survivors.

This is what explains the much sharper bifurcation in the working-class group. These men and women have had a rougher life. They still do. With no more than state pension and supplementary benefit to live on, it is a struggle to find enough for necessities like heating, clothing, or shoes. Other studies have remarked on the appearance of burnt-out 'inactivity' of so many retired working men, their lack of retirement plans or ambitions: 'We've got no ambitions . . . no high-falutin' ideas about what we should do or what we shouldn't do . . . Just settled down to a life of tranquillity. I think you survive longer if you do.'[7] But in fact a sense of purpose is as important in later as in earlier life, and those who lack it are less well defended against depression. Many of these younger working-class men and women will follow their siblings into early death. The danger signs are there, in unhealthy tastes and collapsed spirits. They have been near-broken by the battering they and their bodies have been given. The working-class men and women who outlive them do so just because they are strong people, mentally and physically. They are survivors. They have already made the most of tough times and they know how to go on doing so.

For the middle classes, by contrast, with more money and also more in touch with professional opinion, life has been consistently more comfortable. They continue to enjoy better incomes. While over half the working-class men and women have no car, the middle-class all have their own transport except for two widows who do not drive. They can talk incessantly on the telephone if they wish, whereas some of the working class had no telephone (one couple had just had theirs installed as a Golden Wedding present from their family). None of the middle class could have said, like a retired London lorry driver who spends most of his time 'sitting at home' rather than going out, 'I can't go—where can you go? If you go out anywhere, you have to spend the money and money we haven't got.'[8]

With better incomes and more saved, these middle-class men and women have much more living space. Equally important, they can pay for others—sometimes in their own age group—to help look after it, releasing them for other activities. Alice Cleminson, a banker's widow with a generous index-linked pension is a keen golfer, but her gardener looks after the heavy work outside on Mondays, and on Fridays she has a cleaner for the house. 'She just cleans through for me. It stops me stooping a lot, that's the problem. I know I shouldn't perhaps bother with a help here, she's nearly as old as I am anyway, but she's marvellous, and she'll clean through and hoover. And if I start stooping, it makes my back bad.'[9] Consequently at one extreme of the social spectrum we find a retired business couple living in part of a beautiful country manor, furnished with valuable antiques, and with a spacious garden outside; at the other, an ex-pitman in a bedsitter, sleeping on a folding bed. Where marriages are less than perfect, space to get away from each other and the resources to follow independent pursuits can make for a tolerable retirement, while a couple forced together would live in explosive resentment. The middle-class marriages are not the happiest, but there are none as bitter as several in the working class.

It is easier to make positive plans for retirement when you have resources to realize them. The middle classes had much more often chosen a new place in which to create their retirement life. None lived in the big cities. Without exception, they were to be found close to the sea, or in small country towns, or in villages. With their own cars they could enjoy the countryside, and at the same time the facilities of neighbouring towns. In some of these areas, such as the south-west, there were active networks of cultural associations dominated by older people: 'there are a lot of retired people in our village and you naturally join together . . . We're a very active village. I think we keep each other motivated.'[10]

The working-class men and women, on the other hand, could move house much less easily. One couple, for example, lived in a council house which they had taken over from the wife's parents. They described the estate as formerly 'a very nice neighbourhood,' with 'handpicked' tenants such as railway workers; but now it had many families of the unemployed 'and unfortunately they don't seem to care for the property.' But there was no question of them moving. And the less well-off families who had no car were also much less able to travel even short distances from where they lived, either to visit family or for their own leisure. Thus a couple living on the edge of Edinburgh felt that there was little they could go out to see: for example, 'there's nae pictures noo in Dalkeith, ye'd hae to go away to Edinburgh noo, and . . . it wis pretty expensive to go into Edinburgh, it'd cost me £1.70.'[11]

This ability to move easily is not all gain. It is noticeable how much more difficult the middle classes found it to keep in touch with their children. Only half saw them at least weekly, and several only every two or three months. Three-quarters of the intermediate and working class saw their children weekly, and many of them daily (see Table 2). In the industrail north and Scotland this was an almost universal pattern, although it was less strong in London, where families tended to be more scattered about the city. This difference was especially striking since the middle class, being older, had more practical need for the support of their families. They were now playing the price of earlier success, both as their children moved to pursue careers, and as they themselves moved away from children to realize their own retirement dreams.

Even in this matter, however, the middle classes had more resources to give them choice. If they really wished to, they could move again. One family had specially divided a large old house so that the three generations could live under the same roof, but as separate households. They could also pay for professional caring when one of them needed this. None of the middle class had allowed their own later years to be blighted by personally caring for parents who lived into their nineties.

Yet none of these resources, material or cultural, can guarantee happiness in these later years. On the contrary, just because the middle-class men and women had lived much of their lives in comfort, and had always had relative freedom to shape their own lives, they seem to have less often found later life a time of special fulfilment. It is perhaps no accident that the two most contented among them had both fought their own way from working-class childhoods to their present comfort. The rest took it more for granted. Their social advantages undoubtedly provided a buffer against serious unhappiness—but also expectations hard to realize.

Contrasts in both resources and expectations also shape the differences in quality of later life between men and women. Most older men continue to enjoy higher incomes than women. They can escape on their own to the pub or the club, where women on their own are much less generally accepted. If there is a car, a man is likely to be its only driver. Above all, just as they went out to work throughout their adult lives, most men continue to expect to leave the house after retirement—if only going into the garden—for some form of work or leisure. In a recent study of couples in later middle age Jennifer Mason remarks how 'most of the men talked with gusto about their outdoor activities, but they also spoke of frustration when the weather was bad or during the winter.' Older married women of this ˙generation, by contrast, have typically gone out to paid work intermittently, while remaining continuously housewives and mothers. When such a woman's husband retires she still feels responsible for supporting him and will often put his fulfilment before her own: accepting his pressure—explicit or not—for her too to retire, to be around more, and at the same time for his presence in what had been her own domestic space. 'You can't just go and do things like you used to. You're not free. You have a conscience.'[12]

Such differing expectations have a direct bearing on the greater unhappiness revealed by the women than the men we recorded. Working-class men were battered by work and the loss of it; but women of all classes seemed vulnerable in a similar way to marriage. Marriage is certainly crucial to older men: indeed widowers are markedly more vulnerable to early death than widows. Thus the relative rarity of lonely widowers biases the picture. But it was strikingly rare for men to focus on dissatisfaction in marriage in their accounts. All the unhappy or depressed women, by contrast, described themselves either as locked into unhappy marriages, or as mourning the loss of a husband.

Both the making of a bad marriage, and recovery from the loss of a good one, depend on many factors, from expectations, resources, and opportunity, to individual personality and ability to relate to others. There were successful marriages in all social groups. But it is well established that earlier marriages are the most prone to failure, and worth noting that this was true of these life stories too. The most discontented group had married at an average age of 22; the better adjusted at 24; and the happily married at 25. The difference was much more noticeable still with the small number of second marriages. All were relatively successful, but the earlier remarriages less so, while for the happiest the average age at remarriage was 51 (see Table 3). Both in choosing partners and in adapting to them, those who marry later may gain from longer experience of social relationships.

There were early marriages to be found in all social groups, but there was a slight tendency, in line with national figures, for working-class couples to marry a year or so earlier. Working-class wives also bore more children (see Table 4). In marriage, however, class background is probably much less important than family background. A quarter of those we recorded had at least one of their own children divorced, and these children were overwhelmingly the offspring of the most unsatisfactory marriages. Equally, some of those whose marriages were not happy had themselves suffered in childhood, from an exceptionally harsh father, for example, or from the death of a parent.

One of the most unhappily married women, Meg Jacks, was part of a three-generational pattern. Her daughter Julie has now left a drunken, violent husband. But the roots go back at least to Meg's own childhood. Her father, a miner, had died in his forties, when she was just 14. Very soon her widowed mother

> started going with this fellow. Not long after. Well I thought a lot about me dad and I suppose he spoiled me . . . Well I—didn't like it. I didn't take to it at all. And she married him. And she moved in with him, into his home. And left this elder sister of mine in her home there. But I stopped with her. I wouldn't go over anyway.
>
> Things got—this sister, you see, I only realized when I got older—she couldn't keep me because I hadn't started work then. Her husband was in the war. So I finally drifted back to me mum and this fella.
>
> But I never liked him. And I think that's how you get married sooner than you would do really. Because I weren't comfortable you see with him.

Meg married at twenty. 'I was glad to get away. And then I wished I hadn't have.' Nor did the trouble in the family stop here. The wife of one of her two brothers had a child by another man during the war. 'They drifted back again. But I think she was always ashamed to—you never saw a lot of her, they sort of broke away through that. Like my parents didn't like the thought of her coming back into the family after doing that.' And one of Meg's two sisters has an illegitimate granddaughter, whom she unsuccessfully attempted to mother: the girl was 'knocking a lad' at 14 and stealing from within the home.[13] A family tree, in short, overloaded with bad starts.

Later life is built on the cumulative experience of the years, going back to childhood. It is far from a fresh beginning. Some start with far more advantages than others. But as these stories will show, there are many who have the spirit and the ingenuity to kindle a good fire from a few sticks.

6

As Old as You Feel

'IT doesn't matter how old you are, it's how you feel, isn't it?' said Geoffrey Kedleston, who had worked most of his life as a gentleman's butler, and then bought the village post office and ran it with his son. He was 86. 'I've never felt my age,' he said. And his 57-year-old son added: 'I don't think of you as being old, even though you're 86.' Geoffrey Kedleston thought age depended in part on physical abilities ('All the while I was able to do active jobs, I wasn't old') and attitude ('one person might be old at sixty, and another won't be old till he's eighty, or ninety perhaps'). His son remarked: 'Your father would have felt very old when he got to sixty. I can remember him with a big beard and being very tottery.' The son himself had thought he would feel old at fifty, but having reached that age, he still felt young: 'I think as years go by, you feel younger all the time.' Jackie Stephens at seventy said: 'I don't feel any different than I did when I was sixty, really. I've known people who seemed a lot older than me at forty. It's a state of mind, I think—age.'[1]

Much of what those we interviewed had to say about themselves and their own experience of ageing calls into question commonly held stereotypes of older people. Recent commentators have highlighted the various ways in which 'the elderly' are identified with the decrepit, disabled, and dependent, portrayed as 'senile, rigid in thought and manner, old-fashioned in morality and skills,' or 'asexual, intellectually rigid, unproductive and disengaged,' or as 'insignificant, unintelligent, incapable....'[2] The most common stereotypes of older people were summarized by the American sociologist who coined the term 'ageism' to describe the prejudice and discrimination experienced by old people:

Old people think and move slowly. They are not creative and can't learn, change or grow. They dislike innovation and new ideas. They enter a second childhood and are egocentric. They become irritable and cantankerous, yet shallow and enfeebled.

They live in the past behind the times. Their minds wander and
they reminisce. They are also often stricken with disease which
restricts their movements. They have lost and cannot replace
friends, spouse, job, status, power, influence and income. They
have lost their desire and capacity for sex. Feeble, uninterest-
ing, they await death, a burden to society, their families,
themselves.[3]

Stereotypes of old people are usually negative—'offensive, un-
lovely and obnoxious' as Dr Alex Comfort puts it. But they can
also be positive and still be offensive and obnoxious. Thus there
are stereotypes which sentimentalize old people as 'sweet' and
'kindly'—the 'old dears,' the 'grannies.' Such old people are 'supposed to stay out of the way, sit in their rocking chairs and enjoy
the golden years. They are expected to be inactive, invisible and
happy.'[4]

Whether they are positive or perjorative, the stereotypes create
the impression that 'the elderly are somehow different from our
present and future selves and therefore not subject to the same
desires, concerns or fears.' And they 'allow the younger generation
to see old people as different from themselves, thus they subtly
cease to identify with their elders as human beings.'[5] Stereotypes
create the 'notion that people cease to be people, cease to be the
same people or become people of a distinct and inferior kind by
virtue of having lived a specified number of years.' The reality,
however, is according to Alex Comfort very different:

> old people are in fact young people inhabiting old bodies and
> confronted with the physical problems of reduced vigour, chang-
> ing appearance, and although many escape these, specific disabi-
> lities affecting such things as sight and agility.... Old people are
> people who have lived a certain number of years, and *that is
> all.*[6]

Certainly it would be hard to find a more decisive refutation
of the usual stereotypes than we were given by those we interviewed. Whatever their chronological age, whatever their appearance, whatever their health and physical ability, and whatever
their awareness of all these aspects of themselves, they almost
unanimously did not think of themselves as old.

We asked an open-ended question, 'How do you think of yourself now?,' with a follow-up, 'Do you think of yourself as old?' In

fact, it proved necessary to use a variety of formulations of these questions to suit the readiness or reluctance of people to talk about ageing, as the open-ended question usually did not produce a reply about the person's experience of ageing. It also proved necessary to avoid asking the questions in a way that suggested that the interviewers regarded those being interviewed as old. Because, although that was indeed the category into which they had been put on the basis of chronological age and 'generation,' they themselves clearly did not think of themselves as old. The response to the direct question, 'Do you think of yourself as old?' was an emphatic and virtually unanimous, resounding 'No,' regardless of the age of the person interviewed. Out of a total of 43 people whose ages ranged from 58 to 86, 36 replied with a categorical 'No.'[7]

Only two people actually said 'Yes,' they thought of themselves as old. Barbara Williamson, aged 76, said, 'Touch wood, I'm not too bad in myself really,' but on several occasions when asked if she thought she was old, she said, 'Yes, I'm getting old and fat, I am,' or 'Yes, I've slowed down quite a lot.' She said it was 'my legs':

> I went down the street and I got some things for Mrs Glyn and I came back and I went in her house and I said, 'Dunno what's the matter with my bloomin' knees today,' I said, 'they just won't go.' 'Ah,' she said, 'you're getting old.'

She described herself as only being able 'to hobble' and said that the doctor had diagnosed arthritis. But she had also 'got a bad foot' which she'd had 'all me life,' which required her to have her shoes specially made, one size 3, one size 5, so her limited mobility was not solely the result of arthritis. And although she thought of herself as old, she had only stopped working at the age of 74. She was, however, one of the few people interviewed who said she felt 'more comfortable with people of my own age.'[8]

Louise Barrington, at 82, was the only person out of 43 who was adamantly and firmly negative about growing older. 'As a young person, I didn't want to live to be old. I didn't want to get old.' She had a friend in a residential old people's home:

> I visit a person that's in a home now. That can't do for herself, and yet her brain's better than mine, she's a very clever person, but she's stuck in this home and can't look after herself, and I think, 'That's going to come to me one day.'

She had no particular ailments and was in good health, but had not been able to rebuild her life since her bank manager husband had died. 'A bloody nuisance,' she said when asked for the most significant feature of getting old. She liked 'nothing' about being her age, and she particularly disliked 'being old, and getting old.' And when asked, 'What would you most like to do in the time ahead?,' she said, 'I don't want any.'9

This woman's views about ageing and old age, while they might represent one of the common stereotypes of the 'elderly' as miserable, were in fact totally untypical of the other people we interviewed. And although there were four other people who did not respond with a categorical 'No' when asked if they thought of themselves as old, neither did they answer with an unequivocal 'Yes.' They qualified their response. Geoffrey Kedleston, aged 86, said: 'At times I do, yes,' and described taking it easy and going slowly in the morning on waking, so as not to feel dizzy. A seventy-year-old woman side-stepped the question by saying 'I don't think about age, I think you get a shock sometimes when you begin to think about age, so we don't think about it. That's the best plan.' An eighty-year-old woman said she thought of herself as old 'now and again,' but compared herself favourably with other people of her own age whom she described as being 'old ladies.' 'Children probably think I'm an old lady,' she said, 'and when you're forty, anyone of eighty is old.' And a sixty-year-old woman said: 'I'd describe myself as getting older—it's about what you look like and what have you. I still don't think I'm an old woman. I don't even feel I'm approaching an old woman.'10

Even the ones who qualified their response were basically saying that they did not regard themselves as old, and those who admitted to some sense of themselves as old covered a very wide age range: they were aged sixty, 65, seventy, eighty, and 86. In other words, chronological age could not be said to be the factor that determined what they thought. 'Being old' appeared again to be partly connected with physical abilities and still more to do with how they felt.

Being old also appeared to be relative to people of other ages: it was how 'older people' appeared to young people and people in mid-life: how older people regarded those even older. In these cases, it seemed again to be less a matter of chronological age that

categorized people as old, more their appearance, physical abilities, and the preconceived attitudes and images attached to a
chronological age by others. A younger person may equate eighty
with 'being old,' while an eighty-year-old does not.

The most common refrain of the 36 people who did not think of
themselves as old was 'I don't feel old.' This was expressed in a
variety of forms. People in their sixties said:

> It doesn't bother me, you've got to grow old and that's the end
> of it. (May Drysdale, 61)
>
> No, I don't look on me as old. (Ida Lane, 61)
>
> No, just older. (Fred Doggett, 62)
>
> No. (Fred and Gail Stone, 66 and 63)
>
> No I don't feel old, I realize I am old at 67 because I've got a
> pension book. But I think life just went on at its pace. I never
> thought of getting older. (Brenda Steel, 67, still working part-
> time as an agency nurse)[11]

People in their seventies had a similar response. One woman of
seventy said: 'I'd like to think I'm twenty years younger than I am.
They say to me, "What? you're never seventy." I've got young
ideas. I like to think young.' Another seventy-year-old said, no,
she did not think of herself as old—'Only for the fact they you can't
do what you'd like to do. You want to, but you haven't got the
energy.' A seventy-year-old man said: 'When you talk of age, I
think . . . I don't quite know, how to put it . . . I think you're as old
as you feel. It depends on one's outlook, I think. He said that he
'felt sixty.' Another seventy-year-old said: 'I'm seventy, but I don't
feel it. Only when you see it down on paper, you think, oh, that's
me. I've never been bothered about it really.' A 75-year-old man
said, 'I know I am old, but I don't feel it. I feel younger than I am,
much younger. I don't think about it.' A 76-year-old who was in
very poor health stated, 'No I don't [think of myself as old],' and
two 79-year-olds simply said, 'I don't feel old.' It was, as Rudi
Fine, aged 79, pointed out, a matter of 'getting old without getting
older.'

> You don't feel getting older. You're moving about and doing
> things and you don't think of age then, you see. It's only when
> the parts wear out that you begin to think of age. That's when

you know you're getting older, but you don't feel getting older—
not at all. Getting old is a process and if you're alert and you're
physically well, there's no such thing as getting old.[12]

One might have expected people in their eighties to admit to
thinking of themselves as old, but this proved decisively not to be
the case. An eighty-year-old woman said: 'Not really, I don't feel
my age. It's just my legs that feel old, not me head. I don't feel
nearly eighty.' Leonard Seldon, an 84-year-old, still-active walker,
said: 'No I don't worry about it. I think if nanny [his own mother]
can live to a hundred I can get to ninety or something like that.'
He referred to a Health Visitor and District Nurse visiting him,
chatting and saying they 'didn't believe' he was as old as he was.
This had pleased him:

> It's quite amazing. Because this bloke next door is ten years
> younger than I am and we have an occasional game of golf and
> he isn't in the same street. Not now, even. It sounds a bit
> boastful that, doesn't it? I don't mean it to be. But, no, more
> often than not I don't think of myself as old. People just don't
> believe it and I don't say anything now. I don't think me girl-
> friend knows how old I am, really. Shan't tell her either! No—I
> don't think of meself as old. I don't worry about—I don't think
> age matters and I get this from nanny having watched her so
> much. I might have a very short span. I might have a long span,
> I don't know. As long as I'm enjoying it. At the moment I can
> drive, I can go out and my sight is good and—you know, by and
> large, I haven't got very much to complain about. You get these
> little things that annoy you and you think you're beginning to
> decay a little bit, you know. You get a bit thinner on the top and
> a few more hairs less but—I mean, I'm capable. I can do it. I
> can do me gardening. I can dig. I can do everything, so, it's not
> too bad. There'll come a time when I will have to pack it to one
> side, but I'm not going to.
>
> I think a lot of it is mental—I'm sure it is. It would be easy for
> me to say—I must admit I'd be tempted . . . I've got my set of
> golf clubs out there in the garage and I think well, 'I don't know,
> I might as well pack it in. I've finished with these now, you
> know. I shan't bother.' Quite easy for me to say that. But I
> won't. Because I'm going to play some more golf, I know that.
> But it's a matter of—you know, other people might say 'Well I

know people younger than you who have packed this game in long ago'—well I'm not concerned with other people. I will still maintain my position and I think I'm right.[13]

This soliloquy encapsulates many of the contradictions expressed about ageing by all of the people interviewed, whether they were sixty or seventy or eighty plus. Scarcely any of them thought of themselves as old. There was an apparent contradiction —a kind of disconnection, therefore, between how they looked, how they were, how they felt, and what they thought.

One of the questions asked was 'As you've got older, what changes have you noticed in your appearance?' People's responses indicated the predictable signs of physical ageing. They referred to getting fatter or thinner, or to a redistribution of weight, of getting fatter round the middle, and 'flabby skin' (especially for the women, under the arms). They mentioned more lines on their faces, wrinkles, wearing glasses, losing teeth, thinning hair, going grey or white. Some people mentioned getting smaller, rounding shoulders, slowing down: 'We're not so fast on our feet as we used to be,' said a 63-year-old couple. 'I'm older looking for one thing,' said an 81-year-old woman. And a 78-year-old woman said: 'I think I look a bit older, yes, you look at a few photographs and you think "I've got a big scraggy there."' (She was referring to her neck.)[14]

It was interesting to note, however, that the physical signs of ageing did not fit a rigid chronological pattern, any more than the feelings people had. Physical changes occurred gradually, almost imperceptibly, catching people unawares. 'They've crept on,' said a 71-year-old woman of her wrinkles. People in their sixties were likely to describe the same changes in their appearance as people in their eighties. And the majority of people of all ages over sixty said they were not particularly conscious of the changes in their appearance, nor concerned about them. When asked if they were conscious of their age generally or at particular times with particular people, most people simply said 'No.' Some said, 'I never think about it.' One man replied: 'It makes me wonder sometimes when I find a little depreciation of the body—when I'm not quite so quick to get up.' He was 84. One woman said: 'No—except when I look in the mirror—I never used to have these wrinkles.' She was 71. And another woman said: 'No, nothing, I don't think. Maybe

I've got a few wrinkles to what I had.' She was 65. A man of
seventy said he had not noticed any changes in his appearance as
he was getting older. He asked the interviewer, 'Have I got any
wrinkles?' And then went on to answer for himself: 'I've got a few
under the eyes, I think.'[15] He did have distinct signs of growing
older such as wrinkles, grey and thinning hair, and rounding
shoulders, and he looked like an older man, although he did not
feel it or think of himself as old.

People were also asked if they were happy or concerned about
how they looked. The majority were happy and not concerned.
'I'm not bothered,' was a common refrain, or 'I never let it worry
me much.' 'My family are happy with me,' said a 71-year-old
woman, 'So why shouldn't I be?' One of the few who were not
happy with how they looked (a man of 66) said: 'I don't like it, but
you have to come to terms with it.' Many people responded by
saying it was important to keep themselves looking 'smart' or
'proper.' A seventy-year-old woman said: 'I always try to keep
myself, you know, looking smart and have me hair done and that
sort of thing.' The 86-year-old former gentleman's butler 'liked to
look proper,' changed his clothes several times a day, and was
even concerned about his attire and appearance in the garden.[16]

A desire to look nice was expressed by many people we interviewed. The response of 74-year-old Mary Wesley was typical of
what many people had to say about the way they dressed: 'Comfortably. I'm quite fashionable, but not so much though. No I like
to be tidy. I like a tidy appearance. I don't like a lot of frippity sort
of things, you know.' Or as Rudi Fine put it:

> It is very important to be able to say I wash well, I bath well,
> yes. I care about my appearance. Yes I do care. And I care about
> how other people dress as well. I care about the way my wife
> dresses. I care about that. I like to see her dressed so that she's
> happy with what she's wearing.[17]

At the same time no one was over-concerned about their dress,
and they tended to opt for casual and comfortable clothes rather
than the formal or fashionable.

One rather interesting response emerged from the questions
about appearance and attitudes to appearance. A 75-year-old Scotsman who was not conscious of his age and was quite happy with
how he looked said: 'Well why should I no' be, people tell me I've

never altered.' A 66-year-old woman had similar experience: 'I tend to meet people I haven't seen for a while and they just say you never change.' The people who mentioned their own feelings of not having changed or the fact that other people told them they had not changed tended to use this as a measure for themselves of visible signs of ageing. Agnes Dunbar, aged 79, certainly agreed with not *feeling* that she had changed: 'Deep down I don't feel as if I've changed an awful lot. In mah own self, ye know.' But she was also quite contemptuous of people pretending that she had not visibly aged, for she was fully aware that she had:

> Well I think I'm getting wrinkled. No matter who comes in here, or who I meet at the gate, they'll say, 'Ye haven't changed a bit,' yet I'm that much older and I'm nearly 79. And they'll say 'Ye still look the same Agnes.' Now how can I still look the same? I'm bound to be wrinkled.[18]

There is, of course, a sense in which everyone stays the same as they age, because, as Agnes Dunbar says, they are themselves. Ronald Cressy, the 79-year-old ex-India policeman put it another way: 'We see the world only through our eyes, and the sight I'm looking at now and the sight I would see if I were fifty years younger are the same, you know.'[19] But there are obvious ways in which people change as they age—all the specific ways identified by these older people. And so, as Agnes Dunbar points out, there is an element of pretence behind the not uncommon response which younger people make to older people that they have not changed: as if they themselves required the reassurance, or believed that the older person did. The inability or the unwillingness to acknowledge the physical signs of ageing seems to suggest an underlying ambivalence to the ageing process, shared both by many older people about themselves, and by younger people about older people.

Nowhere was this more apparent than in what people had to say about 'looking their age.' 'Most people say I don't look my age,' said a 63 year-old, who said she wasn't boastful or vain (she'd had 'that knocked out of her as a child'), but thought she looked better 'facially' now than when she was younger. What does looking one's age actually mean? It is a phrase that is used frequently, with respect to people of all ages, not just older people. The impossibility of defining in objective terms what looking one's age actually

means was illustrated by this exchange between George and Maggie
Kells:

> GEORGE [*in response to the question about any change in his
> appearance*]. Gettin' older looking, that's a' . . . well I mean
> you dinna look 65, I mean, but I do.
> MAGGIE. Oh George, I do, of course I look my age.
> GEORGE. You do not, I'm telling ye.
> MAGGIE. You only think that.
> GEORGE. Ah well that's what I think, you don't look 65, but I
> do.[20]

Deciding whether a person looks their age or not is obviously a
very relative assessment, as another woman made clear: 'People
will say to me, how old are you? I'll say sixty. Oh you don't look
that. But someone else might say, "I thought you were older than
that."' Dina Jordan had a similarly ambivalent response to her own
looks: 'Sometimes I think, "Well I don't look 62" but another time
I think "who are you kidding, you do look 62."' 'But,' she added,
'there's nothing you can do about it really.'[21]

Jackie Stephens had been trying to find a hat to wear to a
wedding and her husband Dennis had objected to one because it
looked like a 'proper grannie's hat' and he did not want her to wear
it. He thought it made her 'look old,' and he did not like it.
Neither did Jackie, and she explained why:

> This couple across the way are a good example—Mr and Mrs
> Haskins—they're about 83 now, I think. Now they never looked
> their age. They've always been reasonably smart. Mr Haskins
> had a dressed up job when he was working, and he does the
> shopping and he goes out and he always looks nice and smart
> when he's going out. But its only this last couple of years that
> you've realised they were old. Mrs Haskins has got to the stage
> where she no longer can stand going to the hairdressers, sitting
> under a drier, having her hair permed. She said I'm not bother-
> ing with that anymore. So she just has her hair cut. She has
> somebody come to the house and they just cut her hair and she
> just has a fringe, and it's white, fringe—and straight. And she
> looks a real old lady now.

Jackie Stephens thought attitudes had changed:

> Where, in the past, you were old at fifty and relegated to the
> backwoods, and you dressed accordingly, now it would be dif-

ficult to tell how old anyone was from the way they dressed. I mean when you go shopping for clothes, you're offered the same thing as somebody twenty and thirty years younger than you.

Whether one is considered to look one's age would appear to depend on preconceptions about what people of particular ages 'ought' to look like. Such preconceptions are widely prevalent—and not only with respect to older age groups. Teenagers and people in their twenties are often told they 'look older than their age,' and this is regarded as complimentary. As Jackie Stephens put it: 'When I was young I never looked me age, and I wanted to look older—you know how you do when you're in your teens and people think you're 14 and you want to look 18.'[22] Women in midlife may be told they look younger than their age, and this is usually intended to be (and taken as) a compliment. Older people are often told they look younger than their age. The implication is that once one is past one's youth, looking younger is better than looking older, and those who look younger than their age are fortunate. These evaluations appear to be related to preconceived notions or stereotypes about age and attitudes to ageing, rather than to chronological age.

As well as questions about appearance, people were asked about their health and physical abilities. Their answers called into question not only the common stereotypes of old age as involving disease, disability, and deterioration, but even the picture of old age implied by medical statistics of chronic illness. A recent study, for example, of a large and representative sample of people over the age of 65 showed that three-quarters of the people interviewed were taking one or more prescribed medicines on a regular basis. Half of the sample reported restrictions in their lives because of chronic illness, being unsteady on their feet or having difficulty walking. Twenty per cent were unable to carry out some activities of daily living such as bathing, getting out of doors, collecting pensions or prescriptions, or using public transport on their own. This study confirmed earlier medical information collected by government surveys.[23] It is well documented that with rising age an increasing proportion of men and women become vulnerable to progressive physical deterioration, limited mobility, disability, and inability to carry out some of their daily activities. And each of the chronic conditions identified by the surveys—diabetes, arthritis,

high blood pressure, cancer, heart disease, anaemia, rheuma-
tism—was reported by some among those we interviewed. As
regards mobility, two of our interviewees were disabled by arthritis, and others described limitations from stiffness and pains.

But the picture that those we interviewed painted of themselves
was very different from that implied by the surveys. For the most
part, they did not perceive themselves as old, ill, and disabled, in
spite of being aged between sixty and 86 and having the whole
range of chronic illnesses and disabilities that enabled them to be
so labelled by others. None of them was helpless and incapable;
and their diseases and disabilities appeared neither as major characteristics of themselves and their lives, nor as how they characterized themselves. They gave a very different impression of
themselves and their world. The majority were still active and
able to continue most of the activities they had participated in
earlier in their lives, although on a smaller scale, in more limited
ways. Essentially they perceived getting older—old age—simply
as 'slowing down.'

Most people of all ages over sixty claimed to be, and indeed
appeared to be, physically fit and capable. They might mention
'going uphill and puffing,' but when asked if there were any things
they were no longer able to do because of their age, most people
said no. Ability to do the gardening came up often, unsolicited,
as a barometer of physical fitness. One 86-year-old man, whose
favourite pastime was gardening with his wife, could no longer do
the heavy digging or the mowing, and had a man come round to
help. Another 86-year-old man spoke with admiration of his neighbours of 87 (a man) and ninety (a woman) who still 'did their own
gardening, mowing as well.' And one eighty-year-old woman measured her ageing process by the state of her garden: it used to be
flowers and now it was grass and tended to be a bit overgrown.
One person (aged 86) mentioned being unable to cut his toenails.
An active sportsman, now seventy, could no longer run ten miles,
and an avid walker, now 79, had to walk his five miles much more
slowly. Someone of seventy no longer tried 'to do the roof.' It was
largely heavy work that these older people had stopped doing, or
sports activities that most people of much younger ages were not
able to do either. The 84-year-old walker made this clear when he
said: 'Compared to most people I'm streets ahead. I can go out and
walk three to five miles and come back and not breathe heavily.'[24]

Jim White (aged 66) had suffered from high blood pressure for several years and was on regular medication. In medical statistics he would be categorized as chronically ill, but he was another person in this sample who 'didn't feel old.'

> You don't feel any different than what you did when you were younger. You don't walk about saying, oh, I'm old, I feel old. You just feel the same, don't you, somehow it's something you can't describe.

He described 'ageing' in terms of 'slowing down:'

> You're slower. You slow down a lot, but you don't feel any different than what you did when you were younger, only like I said previously, you're slower. You slow down a lot, but you don't notice it because you're still as tired at the end of the day as you were when you were younger, but you haven't gone as far.

He was quite eloquent in describing the process of 'slowing down:'

> I don't seem much different. Only you can't walk as quick. See I was always in a rush, and I tend to have slowed down that way. But I can still carry me shopping, I can still carry the same weight. When you're doing a job, it perhaps takes you a little bit longer to do it, but you can rest assured that next week the paint pots are coming out in this house. At one time you just said right, get it done, and you do it. Now you got to sorta build yourself up to it. Before I change all me curtains I want all the window frames painted. We'll get cracking won't we. We've got the paint, the brushes are there. It sort of takes you a bit longer to get cracking. I can go and start a job, but I can't rush it. I have to take me time with it. The last time you came I told you about it taking me three days to put 30 odd potatoes in. Normally, I would've done them in a morning. There's only three rows there, twelve in a row, so I only managed to get one row done in a day. That's why I'm so late with me gardening, just now— because I can't rush anything.[25]

Rather than define themselves as 'disabled' and label themselves as dependent, these older people redefined the boundaries of their world and the parameters of what was possible. They measured themselves against expectations that they would now be slower in what they did, and they measured their 'space' in ever-decreasing size in relation to their abilities. At the same time, their opportunities were also determined—and indeed limited—by circumstances outside their control: not only by health, but by social barriers such as exclusion from employment, low incomes, and even poverty, which in turn limits access to leisure activities and social life.

Although the abilities and opportunities of older people are thus to some very real extent diminished, the self-perception of those we interviewed was not necessarily of diminishment, let alone the disparagement of the stereotypes. They did not view themselves as 'other' in the sense that younger people might view them. Their lives are whole and their world is full, *in their own terms*, which is as it should be.

And yet there was still a fundamental contradiction between the experience of ageing and the perception of ageing. By 'objective criteria' (which most people acknowledged) their bodies were ageing (deteriorating or 'decaying,' as the walker referred to it, or slowing down). There were some functional things they could not do, or could only do with difficulty or with help. They all had physical signs of ageing: grey hair, wrinkles, weight loss or gain. They would all—as pensioners, or having been compulsorily retired—be categorized by society as 'old.' Statutory and voluntary agencies that service older people would regard them as elderly, and some of them (those over 85) as the 'old elderly.' They are looked upon by most people younger than themselves, because of their physical appearance, as getting older or as old. They look on each other as old! And yet remarkably, scarcely any of them 'feel old' or 'think of themselves as being old.'

Almost everyone, as we have seen, was honest in acknowledging the physical changes associated with age (looking older, physical decline), but almost no one was prepared to identify herself or himself as old. Why don't they feel old? What does 'old' mean? How is it measured? By whom? Why? According to the majority of people interviewed, whatever their age from 58 to 86, people as they get older do not feel old and do not think of themselves as old, but they do show physical signs of ageing, and other people think of them as old. So are they old? Or are they only as old as they feel? And, if they *are* to be classified as old by some generally accepted objective criteria (such as chronology, or capability, or health), why do they not feel it, or want to feel it, or admit to feeling it?

The fascinating and revealing testimonies of our sample seem to demand a reassessment of our concepts and preconceptions about old age and ageing. Few if any of our interviewees actually fit the stereotypes of old people as being passive, inactive, helpless, dependent, rigid in their thoughts or behaviour, old-fashioned, or unproductive. Instead their lives are characterized by variety, vitality, diversity, activity, energy, interest: by 'youthfulness' in attitude, outlook, and activity (including paid employment), regardless of their age. The people themselves are each unique and uniquely different from each other and from just about every stereotyped image of old people that exists.

The reality of older people's lives is therefore clearly very different from most people's preconceptions: indeed, different from the preconceptions of the older people themselves. Perhaps that is why they are all so surprised to find that they do not feel old for their age, or that they do not look their age or think of themselves as old. As Dawn Roberts, the 73-year-old 'floral champion' put it:

> I could never imagine getting old. I still can't, although I'm old. I still don't feel that I've got to 73 yet, you know what I mean? I still don't realise I've got to 73 because I don't feel 73. I don't feel what I imagine 73 should be like—you know.

It would seem that they themselves have internalized some idea of what people 'should' be like at certain ages and surprise themselves when they discover that their own experience does not fit with the preconceived notions. Ted Keeler, for example, declares:

> Well, I don't feel 71, not by a long way. I mean, often, when I'm out, I go out for walks, I'll go on the beach and walk to Fleetwood and back, you know, along the beach, when the tide's right out, to Fleetwood and back, and in me personal feelings, like, I don't feel nowhere near seventy. I think I'm about middle aged now, the way I feel! I know I can feel I'm getting older, but I don't feel senile in any shape or form.[26]

Most people were pleasantly surprised to find the reality of their lives to be so different from the stereotypes, for invariably the preconceptions about old age and ageing are negative. 'Old age is no place for cissies' is the slogan on a badge worn by members of an organization of older women. Not only is there the gradual loss of physical ability, there are a number of ways in which old people are treated as second-class citizens. Older people are forced to retire at a certain age, not by choice, but by law. They are forced to live on lower incomes. There are attempts to segregate older people socially and medically. Thus the reservations or fears that people have about old age and ageing are not unfounded. The prejudices—the negative attitudes—also have a foundation in the extent to which older people are regarded as inferior, and their individuality is ignored, and they are undervalued.

Given that the stereotypes and associations are largely negative, dissociation of oneself from the category of old age might be a very reasonable position to adopt: for who would want to be associated with negative attitudes or prejudice, especially if one knew they were not true of one's own self or life? From the testimony of the older people interviewed here, it would seem to be not so much their actual age or the actual conditions of being old that are a problem, but the label, the category, the classification, the identity—simply being *identified* as old. In this case a degree of pretence, denial, dissociation, and disconnection would not only be an understandable reaction, but could even be regarded as a commendable form of resistance to the pressures and injustices of the prejudices against the old.

There is further evidence from the interviews that this might be the case. Oliver Ridings, an 86-year-old former businessman who retired in good health at the early age of 43, and who is basically satisfied with his life, admits, like the others, that he does not think of himself as old, but he does not try to maintain the pretence that he is not ageing and getting older:

> No I don't think of myself as old. I've never been old for my age. But there's nothing very good about getting old really. All this about growing old gracefully—you're getting old and can't get away from it. You have to accept it. I feel I'm older. I know I am and I resent it.

Nor does he try to pretend that there's nothing wrong with getting old. He knows there is. And it is not the chronological age or the physical conditions, but the attitudes to older people that bewilder and infuriate him. He resents them: they are not fair. He also refuses to participate in pretence about his appearance:

I haven't got to the stage where I can't be bothered. I think everybody really as they're getting older would like to look younger. I think it's a lot of hooey when they say, 'You look no different to what you did twenty years ago.' Well how can you look no different, it's rubbish.

He was the only person who acknowledged the external social pressures which favour younger people and which encourage older people to want to look or to feel younger. His honesty tends to suggest that there might be an element of self-protection in the majority view, or perhaps an underlying belief that if one does not feel old, then one is not old, even if one might be. 79-year-old Rudi Fine was also more 'realistic' than most people:

I wish I was—was physically better off, because I would like to be a little more adventurous, you see, I know that I can't travel and I would like to travel and I know I can't because I can't— can't walk a lot. I get tired and that's one of the things that I know about old age is that it takes a lot of enthusiasm away from you. You see, when I go to put my socks on, I put one on alright, but I can't get the other one on and then I know that I'm old and I can't bend down and really get it on properly—you know, that's the sort of thing. Old age is not really—is not such a marvellous thing.

Even Jackie Stephens, who led such an active and youthful life, had to admit:

I don't think there's anything to like about getting old—to be quite honest, I don't. What's to like about being old? You're at the end of your life more or less. Near enough. There's nothing to like about it. I feel grateful that I'm still capable of being active.

Ted Keeler, aged 79, offered a very creditable explanation of one reason why older people, at least, might think that they have not changed as they have grown older:

The people mainly I'm connected with are getting older with me, you know, the difference is together, if you can understand what I mean. The people you know of your own age are growing old with you and you see them more regularly, so therefore you don't see any change as if you haven't seen them for years. If you haven't seen them for years you probably notice it, but being in contact with them, you grow old together.[27]

People were also asked: 'Are there some things you'd like to do but don't because you think it's inappropriate for someone of your age?' Most people said 'No.' There are, however, a variety of sanctioned age-appropriate behaviours. For example, a number of people mentioned 'growing old gracefully' and not wanting to look like 'mutton dressed as lamb,' phrases that are used respectively to refer to prescribed behaviours and to demonstrate contempt for older people who appear to be trying to dress or to look 'younger' (implying an age-appropriate way to dress and to look). 86-year-old Oliver Ridings replied 'No' to the question, but then added: 'But we don't try to be 25 instead of 85.' And the wife of a 66-year-old man said, 'I think he still likes to feel young. He wants to do things his sons do and wear the same style of clothes. He would if he could.' Rudi Fine referred to wearing 'clothes that are desirable for the age—quiet clothes for the age,' implying that he had a precon-ceived notion of how people of his age 'ought' to dress.[28]

Sixty-year-old Verity Hampshire talked about still liking to do 'everything along with the kids, but you feel sorta prohibited a wee bit because of yer age, you know, people say, "Look at her, at her age, you know." Which implies such a lot and you're itchin' to do something you know. It's very unfair. And yet they're always advocating on the telly and the radio that you should just act yer age, you know.' 61-year-old Ida Lane said, 'At parties, dances, that's when you feel your age, when you know you can't do them.' She was certainly physically capable (she had only recently retired from full-time factory work), and was obviously responding to the belief that dancing was not appropriate to a woman of her age. The seventy-year-old man who had wanted to know if he looked his age and was not sure if he had any wrinkles, said: 'I've got a lot of young friends, as well as middle-aged and old . . . and they like to pass remarks—"Oh, you're too old." '[29] So although almost every-one denied constraining their behaviour, it seems possible that some people might have unconsciously adapted their attitudes and behaviour to conform to some of the stereotyped images of ageing.

Certainly, their attitudes were an accurate reflection of society's negative attitudes about older people.

People were asked the question: 'Does anyone treat you differently than when you were younger?' Most people said 'No,' and then quite a few qualified this denial with comments like:

> More respect. (Gail Stone, 63)

> Little boys get up and give you a seat sometimes. (Vera Stonehithe, 80)

> They've respected me more. I like it. (Geoffrey Kedleston, 86)

> Strangers might think, 'There's an old lady,' but not people I know. (Alice Kitchin, 60)

> My nine-year-old granddaughter helps me up steps. (Annie Mimms, 78)

> Our sons call us OAP's, in a comical way. (Esme Hibblethwaite, 70)

The most revealing comments however, came from Fred Doggett, (aged 62) who was still working as a docker, and who replied, when asked when he began to think of himself as getting old:

> When you, I suppose, have to face the possibility of retirement—when it's talked about. Like specifically with you included, not someone else. Well of course you know that you're getting older, in that the difficulties with doing jobs at work, which you could sail through, certain lifting jobs that are a chore, where you could do them without a moment's thought. You could do the job, and now it actually becomes difficult to do that job. . . . One thing that struck me about the old age part, is that I can now understand the employer who does not want to employ people when they're getting older, or getting old. I can understand that, cos I can realise that as much as I might think I'm good as I used to be, I know that I am not. I've accepted that.

Then in response to the question about being treated differently, he said:

> At work, some of the chaps are inclined to—without, say, asking, they would step in and do something that they know in their minds that its easier for them to do, and they will help.

But you don't always receive that offer of help. Do you know what I'm trying to say, I can't put it in the right words. But sometimes you'd rather they didn't, because you can manage.[30]

Fred's experience illustrates both the way that other people hold ideas about what older people *can* and *should* do, and also how individuals come to hold these ideas about themselves. He makes it clear that there is more to the process of ageing than a decline in physical capability: there is also a change in attitude. His experience also reflects the ambivalence felt by many people when it comes to the point of compulsory retirement. As we saw earlier, some people looked forward to their retirement, but some dreaded it. A number of people took charge of choosing when they retired, even if only by days or weeks, and felt empowered by doing so. And many people remained economically active after retirement. For men, especially, the sudden enforced end to a working life, which had provided meaning and identity as well as income, could be a difficult hurdle. It would be made no easier by the simple equation of retirement with old age.

George and Maggie, when asked if there was anything they regarded as inappropriate for their age, mentioned sex. Surprisingly, they were the only ones who did, given the power of the stereotype of older people as 'past it' sexually—of being asexual, or not interested in sex, or incapable of sexual activity. This, as we shall see later, is another common stereotype of ageing not borne out by the experience of most of those we interviewed.

When asked if they felt more comfortable with people of their own age, almost every person interviewed said 'No.' All but one said they enjoyed the company of people younger than themselves and took opportunities to socialize with young people. Most people said they had friends of many different ages. This is a typical response:

When we go down and see Tony, Lizzie's niece, they're all young, but I feel quite at home with them. They don't treat you any different, that you're older than they are. You don't feel different, older, they treat you the same as what you are your-self, and they treat me the same as what they would each other.

Most people were equally emphatic in their reservations about socializing with older people, and many said they did not—and would not—belong to over-sixties or Derby and Joan clubs. This was not true of everyone. Eighty-year-old Vera Stonehithe was an enthusiastic member of her village Derby and Joan club, but as she said:

> I mean, a lot of people won't join it. I had a friend down the road—well she's dead now—and I used to say why don't you come to the Derby and Joan? She'd say, Oh, I'm not an old age pensioner, which she was, she was just a little younger than me, not very much, but she wouldn't come.[31]

There was some apparent reluctance for an old person to identify with other older people, for fear of having to admit to themselves that they were old, or out of a desire not to be identified as old, or perhaps simply to protect themselves from being placed in a ghetto or segregated from younger people.[32]

A fear of being confined to a ghetto in that worst of all possible places, residential care or an Old People's Home, was communicated by Leonard Seldon, the 84-year-old active walker:

> The idea of a Home scares me stiff. I've been to these places and they just sit and they've got their own chair, you know. Back-to-back and then they're looking at who comes in and who doesn't and they just sit and look out into space. I couldn't—I couldn't, I would have to do something. I just couldn't stand that, I'm like Nanny. She didn't and I won't.[33]

Of course, not all old people's homes are like the one Leonard Seldon described, but some are, and few are altogether free of the aspects of institutionalization that would be offensive to many individuals, and a source of some justifiable fear.

Given all these oppressive aspects of old age and ageing, it would not be surprising to find people wanting to avoid it altogether: to deny to some extent their own ageing, to detach themselves in some ways from themselves as older people, to dissociate themselves from other people who are also old or growing older.

At the same time, there is a very strong and clear message about the actual experience of ageing which may not ever have been revealed so clearly as in these life stories. And that is that the actual experience of ageing is nothing like as bad as it is represented or imagined. People were asked: 'When do you think old age begins?' and whether they knew people whom they *did* think of as old. Most people were in agreement that it was not 'actual age' that determined whether someone was old, but 'physical ability:'

> When people are incapable of doing what they used to. (Helen Burnsall, 70)

> It's not what you look like. There's nothing nicer than an elderly lady with white hair. It's senility, when you lose control of your faculties. (Gail Stone, 63)

> No age when people get old. It's to do with health. (Verity Hampshire, 60)

> When one becomes unwell. (Mary Wesley, 74)

> Depends on health and physical ability. (Vera Stonehithe, 80)

> Well I think old means when you are incapable of doing what you used to do. I think of this one as old because she's a bit helpless at times. But there's another lady more or less as old, but she's capable, so I don't think of her as old. (Edna Rourke, 73)

There was a tendency for people to think of 'old people' as 'other' than themselves, someone else at some other age, never oneself at whatever age one might be. A 66-year-old man said he thought old age would begin 'in a few years time, in the seventies probably.' He would not have thought so if he had interviewed people in their seventies, who were virtually unanimous is not having 'an old outlook.'[34]

The majority of people of all ages in their sixties, seventies, and even eighties believed that old age was not defined by chronological age, nor by the social category of retirement, but by health and physical ability. By far the most universal and unanimous definition of old age was therefore a combination of incapacity, inability, and ill-health. This accounts for the common tendency amongst people whatever their age to believe that 'other people my age are old but not me.' 74-year-old Mary Wesley said: 'I'll say "that old woman," and they'll say "Oh my, she's just about the age of me," you know. You say that, "Oh my, that old woman." And then you think, "Oh my, I'm that age too."' And Dawn Roberts, who could never imagine getting old and who did not feel 73, said:

I mean, you see people walking about the street, and they're absolutely bent double and they're creaking along and—to look at them you'd think they were about ninety, and then you find out they're not as old as you are, and you can't believe it, you know—you just don't know what's made them get like that. How did he come to be like that?

86-year-old Elsa Mackay thought people were old if they were 'infirm:'

> See a poor old soul wi' a walkin' stick . . . you know you do see some terrible poor old souls . . . Oh I've admired many an old body, the age of them and what they do and so forth.

She, however, did *not* think of herself as old—'and I've no intention of doing it,' she said, 'I have intentions of staying as young as I feel;' and she concluded: 'I don't feel my age.' 72-year-old Dick Tiverton identified the conflict between physical ability and mental attitudes:

> There are going to be times when you think of the sort of things you used to be able to do and you knew perfectly well that you can take a shot at it, but you couldn't really do it. Then you realize your body has aged. Mentally, I don't feel very old at all.[35]

Men were more inclined to define 'old age' in relation to retirement. 75-year-old Scotsman Bill Duncan said:

> I would say old age begins when ye're forced to retire. I mean forcibly retired. I mean, ye don't want to retire, but ye're forced to retire. I would say that's when old age begins.

He had staved off old age (in his terms) by continuing to work, and he was still looking for jobs. The docker, who was coming up to retirement age and having to face the fact of his *own* retirement was another man whose definition of old age was linked with compulsory retirement. But this was by no means true of all the men. Among the women, Verity Hampshire, a professional nurse now aged sixty, explained in some detail how she saw the next 35 years of her life:

> Well I recognize that I'm pretty near what they call retirement age. Pension age, but I feel that I have a lot of years ahead of me

yet. So instead of laying down everything at the age of sixty, I think I'll just continue on the way I'm doing. Until such time as the body begins to wear out or maybe . . . well there comes a time that you have to stop. But in view of the age of my parents and that, they're all long living people. I have a good twenty years ahead of me yet and more. Because my mother was 95 when she died. That's thirty-five years I've still to go till I reach her age. So there's no saying what I might do yet.

So I'm not really, I'm not stopping if you know what I mean, I'm just going to continue on, I can see a lot of things that I can do yet, voluntary in the community. And I would like to keep active that way, rather than sayin', 'Right, I'm finished, now I'm sixty I'm stopped.' I could ultimately feel that there's a lot of things, a lot of work that could be done to help people in this community . . .

I would say old age begins when you begin to feel really old. You know there must be a time in your life when you say to yourself, 'Well I'm not able to do that any more.' I would say that is the time to say you're getting old . . . I don't think it really goes by the calendar at all. I think it goes by yourself, your own attitude to life.[36]

So to her, old age is largely an attitude to life, an attitude of mind: and to judge by the life stories and lived experience of these 43 people in their sixties, seventies, and eighties, the social attitudes and stereotypes about old age are definitely not the attitudes held by older people about themselves. According to Jack Hands,

People are never old, it's only when they look upon themselves as being old. It's attitude of mind all the time, I think. You do realise you're getting older when the stairs get steeper, and the mile gets longer, but I can climb up a ladder and paint the roof.

Although he was chronologically 71, Jack said he still felt 21, and could not see any reason why he should not feel the same in another ten years' time.

I don't expect any changes. I expect to go on as I am. When you feel like I feel at the moment, since I retired, you don't expect something to happen to you, and you can't do this and you can't do that. I suppose it's stupid, but you think life's going on as it is. It's gotta stop somewhere, but I can't see it.[37]

The reality is that—however one *feels*—life does come to an end in death. Everyone dies at some age—and statistically, of all the men and women aged over 65, 63 per cent are under 75, 31 per cent are aged 75 to 84, and only 6 per cent are over 85.[38] The longer one lives, the likelier one is to die soon, the more imminent is death.

People were asked: 'Do you ever think about dying?,' and the general response again indicated a substantial degree of denial (of death) and disconnection (from their own eventual experience of dying). This attitude of denial and disconnection with regard to death and dying is in fact common to people of all ages. What is interesting is that it should be maintained into old age when people have come so much closer to the likelihood of their own death. For those we interviewed did not show a significant concern or preoccupation with death. When asked, most people of whatever age said they did not think about dying. 'Not really ...,' 'I don't think much about it,' 'Not much,' 'Don't give it a thought,' 'It doesn't worry me' were typical responses from people varying in age from sixty to 81. Derek Hibblethwaite, aged seventy, said: 'We don't talk about it, no. I mean we've made arrangements we think are suitable, we've made wills.' And 75-year-old Bill Duncan was equally matter-of-fact: 'I'll accept it when it comes, if I have to die I'll die. Ah mean I'm no' afraid t'die. I never give it a thought. No way, not.' Ben Bradgate, who was also 75, did not think much about dying, but that was because he felt he was going to miss life too much:

Well, I don't think much about it, because I know when I go, I'm going to miss a lot of things that I like, won't I. I'll miss rugby for instance, as I'll have to go, and I don't want to live long, I don't want to live until I'm incapacitated to an extent as I can't do nothing for myself, but having said that, it might just happen to me, through having said it! I don't know whether He's listening to me or not but, it would please me if when I was at rugby one day, something happened and they had to take me away and I was gone.

76-year-old Barbara Williamson, on the other hand, *did* think about dying, precisely because she was going to miss life. In response to the question, she said:

Well, a funny thing you should say that, but I do. I think, well, I don't wanna die, I don't wanna leave all my kids. I mean, I know it's gotta come to it, but, yes, I do think about it.

Alice Kitchin, aged sixty, did not think much about dying, but like a lot of people she hoped she would 'go' quickly and easily. She replied:

Not really. I mean not to the extent that I'd lay there or sit there and think 'God am I going to die, when am I going to die.' No, not really. I think every now and then you think to yourself 'God, I'm this age, I've not got that much longer, to what I had a few years ago.' Not something that worries me. I mean like anybody else I must say I don't want to, but you've got to someday, and when that day comes I just hope it's as easy as is possible.[39]

Most people certainly accepted that their lifetimes were limited. One man commented: 'I'm a fatalist. It's bound to happen.' A woman declared: 'The sooner you come to terms with it, the easier it is for you . . . It's something that you've no control over.' In that sense, they have come to terms with death itself. More often, they fear the manner of dying. 'I wouldn't like to die a death of agony.' One woman, unhappy in many other ways too, was haunted by her fear of renewed cancer: 'I can never get it out of my mind that I won't get it somewhere else.' Others are more worried about outliving their independence. One man stated: 'I don't want to live long. I don't want to live until I'm incapacitated.' A woman remarked:

I don't want to be an invalid. I don't want to lay a cabbage, like I've seen them laying in hospital, where they've had seizures and they can't speak, and they can't feed themselves, and all their bodily functions have to be attended to by somebody else. I hope they shoot me if that ever happens. It's a lowering of people's dignity. To me that is infinitely worse than death.[40]

Whether or not they wanted to talk about it, death was an ordinary presence in their lives. Some couples talked about it. 'I'd like to see both me and Freddy go together, I really would. I think if I go first he'll be like a fish out of water. If he goes first, I'll cope better, I think. But I wouldn't want to.' Afterwards, the memory could be a comfort or a challenge for the survivor. One widower's wife 'used to say, "I don't know what tha'll do, Ben, when I die . . . I don't know what tha'll do, you're useless." So I'm not useless now: I'm not a cook, I can't bake or anything like that, but I get a meal ready, I go to butcher's and I cook.'

Other couples, more typically, accept the fact of death but talk of it rarely:

> WIFE. I don't think we do discuss it, not really much, no. We— that's something that's inevitable. It will come, so leave it alone, aye?
> HUSBAND. Leave it alone. Finish.[41]

Some people indicated that they would *like* to talk about death and dying, but no one asks and no one listens. Belinda Simonson, aged 65, has thought about how she would like to die: 'Oh yes I have. I don't want to be a bother to anybody. And I'd sooner drop dead than suffer a lot.' She would like to talk to her husband, but he 'won't discuss anything like that, because he doesn't like to talk about dying.' Louise Barrington (83) tried to talk to her daughters, but gave up because they did not want to hear. Although she is suffering from a debilitating, long-standing illness, her son persists in calling her 'as fit as a butcher's dog.' In this middle-class family the son, who was a medical professional, seemed even after the death of his father brusquely unwilling to admit face to face with his mother that sooner or later she would die too. Is it to protect their parents or themselves that children find it so difficult, even disloyal, to talk to a parent of his or her death? Dick Tiverton, also widowed, reflects:

> It never worries me talking about death. I think anybody who is scared of it is silly, because they must know that it's going to come sometime. . . . All I hope is that when my time comes, it will be nice and quick . . . I think most elderly men, that I've spoken to, seem to have the same idea . . .
>
> I'll quite often, if we're discussing something that's being done, shall we say this new town centre, say, 'I shall probably be dead by the time this place is finished.' And they'll say, 'Oh, don't say that!' and I'll say, 'Well, what do you expect?'
>
> No, I think a lot of the younger generation get really worried if anybody mentions it.
>
> I wonder whether it's a reaction to the Victorian attitude,

where people talked of little else. Death was so common then, amongst children and middle-aged people as well, and they made this great thing about it—with black-edged notepaper and black-edged cards and special funeral biscuits and all the rest of it. Everybody going into mourning. I think maybe it's a reaction to that.

People say, 'Let's live, let's not talk about that.'

But I think there are some people—young to middle-aged—who are genuinely scared of talking about it.[42]

Often it is the death of a parent or a sibling or a spouse that brings an awareness of our own death. Dawn Roberts, aged 75, described this happening to her on the death of her husband:

He just looked at me with his eyes wide open and they were smiling—his eyes were smiling and he was smiling—and they were the clearest words that he said and the very last he ever said to me or that anybody could understand. He looked at me and he smiled and he said 'You're looking after me, aren't you, Dawn?' and smiled, you know. And it went right through me. It was then I began to realize what we'd meant to each other since retiring and what I was losing. Because I knew he'd never recover. And I just prayed there and then that it wouldn't be long because I knew he wouldn't want to live like that and it was only a day or two. I know it was awful to pray for him to die, but I couldn't pray for him to live like that because I knew it would be the last thing he would have ever wanted to do. And it would be the same with me.

74-year-old Mary Wesley provided an equally detailed and moving account of her husband's death, but her experience had not made her think more about her own death: 'I just think if I die, I die and that'll be it, you know.' With others it is the death of friends and neighbours that reminds them of their own eventual death. 84-year-old Leonard Seldon's response to the question was:

No, not really. Well, I won't say—of course, you do. I—there are one or two people here roundabout—there's one up here and there's one up there and there's one just down here, three men that I know—and they've all just had little strokes. It's enough to sort of warn them, you see, and that makes me think a bit and I thought I wouldn't like that. Then I hear of somebody who, like this chappy who lost his wife, you know, he had about two months on his own and he suddenly goes to bed and that's it, he's gone. That would be lovely.

But I must admit, when I hear about these people, round about my age, some younger, some older, that are having these strokes and they're incapacitated and some of them don't recover. There's one not far away who doesn't recover at all. He's younger than I am. It does occur to me and I think well, blimey, I haven't got any choice, but I hope it doesn't happen to me. I wouldn't like that at all.

I believe in heredity, of course, a tremendous amount. I think that's where you've got to go back. Habits and all sorts of things are hereditary and I think it's a very important factor. So—if you mean, do I worry, I don't worry because it's not much good worrying but these things do bring it home a little bit and I'm a bit apprehensive and I just think—not for me, I hope.[43]

A few people did admit to being frightened of death. Dina Jordan, aged 64, said: 'I'm frightened of it. I worry about it, 'cos I don't think I've got any faith, you see. I mean, you know, to me death is that, that's the end of it. It's because its inevitable that it's so frightening. Nobody can do anything about it, can they?'[44]

Some people had what can only be described as a 'sensible approach' to death and dying. Elsa Mackay, 81 years of age, simply said:

We've thought about it and talked about it but that's it. I don't think anyone should think about that. You know, you can look at it sensibly, if you just sit down and talk it over. What's t'be done this way, what's t'be done that way. You know, if you go first, if I go first, what's what. And it really doesn't . . . it may do later on, I don't know, if you was taken ill or something like that. But at the moment it doesn't worry me.

79-year-old Rudi Fine had perhaps the most 'relaxed' attitude and readily admitted to thinking about his own death:

Yes. Very much so. Oh yes. I know that there's a limited time now. Oh yes. No question about it. How it'll happen, I don't know. But there's a limited time. All things are ready for the occasion. A Will is made. You—you talk about the thing. You talk about it so that you know it is an inevitable thing to happen in due course. You talk about it. 'I won't be here for ever,' you say, and everybody says 'well, don't talk like that,' but then that's what it is. You won't be here for ever and what will you do about so-and-so and you'll speak to so-and-so if you want to know anything more. Whereas I'm doing the thing now—somebody will help you a little later on if anything happens and such—this is—this is what it's about. A sensible approach if you—if there is such a thing—try and do that—as much as possible.

Dick Tiverton, aged 72, had a similarly pragmatic point of view:

I'm quite honest about it. I won't say I'm prepared for it, but on the other hand, I know it's going to happen some time and I try to be as realistic as I can about it. . . . No matter how it comes, it's going to come.[45]

7

Meaningful Work

WORK, paid or unpaid, is one of the commonest ways in which men and women make sense of their lives. Work both gives purpose to daily activity, and generates meaningful relationships. The possible absence of work is consequently amongst the most central challenges of later life.

None of the thirty-five women and twenty men whose life stories we recorded had never been in paid work, and although few women had continued working without interruption through the period when their children were young, most had gone back to at least part-time employment as their children became independent. Louise Barrington, the Lancashire bank manager's wife married in the 1920s when 'it was considered beneath your dignity if you worked' was unusual in not responding to later changes of attitude to married women's work. But the neutral stance she exemplifies—'I didn't dislike it, it wasn't anything I was fond of'— remained much more common among married women, partly because their jobs were typically low in pay and status, and also because they were socially encouraged towards an alternative sphere of work as housewives and as carers.[1] Retired men could become highly domesticated, and some have taken this on as a new work role; but up to his sixties a man was expected to be in full-time paid work, the family breadwinner.

It is thus men above all who may thread their whole story around winning a living. Oliver Ridings, now in his late eighties, feels 'I've had a grand life. I've had one of the best lives that's ever been.' But behind that satisfaction lies a double triumph. He has fought his way up from a childhood in a Lancashire mill-worker's family to a life of financial ease and security: 'independence is worth a lot to me . . . If you haven't a lot of worry, you'll live a long time, I'll tell you. I've no worries. I might live till I'm ninety!' But he has not only risen from his class, but far surpassed the older brother who, in his boyhood, was the family favourite. This brother was a model son, 'one of the best,' helpful at home, 'brilliant' at school, continuing to a technical college and finally reaching the level of mill under-manager before he was killed in the First World War. Oliver by contrast was 'a bit of a scarecrow,' fond of his mother but never helping her: 'I had to be out and away,' fishing, cockfighting, or up to other adventures. He collided frequently with his Methodist choirmaster father, who had 'a nasty temper' and 'wouldn't think nothing of giving me a good hiding.' 'Me dad and me wasn't the best of friends;' and his father used to warn him sternly, 'me father used to say, "You'll never be anything."' When he first started work, it looked as if this discouraging prophesy might prove all too true. Oliver tried the mill, but could only stick it for two weeks: 'I said, "Well, I can't stand this. I'm finishing with this."' His father and mother had 'wanted us to get on, but I didn't want that at all. I wanted to go out and have a gamble.'

The gamble paid off. Oliver got a job as horseboy for a grocer, and succeeded in marrying his daughter. He was then able to take over a fish wholesale business, managing it while the owner was in the war, and raising the takings fivefold: 'I was always very progressive as far as doing my job.' Then he took over one of his wife's family's shops. He combined this with speculative dealing, sometimes borrowing from his father—'he'd charge me full rate, oh aye!... He said, "When he's spent it, he's back to clogs."' He would deal in houses, horses, shares—property of all sorts wherever he could smell a bargain: 'buying and selling it, you see—that was the most important to me ... It didn't matter what it was, I'd buy it. No matter what it was, I could make some money out of it. That was my job.' Through these years he was a fanatical worker. 'I was a slave-driver in them days, because when I started to do a job, I did that job to the best of my profession. I used to be working at half-past five in the morning till ten o'clock at night sometimes.' And then suddenly, quite early in middle age, he threw it all up. He had been warned by a doctor that he might strain his heart if he went on at the same pace. 'I retired at 43. Well, I didn't want to work no longer, so I gave it up!' Not completely: he and his wife still pore over the *Financial Times*, actively caring for their stock-market shares. But he had already won sufficient to feel fully vindicated. 'I often think about my brother. He was so smart. He couldn't make money and I could make money. And my father used to say, "You'll never be anything." '2

Both in his success at work and his very early retirement, Oliver Ridings is exceptional; but the importance which he places on work is not unusual. Among the men, only a minority—seven—felt that they had been glad to retire from paid work. A lorry driver seized redundancy gladly—'I wanted to retire;' a school caretaker, formerly a miner, was distinctly 'narked' when not allowed to take redundancy at 64; and another ex-miner, a store clerk, thought his redundancy at 63 the 'best thing that ever happened ... No, I think if you're worked fae ye're 14 till ye're sixty odd, I think ye've done enough o'it. Forget all about work.' Derek and Esme Hibblethwaite, who had run a farm single-handed with Esme responsible for 'all the tractor work' as well as the accounts, welcomed the release from their incessant tasks. 'You were glad to sit down.' Even six years later they still felt an oddity about 'being able to do as you please ... We always had to get back in time for feeding stock ... Oh aye, we slept for about a month after we left!'3

All these had worked in notably tough manual work, but a linotype assistant was also keen to retire: 'he retired on the day of his birthday. He never even finished the week. He was that eager, he couldn't wait. The day he was 65, he retired. He says, "I'm not going in till Friday. They'll be making a fuss and giving me cards."' A factory coachtrimmer was glad to see the back of supervisors, whom he saw as 'the reason why British industry has gone down the drain ... I don't have to cope with these people anymore ... I've had enough hassle.' The last of those who had welcomed retirement was a teacher: Dick Tiverton retired a little early because he could see his job conditions were deteriorating, and also 'I began losing patience with the kids;' 'I got sort of fed up.' So at 63, 'I reckon I deserved a rest. And I knew I could go on a reasonable pension.' Although he still mixes mostly with former colleagues, he does not miss work: 'not at all, no ... I think some people get so wrapped up on their jobs that they can't think of anything else. That's it, that's their life. I think these are the sort of people who don't do very well when they retire. They feel absolutely lost.'4

It is noticeable that all these men retired by choice, at their own chosen time—even if this only made a difference of a matter of months, or in one case, days. Three men who were forced to stop

work early, on the other hand, present a striking contrast. Two had
suffered from serious depression while at work, and one of these,
last employed as a bus conductor ten years ago—'he can't take
responsibility in a job'—goes through 'recurrent troughs in which
he does not speak. The third was a skilled car worker who had
been made redundant, with a works pension. Bob Jordan described how 'deflated' he had felt:

> For a bit you go quiet. And you go and look for work. And you
> get rejected. You fill in application forms. You don't hear any-
> thing; or if you do . . . and you're accepted for interview . . . and
> you go all through it . . . then you get a letter saying unfortunate-
> ly there's no vacancy at the moment . . . And you do this—after
> half-a-dozen times, a dozen times—one day I tried six different
> firms and I didn't get anyone in authority: 'no, we've got no
> vacancies.' And I did feel like throwing myself under a bus. I
> was that down.

He still suffers from sleeplessness: 'sometimes I get very melancholy now I've got more time on me hands, being unemployed;
and I get depressed.'[5]

Nine out of the twenty men were able to continue in some form
of paid work, usually part-time, after they reached the point of
retirement—four of them into their seventies. Almost half the
women too still have paid jobs, including four in their seventies
and one of eighty. Thus the life stories, by picking up the inci-
dence of part-time work which is not well recorded by census,
shows older men and women to be far more often economically
active, at least in a small way, than is generally thought.[6]

Nor is the reason for this primarily financial. One of the most
affluent of all the men we recorded only stopped working at his
business at 75:

> I worked hard—really hard, until I was 75. And then I thought
> I'd had enough. In fact, I had to pack it in. My back more or less
> folded up on me . . . I didn't want to retire. If I was fit and well,
> I wouldn't have retired.

But he could retire to a rural manor with a full sense of satisfaction:
for 'if I've achieved one thing I wanted to achieve, then that is a
nice home in the country.' Among the others, one man who had
gone back to work had felt himself 'financially fairly well set up'

with his Civil Service retirement lump sum and pension, while a working-class couple who felt 'no money worries' with no more than the state pension had both taken on new jobs. A woman who worked once a week in a chip shop was contemplating giving it up because 'I'm tired when I come down,' but hesitated because 'there's all people as come in and them girls as I work with, I enjoy that.' Money would certainly not be the deciding point: financially, 'you can always adjust.' With three-quarters of these households depending mainly on state pensions, adjusting cannot be easy. But in fact they have little choice: not only because most jobs open to them are ill-paid, but also because of the trap set by the social security system. For ironically those most in need, living only on state pensions boosted by Supplementary Benefit and rent and rate rebates, could do least about it. If they did find paid work, most of their earnings would be counted pound for pound against their benefits, leaving them scarcely any better off. In fact only three women—one on her own—suggested that earning was important in their continuing paid work. One felt the pension was not sufficient—'definitely not;' another could just 'get by;' while a third, who had continued as a nurse into her late sixties, had 'always been careful,' saving from her earnings, and was eventually glad to stop, now thinking the best thing in her life 'Not having to work! Do what I like, when I like.'[7]

Among those who were no longer earning, on the other hand, the attitude of the Hibblethwaites was typical: 'we just have to be careful. There'll be no holiday this year, we've had new windows put in.' As a retired Scots worker put it, 'No, when ye get older, it's no got the same glitter . . . The amount o'money, it disna dae anything to ye. Ye're comfortable; ye ken it's there if ye want it; ye never think of spending it.' But there were others who undoubtedly felt themselves financially pinched. One northern working-class couple had instead of saving practised for retirement by overspending on house furnishings and managing on less. The wife, Meg Jacks, felt in part resigned—'as long as there's enough to pay the way and have a little holiday and food, I'm not bothered'—but also that managing had been a fight 'all the time, and we're still doing it. Yeh, it is, it's an uphill struggle. It never changes. Money was always tight.' Yet neither of them were employed, from choice. She had not originally wanted to leave her job, but was persuaded by her husband: 'I was a bit reluctant . . . He had to talk to me a long long time before I said. I kept saying, "Oh, I'm going to miss this."' And afterwards, at first she did: 'you miss the companionship of other people.' But when her employers asked her to come back, she refused.[8]

In the past the old worked because they had little choice. Today's employment and welfare policies mean that both men and women up to their late seventies, provided they are fit enough, and provided they have the chance of a job, work principally because they want to. In imposing retirement as a universal goal for all at work, contemporary industrial societies not only have unwittingly extended poverty among their older citizens, but also are throwing away an economic contribution to their general prosperity which many of them would gladly make. The dream of retirement makes good sense to many, but there are an almost equal number to whom it seems an empty reward for a useful life.

Men who resent retirement can sometimes continue in their existing occupations: especially (as often in the past) the self-employed. A Lancashire tailor, for example, evidently lived for his work. Walter Roberts

> was always dressed up. He was always smart. He'd got about half a dozen suits, all hand-made Saville Row; beautiful designed material, pure woollens and cashmeres . . . All what he made himself. Always expensive shirts to match. And always the same socks, Argyll socks. And he had shoes to go with everything. He was a particular man like meself . . . I suppose when we went out, we thought we were the cat's whiskers, the pair of us.

He found retirement intolerable, and went back to work after only three weeks of it.

> He couldn't stand that three weeks, it nearly drove him round the bend. So he went back to work. I think it made him feel old and useless . . . He just went back to what he wanted to do. He always went out early in the morning and he had no need to whatsoever, but that was a habit he couldn't break off.[9]

Only a few men, however, were able to continue their old work, or keep it open for possible return. Most had to accept lower ambitions. One man approaching retirement expected to 'see the winter through, then to look round and find something to do. Just a small thing. Just to force yourself into a routine.' John Bridges, a

factory supervisor who retired at 65, had 'wanted to go on and on,'
but had no choice but to leave. Afterwards he felt 'very down . . .
I miss the complete involvement. . .; the responsibility; keeping
your brain active. I miss the people that I worked with . . . I
thought, "Well, what on earth am I going to do now?"' So he took
a part-time job delivering specialist equipment; but soon, 'because
I am not a very keen driver,' he was looking out for other work.[10]
Finding suitable employment as an older man is, however, ex-
tremely difficult. Road transport, because it is dominated by small-
scale enterprises and poorly regulated, is in fact an unusually
promising area.

Bill Duncan, Lothian ex-miner, is the extreme instance of an
unstoppable worker. He had followed his father into mining, and
'I'll say this about the pits, as far as comradeship was concerned,
the pit was the best thing I was ever in.' But he was forced to quit
after an accident when he was in his forties, and he then took up
hospital work. He was obliged to retire at 68, told 'my time was
up,' and almost immediately afterwards was suddenly widowed.

> And—eh—I was fed up. I was saying to myself, 'I'll go up the
> street a walk.' I was up the street at the crossroads and looking
> round, seeing all thir layabouts that's no intention of ever work-
> ing in thir life if they can get away wi' it, going back and forward
> fae the bookies to the pub and fae the pub to the bookies, then
> back to the corner to wait for the result o'the races coming in. I
> says, 'Good God almighty, I hope I'll no come to this.' So I went
> down and got hold o'the *Evening News*. The job was advertised.
> I says, 'Right, I'll take a chance.' And I got it.
> They were advertising for a driver for a van, a light van . . . So
> I phoned the manager and I told him, I says, 'Have you any
> objection to anybody that's retired?' He says, 'No.'

So with his age overlooked Bill was able to start on a third career,
as a van driver delivering motor parts. 'I was fully five year wi'
them and I did a lot of travelling—Inverness, Aberdeen, Glasgow,
Perth, Dundee, Newcastle, Chesterfield—all over. Done deliver-
ies east coast, west coast, all round about.' But eventually his firm
was taken over by a much larger company, 'one of the biggest
firms in Britain, and they were clamping down on older men. In
fact the man that was manager at the time tried to talk them out of

it, but they wouldna listen to him. So eventually I had to leave there.'

Undeterred, although now 73, he called the following week at a garage for petrol.

> I used to deliver stuff to them and George came oot to talk to me. He says, 'How are ye doin', Bill?' I says, 'Oh not too bad, George, but I'm looking for another job.' He says, 'What d'ye mean, ye're no leaving?' I says, 'I'm no going to leave, I got paid off . . .' 'Oh,' he says, 'I see. Can ye start here Monday?'

The upshot was two more years' work, 'taking the wee van to pick up parts;' until George gave up the garage.

> So that was me finished after that. I couldna get another job. Actually . . . I did get another job. You know the Rosekirk Dairy? My grandson was workin' wi' them and they wanting a driver, so my grandson phoned me up and told me. So I went over to see them.

He started delivering to shops and cafes in the city. But on the Thursday of the first week, the boss summoned him.

> He says, 'Bill, I've got trouble.' I says, 'Oh, what kind o'trouble like?' 'Well,' he says, 'apparently my insurance company won't insure anybody over seventy for a commercial vehicle.' 'Ye've no got any trouble,' I says, 'It's me that's got the trouble. I've got no job.'

For Bill Duncan, the ability to work through these later years has been the best thing in life: 'to think that the people I was serving had no more time for me, and I could get another job in another station and be accepted and carry on.' He is still not resigned to retirement. 'I'll tell ye the noo, if I got a job I'd take it . . . Not for financial reasons . . . You miss the company . . . I would say old age begins, when ye're forced to retire.' Bill believes you need to be active while you can: 'Let's face it, ye're a long time deid.' Given the chance, he would be back at work tomorrow. 'I could fill time up now, oh aye. But if ever a job come, I would definitely take it.'[11]

For most men, however, even if they want to work, a more modest fulfilment seems the only viable option. Characteristically they talk about general manual skills, making and repairing things, sometimes paid but quite often free. As a former factory quality controller put it, 'I'm the handyman. Any small repair jobs.' Like several others, he also took on extra gardening. Jack Hands, retired foreman patternmaker, who had been unable to find a part-time job, had turned to house improvement in his own home.

> You do so much in the house, but you can't keep on working, painting and decorating and painting. So I do odd jobs, if anybody wants a job. Naturally for money: but its fifty-fifty—I do it cheap, because it keeps me occupied. I'm happy doing it, and they got a good job for a cheaper price.

A retired printer looks after a church garden, and 'mends hoovers, anything electric. He does everybody's window outside—save them paying window cleaners. He's got all the tackle; he does all along the road . . . They bring things to him to be done—even filling lighters.' Sid Simonson, an accountant who had once been a carpenter, took up his earlier craft again: 'he's worked since he was eight years old . . . And he's still working.' He finds himself in continual demand, with people 'ringing up and asking him, lots of young people, "Will you do this for me?" He made that table, the set of tables; he made my unit in the back room; he does fitted cupboards . . . It's got a professional touch.'[12]

Part of the appeal of work is that it can give regular routine to daily living. John Bridges, former factory worker, allocates three days a week systematically to work tasks.

> There's normally something every week that somebody wants done. I've got a list of repair jobs: domestic work; car repair— which I do a lot of; general house repairs—internal, not external—decorating, electrical breakdowns; shelving, reorganization of kitchens, fitting units. All those sort of things [for] friends, relations.

For some men, indeed, the thought of previous work alone is enough to order the day. An ex-Indian policeman and administrator was still 'an early riser':

> I always have been an early riser. I remember the poor old superintendent telling me, 'In later life you'll rue all the hours you wasted when you could have been out and about, when you're housebound.' It's true. No, I get up very early. As soon as the sun gets up, more or less.

A former gentleman's butler, now 86, still only feels comfortable over forty years later if he changes his clothes three times a day: 'Oh I like to look proper; properly dressed . . . I've always had to change two or three times a day. In service, of course, you had to.'[13] And as we shall see, other men generated new work patterns for themselves from housework, which up till then had been overwhelmingly the task of the women of the family.

For this generation of women, encouraged to see themselves primarily as wives rather than as workers, retirement from paid work was much less often described as a dramatic turning-point in life. The most striking exception was, significantly, a professional woman, a widowed nurse, who had found retirement

> a traumatic experience. Well—suddenly—you have no company any more. At work you've got other people, lots of company, a lot of chat. And you miss that terribly . . . You are alone. And you just have to think of something to fill the day: give yourself a little company . . . Terribly boring.

More typically they recalled the impact of retirement as much more mild: 'I'm quite happy to be at home . . . I missed the company of the girls, perhaps,' as a former clerk who had retired at the same time as her husband put it.[14] None were thrown through loss of work into the deep depressions suffered by some of the men.

This was not only because most of these women could see an alternative continuing work role for themselves at home, but equally because for those who still prefer paid work it is much easier to find. There is plenty of part-time and usually low-grade service work about, with few restrictive regulations and mostly with low wages in traditional women's occupations, often the sort of work they had been accustomed to earlier in their lives. Two women work for shops, five are cleaners, and five are private nurses. Two others have knitted or made clothes for cash, although as one remarked, it 'pays so badly that I've decided to give it up.' In contrast to the men, some of the working women do seem to have been concerned about their meagre earnings, and one nurse made quite a shrewd business out of her caring activities through the legacies she received. Nevertheless, as with the men, money was never described as the main motive for continuing work. Two couples had been taken on jointly by a church, the husband as caretaker and the wife as cleaner, and this brought the pleasures of company: 'I enjoyed that. I enjoyed the weddings: you met people, and oh, friends that you'd never seen for years . . . It was an interesting job . . . You missed it after you left.' The nurses especially felt their work valued. 'People that are needing help—they just contact . . . I prefer working cause you've got some object.' As another, now nursing much younger invalids, put it: 'I'm glad at my age to be so very useful, this is the thing.' A 76-year-old nurse had been told off by her son for agreeing to look after another 'old lady,' as she called her patients: 'he says, "You're not fit. . . ." I says, "I was put on this earth to do good, and I'm going to do it till I go." '[15]

These women bring food, clean, and day- and night-nurse for clients as professionals. But servicing and caring for others, paid or unpaid, is a socially approved way of life for women of all ages—more than that indeed, a way of life into which most women, whether mothers or daughters or wives, are propelled whether they like it or not. The unpaid servicing of others differs from the defined limits of work for an employer in being a seemingly endless task. It can impose habits of mind, rhythms of daily living, which like those of paid work often survive long after they are needed. But they are distinctly different rhythms. Elsa Mackay, farmworker's wife, mother of three children, now in her eighties, was still battling against dirt as if she had a complete houseful to mind. Her day still pivoted firmly on dinner at 12.30: 'never changed the dinner hour. Just kept it the same.' But her working hours had no boundaries at all. 'I always find something to do inside, you see . . . No resting . . . I can't, I must be on the move . . . "Don't sit—keep going," that would be my recipe . . . I still don't feel retired.'[16]

One reason which some women gave for feeling less strongly about their retirement from paid work, apart from the limited satisfactions of typical catering or cleaning jobs, was that they could see a continuing unpaid work role for themselves in the home. 'It's not so bad for a woman to retire, because she's got plenty to occupy her in the house.'[17] We might see this buffer in later life as a small, belated compensation for the price they pay for the role earlier in life, which has been rightly emphasized in recent feminist writing: the breaking of careers through childbearing, the waste of women's full creative talents, the long years in which even to concentrate on a single objective for an undisturbed hour is a strange pleasure.

Yet the caring role can be even tougher in later life. Servicing others, and especially looking after seriously ill parents or spouses, is the most physically demanding and emotionally exhausting task to fall on many older men and women. One couple, Jim and Gloria White, have certainly had more than their fill of it. They take it in their stride, without any resentment at all, that they have a working son still living with them who expects his mother to cook and clean for him and make his bed and leave food in the fridge if she is ever away. Their whole daily routine hinges on making sure his dinner is ready as soon as he returns from work: 'David comes in at about ten to five and it's ready.' What has upset them, however, is the fact that they had barely retired when they found themselves responsible first for Jim's parents, both of whom lived into their nineties, and then for Gloria's mother. The last ten years for them have been 'heavy going.'

Jim's father had been a lorry driver, and he had 24 years of retirement, the last phase in a council old people's bungalow with a warden, overlooking a bowling green.

> He used to potter in the garden, and me mum just saw to the house . . . And that's where they spent their time, me mum and dad, on the bowling green. Me dad taught me mum to bowl. In fact she won a cup one year . . . They were together all the time.

For many years their two children co-operated in a regular pattern of daily visiting and weekly shopping for them. Then eventually the old man died, aged 94. His last words to Jim were, 'Look after your mum, won't you.' But from then on she declined, slowly. 'She never went anywhere, unless just to the front door to sit on the bench in the summer, watching 'em bowling. But she didn't go on green, after my dad died.' In the winter 'there was nothing— only to sit there by the window, with a big radiator underneath it, her hands on the radiator, and just get up to go to the toilet and back again; make herself a cup of tea.'

She became seriously ill and, amazingly, survived two severe operations. Her children were now struggling to sustain her. 'There's not a day gone by without some of the family had gone to see her . . . Somebody went in her house every day, out of the family, to see she had a meal.' But she had become increasingly difficult in her own troubles. She refused meals on wheels, 'sent the lot back;' and she would not allow a home help to clean for her. '"No, I'm not having home help. I've had 'em, and they don't move your wardrobes to dust behind 'em." So she wouldn't have them.'

Eventually she started to have serious falls. A nurse reprimanded the family: 'You're not doing enough.' So the children tried to organize a shift rota to look after her at night. Her doctor, however, intervened at this point, telling Mrs White senior, 'You know your children are being pulled to pieces by you, you should agree to go into a home,' and explaining to the nurse, 'What you have to realize is that Mrs White's children have all got pension books. They're at the stage where they want help, not having to give it.' Mrs White was coaxed into a home; the nurse apologized; and the children continued visiting, one every day. She died there, aged 99.

Almost at once, Gloria's mother fell ill. She too had been visited daily, but since widowhood at the age of 86 she had deteriorated: coming back from the funeral, sitting at the back of the car, 'she said, "Well, that's it now, he's the last of the big family. There's nothing left now." It wasn't what she said, but how she said it. And we thought she'd given up then.' She was now 'going a bit aggressive, lashing out with her tongue, and she's fallen. She's incontinent, and she's hopeless remembering anything at all.' The task of caring had again become overwhelming. 'I got exasperated with her a time or two, I must admit.' At last she too was moving into a home. 'We've been emptying her house.'

The Whites felt 'a bit rotten' about this, even though she is now much safer: 'she's got the attention.' 'She said, "I don't know where I live, but I want to go home" . . . It's just so sad.' Yet they also feel, for the first time in their lives, the freedom to put themselves first. They had dreamt of day outings, 'bobbing off on the moors, when weather were nice . . . but with me mum being like she was, it didn't materialize.' In the whole ten years, they had only taken a single holiday, and that secretly: 'one year we went away for three days, and never told anybody. Went to Cromer and never let on. It was awful. We felt very guilty— dead guilty—at our age!' Retirement so far has been little fun for them. 'It's been spoiled for us . . . Makes a right pig's ear of your life, you know, the demands on your life. . . . That's the thing that really spoiled our retirement, having to look after me mum and dad to the extent we have had to.' They will never be able to make up for those lost years. All the same, for the Whites, 'the best has to come.'[18]

The Whites have carried the most prolonged burden of caring of all the lives here. But with the lengthening of life it is no longer rare for those in their seventies to be looking after parents in their nineties. Another widow spent eight years with her daughter, the last three bedridden, until she died at 95.

> She got to the stage when she couldna be left all that long. It was one of my regrets that—eh—my husband died before her you see. And we had planned to do different things. We used to go up to the Magnum at Irvine and we used to say, 'Well sometime when Granny's no here, we'll take up this carpet bowling.' And we had plans to do different things. But we never got any of them carried out.[19]

It is a characteristic of caring that it waxes and wanes unexpectedly, and at many different points in life. There is no neat way, for instance—as some family sociologists have suggested there should be—of identifying a certain point in each of these life stories at which a woman whose children have reached independence enters the 'empty nest' phase. Grandchildren may arrive to fill the gap even before the last child has left the home; and sometimes, for example when a child's marriage runs into difficulties, may more than fill it. Bob and Dina Jordan felt sorry for their grandchildren and had tried to be a bit of an anchor for them.' But when their son moved back in with the Jordans, they were uncomfortable with his rough way of handling the grandchildren, and still more with his bad temper towards themselves. They came to the conclusion that they preferred children 'in small doses.' When their grandson, whom they had had for his first seven years—'we practically brought him up as one of our own'—wanted to stay on with them, they refused. 'We know we couldn't accommodate a young mind now . . . I wouldn't go through the boys' teens for all the tea in China again . . . We wanted to be like other families and see the grandchildren now and again.'[20]

For a woman to be able to make such a conscious choice against a continuing caring role is exceptional. Typically it is an expectation difficult to avoid. And equally seriously, for those women whose lives are largely or solely built around a caring role, its withdrawal is just as arbitrary. It was indeed when they had suffered a sudden and involuntary diminution of domestic responsibilities that this generation of women most often showed the feelings commonly expressed by the men at retirement from paid work. This sudden change may come about in three ways. The most intractable—which we shall consider later because it is a loss of so much else too—is widowhood. Almost half of those whom we recorded had lived through this traumatic experience, and several had still to recover from it. It is a loss which may occur, often unexpectedly, at any point in later life.

A second way is more predictable: it comes from a man's retirement. It was noticeable that a good many couples retired together, sometimes due to explicit pressure from a man who clearly expected the supportive presence of his wife at home during the day. One woman who continued working as a caterer was able to do so in part because her unmarried, retired sister had moved in to do all the cooking, but her workless husband remained unhappy: 'me going to work, and him not being able to work, that goes against the grain very much.' But a minority of men, choose this same moment to take on a much larger share of domestic responsibilities. Sometimes this can be wholly positive. Ted Keeler, former fisherman, for example, who had no doubt got used to caring for himself at sea, had moved in with his son after being widowed, and decided to retire early when his daughter-in-law had the chance of a better job, full time: 'so if I retired to look after the kids, get them off to school and that, she could get that job. So I did that.' He is the one who is up first, at 5.30, to get one now teenage grandson off to work; 'and then when they've all gone to work, make the beds, do a bit of vaccing and dusting, go out and do some shopping . . . I do a bit of cleaning up, messing about ironing, and do the garden. Which keeps me active, which is what I want to do.' He was glad to have taken early retirement: 'I thoroughly enjoyed it! I had two little boys to look after.' A Midland man, who was equally 'housetrained,' and believed housework should be a joint task—'not mine, not hers; it's ours; who does what, doesn't matter'—had a well-matched spouse. As she put it, 'I've always hated housework and I married the most tidy man on earth.' For him, unwillingly out of paid work, with days typically 'very boring,' domestic tasks were a lifeline: 'that's what keeps me at full vigour.'[21]

It is a much less happy solution when the retired man unknowingly cuts his wife's lifeline. Maggie Kells had earlier worked herself, sterilizing bottles, and had not wanted to give up her job.

'I loved my job, loved it.' Her husband George is a retired Scots
worker, whose many jobs included fourteen years in the pits. He
has always taken a share of the housework—'he's always been
good.' Made redundant when his store closed down, he did not
look for more paid work, being convinced it would be fruitless to
try: 'ye'd never get one at 63-year-old . . . Ye've no chance.' Instead
he threw himself into domesticity, treating it as a job. As Maggie
remarks to him, 'Ye dinna forget aboot work, George, cause ye
canna sit still for five minutes.' He took over the garden as if it
were a necessity to grow their own food. 'I wouldna do it if I didna
have to, ken it's really, I hae to dae it. I dinna like it, but I've gotta
do.' Maggie interjects, 'It's bonny when ye see a' the stuff growing
in and coming on. Ye like it when ye see the carrots and cabbage.'

The garden, however, was certainly not enough to occupy him.
He also does the daily shopping: 'went oot to dae the shoping this
morning, he's quite happy going shopping. He loves going through
the shops.' And he does most of the cleaning and much of the
cooking. To George, this was a just reward for Maggie for all the
caring she had done while he was out on a job, but to Maggie it is
more than she ever asked for. As George sees it,

> She's done it all they years when the hoose wis full, and she
> used to rise at five o'clock in the morning and go away to work.
> And my way of thinking is this: she deserves to get the benefit of
> it noo. And that doesn't suit her, cause she can't accept that she
> should be sitting doon and taking it easy.

So George's very eagerness to help creates friction. 'I canna get
in the kitchen fir him.' She cannot get on with cleaning, partly
because she is less fit—'I canna stand up on a table now'—but also
because she hardly starts before he intervenes with '"Leave it,
that's my job, I'll do that." He thinks I shouldna rise in the
morning and polish the grate and do the fire. I'm no allowed to,
right?'

Maggie, in short, has been made redundant as a carer by her
retired husband's helpfulness, and she does not like it. 'It's
murder . . . I'm bored to tears.' He has taken from her the regular
routine which used to structure her days:

> I had a set routine. The time I got up—I had to wait till George
> wis just oot the door, and as soon as he wis oot the door, I got

up, dressed, and got the heater on in the winter, the cooker on,
the kettle on, all curled up in a chair, did ma crossword. Always
did ma crossword first. Then I'd maybe, half past nine or nine
o'clock, I'd say, 'Right! Away!' an' start work. An' I occupied
myself wi' hoosework all day, daeing this and that, all the jobs,
all the skirting boards, all the glass work, all day, all the
jobs. . . . I hardly ever had a spare minute . . . I had the wireless
on and I used to dae an awfy lot o'washing and ironing and
baking. I had—Monday wis washday, Tuesday wis ironing day,
Wednesday wis may baking day, Thursday I did the bedrooms
and the bathroom and the lobby, Friday I did this place
thoroughly—I had a day fir each thing . . .

But see noo, I've got that much spare time that I dinna know
what to be at.

Maggie suffers like a paid worker forced out of work. She finds it
hard to leave the house and face others; yet it 'gets on my nerves
noo there's only the two of us . . . I would rather be busy than sit
like this, aye, I've never been used to sitting. Very depressing. I
tell ye if thir wis a wee bairn to come in and run aboot, I'd be
quite happy.'[22]

The loss of a caring role here is not a stark result of demography:
of childlessness, or death. Compared with many women of her
age, Maggie is surrounded by family. Her own mother is still alive,
in her eighties, although she has little to do with her; Maggie has
her husband; she has children, including a daughter 'very near,' to
whom she feels close; and she has grandchildren. The arrival of
grandchildren, for whom she makes clothes and babysits, has been
wholly positive. Both of them felt 'over the moon' when their first
grandson was born: 'It keeps the family going.'[23] Yet there can be
no doubt that Maggie suffers from her sense of an empty home.

The departure of children is the third way in which the caring
role can be taken away. If demography alone was the main deter-
minant of an 'empty nest' phase, every woman should suffer when
her children leave home, and those with the fewest offspring
should suffer most. This turns out to be entirely false.

In fact only very few women feel a continuing inner emptiness.
Far from having the smallest families, these mothers have been
among the most prolific, with an average of more than four children each. Three out of the four are still married, and all are in

regular contact with both children and grandchildren. Their feeling of need clearly comes from the very centrality of children to their own sense of self and the exclusion of interests or work outside the home. One couple, who worked at tailoring in their own home, had six children, and were so used to the noise of them and their friends—'we always seemed to have a crowd, children, or somebody in at weekends'—that later, although the youngest was still living at home, 'the house seemed empty and I remember my husband saying, "Why don't you go and fetch some kids from next door? It's dead here."'[24]

Agnes Dunbar, married to a former Scots miner and then engineer who became ill and unemployed, feels equally empty without her five children in the home. 'You miss them out the house, you miss the company.' In fact, she sees all of them regularly, and every day two call in for an hour or so. Being visited does not solve her central problem, which is lack of purposeful work now that the children no longer require her care.

> I've just got Mr Dunbar to look after now. And it's a long day. It can be a long monotonous day . . . and sometimes you get a bit depressed . . . I've lived only for my family . . . It's a lonely house now, a quiet house . . . Very dreech day actually. Aye, well sometimes I lie and wonder in the morning if it's worthwhile getting up.[25]

It is thus the very abundance of earlier family life and the dominance of childrearing as a source of life purpose to the exclusion of other interests which makes its waning most difficult to accept. It is notable that—partly because family created a social life for them—these women and their husbands have few other social activities and no close friends. As busy mothers they were not able to develop work careers, and they have also been unable to develop special interests of their own since. Nor were they and their husbands as close to each other as many retired couples seemed to be.

For such women the best strategy in later life may seem to be to recapture a meaningful caring role. Jean Macpherson, for example, had moved north as a young Englishwoman to marry a Scots labourer whom she had met as a wartime sailor, and settled only slowly and with difficulty into the Clydeside community: at first it was 'terrible.' After her children had left home, she found an unexpected new fulfilment when one of her sons divorced, leaving her with two granddaughters to bring up: 'I reared those first two when they got divorced. Aye, they stayed wi'me, I reared them till about four year ago.' But once they left to return to their father, life became difficult once more. 'It wasn't a best time at all. No, because I missed them, and I didn't have as much to do. Although even now they've left home, I can't get used to shopping for two of us.' Her weekdays seem empty, 'boring:' 'once this house is clean there's nothing else for me to do . . . The days get longer and the years get shorter.' So Jean's consolations feed on a fuller past: 'I loved the wee anes and this place is empty when there's none here. I don't know what I'd do if my grandchildren didn't come down and see me.' She has eleven grandchildren, and the highlight of her week is on Sunday: 'the feeding of the masses . . . The meal that I enjoy most is a Sunday dinnertime . . . I can't get used to cooking for two . . . I still enjoy working out here in the kitchen and specially if I know the family's coming.'[26]

For the majority, however, the experience of children leaving home proves more positive. Their aim is to see their children independent, and they speak of only brief pangs at their departing: the focus is much more on pride in children's achievements, and pleasure in grandchildren. As one mother put it,

> When the last one goes it's a bit funny, you think to yourself, 'Well, there's nobody to run around after now,' and there's just the two of you, you're left on your own. But you see they come back, they come back and forth, whatever jobs they have, they come home.

Relationships could indeed deepen as children grew into adulthood, as a former nurse, mother of four, explained: 'They were more companions to me, that I could talk to them and discuss different things . . . We could go out together . . . As they grew older I grew up with them and yet I stayed on a level with them.'[27]

Most important of all, many could quickly see that the changes in their responsibilities could bring compensations. Shedding a work role, whether paid or unpaid, is one of the most difficult adaptations which later life demands. But it can be a release too, bringing new opportunities. 'It was a different time: we began to get closer, my husband and I, because we were more on our own . . . We both had to adjust to a new way of living . . . I was freer . . .'[28] And it is to the use they make of that freedom that we must next turn.

8

Freedom and Fun

QUITTING work has two kinds of attraction. One is release: from the burden of work, the anxiety of responsibility, the physical effort and exhaustion, the constraints on personal choice and time. 'It's less stress,' one couple put it, and 'for the first time in our lives, we're able to please ourselves, more or less, what we do, and when we do it; and we were never able to do that, never.' And many others felt similarly: 'I can do what pleases me;' 'I've got freedom—it's the freedom I like;' 'I always reckon my life's one long holiday. We can do what we like, and have a cup of tea when you feel like it, have a walk round the garden....'[1]

For a very few, the sense of freedom was enough in itself. The Hibblethwaites were leading a very quiet life, only occasionally going out to dinner with friends, or to a fortnightly farm club. They had no relatives nearby. Their main entertainment was television: 'most nights, I'm afraid.' But simple relaxation suits them. She knits; he mends the car. 'Oh no, we're enjoying retirement. We're mostly at home, aren't we?' Twelve others also had very few leisure pursuits; but none of these were very happy with their lives. One woman was a recent widow, acutely depressed. The others were still married, but all somewhat discontented couples. Among them were two mothers still missing their children, whose only pleasure was a weekly club or bingo evening; two wives with uncommunicative husbands, who read a little, while their men went now and then to the pub; and a frustrated, captive housewife who dreams of activity but cannot get her man to go further than the pub—'he's a man as has no sort of hobbies or interests. I like everything. I'll go to anything... theatre... snooker... swimming... I can't just sit somewhere having a drink, and nothing—no.' One other husband, who had been forced to retire early, tried to take up a new interest but was too depressed to sustain it. 'He did set himself up with two boxes of Meccano when he retired. He got through the first easy one, he didn't mind that, but when he bought a more advanced one, he kept getting impatient with that and it was "too fiddly" and he "couldn't do it." So it's all been abandoned now.'[2]

In most of these homes television provided the most regular entertainment. They were not unusual in mentioning watching television as a leisure activity; two-thirds of those whom we recorded did so, and some also listened to radio. One lonely widow used the television simply for company: 'it's on all day and night. Sometimes because it's just a noise in the house.' But most people watched television selectively: sport or soaps, plays or music. As a widowed nurse put it, 'I choose my programmes. I like documentaries and nature programmes. I don't like stuff like "Dallas," I just get annoyed at it.' A couple, both retired from factory work, 'watch documentaries, interesting things. We're not lovers of soap, although we don't mind a thriller, a good picture if it's a thriller. But we do like documentaries and we like horse-racing. He likes boxing, and I like snooker and golf, watching it. I love the horses; I have a bet every Saturday.' Those without special interests of their own, by contrast, are much more passive also as viewers: 'it's never off;' 'I watch nearly whatever's on.' As nothing else can, it fully absorbs them: 'once tellie's on, he's mesmerised. Can't get a word out of him.'[3]

No other home entertainments matched the media. A third of both men and women mentioned reading. One couple do crosswords together, and a few listen to their own music. Some of the women enjoy cooking, but none mentioned it as a special interest: it is a rewarding part of the job of being a housewife. Making clothes, on the other hand, and especially knitting, was mentioned as a leisure activity by one in three women. They continue a skill learnt from their mothers in childhood, when making clothes was a necessary saving for most working families; but they now use it mainly as a practical way of showing their love for their grandchildren. Yet although it is skilled work, like cooking, they show no pride in it. It is more likely to be dismissed as 'the needful sewing; but not in the way of hobbies.'

There is only one exception, Annie Mimms, a London ex-cleaner and nurse married to an electrician, happily retired to a Green Belt village. She remains active both in the village and back in the nearby suburbs. She used to assist the Red Cross nurses at an old people's day centre—including helping to 'bath the incapacitated people.' She still helps organize the village Horticultural Show, exhibiting her jam and marmalade, pickles and sewing; twice recently winning a cup. She is a regular at a bingo club and the Women's Institute. But above all, she has made a new life around sewing and knitting. It gives her fun, and she earns a little cash from it too:

> I've got a friend over at Chipstone-on-the-Hill, I've done all her curtains, all her lined velvet curtains and other patterned curtains, and covered her settees and chairs. Been over there three or four days at a time to do all this sewing. And she'd come and get me and bring me back when it was ready, and feed me while I was over there.
>
> And then I've got another friend at Hicklow, who used to live at Bexley, and then she moved in the December, two months after we came here. And I've made all the curtains in her house, all her lined velvet curtains, nine foot lengths, and covered her chairs. This friend I've known for forty years ...
>
> A friend across the road came in in the mornings ... and one day she said to me, 'Oh Mrs Mimms, you do sewing—you like sewing?' I said, 'Yes.' And from that day till now, I've done all her sewing, all her mending. All the boys' mending; knitted all their school socks, knitted all their woollies ... I've patched all their jeans ... Now Luke's just come home from university, he's 20: knitted pullovers galore for him, knitted his socks because he's got such big feet ... And Jack is 36 in November: he brought me a couple of pairs of trousers the other week and I shortened them for him. Made all their things; so I've been mixed up with it years and years. And I've just knitted her a couple of baby cardigans for her daughter's little baby girl that was born last Friday. I've done any amount of knitting ...
>
> This is for my great-grandchildren, toys and things now. I've knitted this little chap round here, this little scarecrow. And I've knitted one for Helen's little boy; and now my great-granddaughter wants me to knit her one ... I'm always knitting.[4]

One other domestic activity is almost as common as making clothes, but this time outside the house, and enjoyed by both sexes: gardening. Most really serious gardeners, however, are men. The exception, to whom we shall return, is the floral champion—but for her the garden is a means to fulfilment beyond it.

Annie Mimms herself is typical of those who pursue their leisure
most vigorously through having a great range of different interests,
and gardening is among them. But she and her husband divide the
work up in a very typical way. 'I can do a bit of gardening. I've
been pottering around and putting the plants out, the begonias,
and potting up a lot of things.' But for Walter Mimms, gardening is
a much more consuming passion. 'He lives out there, you see, he
loves the garden . . . My husband works out there all the time. He
really does work hard out there, but he loves it.' Several men have
thrown themselves into gardening as if it were a business. A
retired under-manager laid out the garden and lawns himself: 'I
did all that and I built myself a greenhouse and a shed so that I
could get my own work on the bench up there.' Another man built
two greenhouses for his retirement. A Scots wife recalled how her
husband was fully occupied after he lost his job: 'he wasn't any
bother then, because you see he did the garden. Oh, he loved
gardening. He'd do the best potatoes, he grew the finest tomatoes,
and he had them ready every year, Fair weekend. Beautiful tomatoes.' A businessman had an orchard and a kitchen garden where
'we used to grow all our own vegetables . . . So we have a busy
life . . . We cut down the trees and we trim everything up. It's
getting harder work now . . . I'm a bit of a fanatic. Everything has
to be right.' Like making clothes, gardening is an activity which
was once a vital support for the standard of living of ordinary
families. But these men have few people to feed, and they do not
seem to make social relationships through gifts from their gardening. The one exception is Ted Keeler, the domesticated fisherman.
Gardening was a new pleasure for him, and he not only keeps his
own garden, with its roses, orchard, and greenhouse, but also
helps out two neighbours. He looks after a headmaster's greenhouse when he is away, and permanently cares for the garden of an
old lady opposite: 'which is a fairly big one at the back, and I like
it. I like keeping busy.'5

   Gardening not only provides purposeful activity, but also regular
exercise. A difficulty is that because it requires a lot of bending
and heaving, it really only suits those who remain strong. Ted
Keeler complained, 'a couple of hours in the garden, and that's it
now, whereas I used to work 24 hours on the sea at a spell.' But
only a quarter of those we recorded took any regular exercise for
the sake of it. One remarked, 'There's far too much nonsense
talked about it. I often wonder what people are keeping fit for.'

Those who do take exercise often combine more than one form. None play games more energetic than bowls or golf. The players include a widow who met her new best friend, a retired civil servant, at a bowls club. 'She sat there, not a person spoke to her. I said, "Oh come on, have a game of bowls with me."' They now go every Friday. Four others swim. Four couples and three of the widowed still dance, so that dancing is almost as popular as gardening. It certainly keeps them in trim: as one couple remarked, 'we finished at the school being the only ones on the floor doing a jive.' But dancing is much more than a form of exercise, as we shall see. There are also twelve who walk or cycle regularly, or both—for a variety of reasons. The ex-policeman had always been riding or walking in India, and kept up the habit: he had no car on purpose. 'I'm not one of those joggers . . . I'm a terrific walker, you see . . . Here, I walk everywhere.' One man walked six miles regularly to see his brother; and a cyclist had managed a 22-mile sponsored ride. A Chiltern widow is out on any decent day: 'I put a coat on and I climb all the hills . . . Generally go for a couple of hours over the hills. It's beautiful out there, can see for a long way. And talk to the villagers . . . So I go out and meet people, talk, pass the time of day.' One couple, who are regular dancers, also 'like walking; we like going in out-of-the-way places in the country, where it's quiet, and watching the birds and the wildlife.' Leonard Seldon, widower, who before retirement had dreamt 'of all the golf I was going to play—I did play a lot too,' and managed a golf club for a while, also took solitary pleasure in walking with the company only of his dog. Although some others kept a cat, none had the same enthusiasm as he had for his pet.

That dog, she was super. She was. Oh-ooo . . . I went up over the hills and walked up there with the dog and I thought, well, this is lovely. I have no allegiance to anybody now, except my wife. And it was lovely. I did enjoy that, yes, and I have ever since.[6]

Another way of getting out of the house is to take an outing in the car. This is as popular as the various forms of physical activity. A part-time office cleaner married to an ex-patternmaker described how she had become

not so fussy with my housework now as I used to be . . . It used to be dusted and mopped and carpet-hoovered, every day I used

to do that. Then there's washing. But he's got me out of that a
little bit now. "Come on, we're going out, leave it...." Sometimes we go and pick up our friends . . . We like to find a country
pub and have a ploughman's. Go out for a ride in the country.

A widowed nurse goes out in a friend's car, perhaps to a pub or to
a hotel on the coast for a meal, or 'to one of the stately homes.'
These are typical objectives for outings. Some go out with local
preservation or arts associations, but only one couple went regularly to the theatre and concerts on their own. Unless a special coach
has been organized, outings are a daytime rather than an evening
activity for the retired. As a result, they are not usually far afield.
Certainly some still take regular holidays, both in Britain and on
the Mediterranean. A banker's widow was just off to Tunisia at
eighty—with her older brother. And a few have made ambitious
trips to see far-flung relatives in Canada, Australia, or New Zea-
land. But these travellers are a small group. It is not only a
question of the cost and the strain of travel; also that those who
are not working do not centre their dreams on a brief annual
break. Holidays are like a series of day trips from a different base:
equipped with camp stove and picnic basket, 'we tend to be
out all day.'[7] Their essential enjoyment is their regular pattern of
living.

The most individual forms of leisure activity are those with a
special creative aim: the painter, the collector of pottery or antiques, the photographers, the man who is writing poetry. One
couple 'belong to the Wine Circle now . . . There's a competition
next week—I've made the mixed fruit wine.' A Scots widow had
thrown herself into self-improvement, taking a succession of
courses from Gaelic to astronomy, lampmaking to leatherwork:
'every year there was something else I went to.'[8] But those who
most stand out are the dancing couples, and the floral champion.

Dawn Roberts is a widowed ex-laundress with a new vocation, 'a
new lease of life . . . When I retired, I went flower arranging. Now
that's a very expensive hobby, but it's very satisfying.' For her first
four years of retirement, she went to weekly flower-arranging
classes by Bill Lomax of Knutsford, 'one of the most famous
teachers in the world,' who offered a special low fee for pensioners. At the same time she started gardening, to provide the mate-
rials she needed for her new art.

My garden has lovely coloured shrubs in it. Some are evergreen and some are deciduous. They come out at different times . . . White blossom, that'll be out in a couple of weeks, and then I have other shrubs with a great pink bell and light grey velvety foliage, and berberis, all tiny vivid red berries, and a golden privet, which is a special one, a green stripe down the middle— all for texture. And then this one out here, all lovely yellow and red, a big one, and then I've got a eucalyptus which is all grey, and I've got a lovely honeysuckle. I've got clematis up the wall and intermingled through the trees . . . I have a little fish-pool with water lilies on it, because it's only a pocket-handkerchief size garden, and grey and white foliage that grows low down on the ground and tall big lilies . . . The front's all roses . . . I've got winter heathers, spring heathers, summer heathers and autumn heathers . . . so there's colour all round . . . You can buy yourself a few flowers, but you can't buy foliage, and you can't make flower arrangements unless you can back it up with foliage.

She specialized in the Japanese style of flower arrangement. 'You've always got to portray something: you've got to represent something.' And a colour sense is essential. Her teacher immediately spotted her gift for this, and from the first year on she has been a regular prize-winner. 'Each year that I've entered I've won something.' She now belongs to two flower clubs, which hold regular open days as well as shows:

You make lovely friends and you go on all trips out in the summer to big houses that demonstrators live in, big farm-houses, and they show you all the different plants and some sell them and you can buy them for your own garden: that's how you accumulate things. ⚓

At Christmas she makes floral wreaths.

I used that tree and me own variagated holly and then I have some artificial which I put in as well, and big silk poinsettias, white Christmas roses. And I make very big arrangements, great big ones . . . My daughter-in-law, she likes one of these holly wreaths that you put on your door, it's on the porch there, and I always have one.

One year she made some extra wreaths for sale and her son did a roaring trade in them at his butcher's shop: 'on bark, and Father

Christmases stuck in, and little robins stuck all over the place.'

Her repertoire does not end there: when her teacher presented
the class with a box of cardboard tubes and asked everyone to
compete in designing a 'modern' arrangement she made two, one
including plastic oilcloth and the other pebble-dash wallpaper.
'I've never gone in a show yet that I haven't taken something.'[9]

Some of the dancing couples have also developed special skills of
which they are understandably proud. One pair go to twice-weekly
classes in sequence dancing. Another regular dancer 'can dance
with anybody. I love dancing. And the clubs I go to, they all say,
"She's one of the best dancers here"—whatever dancing it is. If it's
the mod stuff, I can do it with anybody, besides ballroom dancing.
I've been dancing since I was eight years old.' For the handful of
regulars, dancing is indeed a consuming pleasure: it is exercise,
and a skill, and companionship, and a romantic echo of youth, all
in one. As Bill Duncan, the unstoppable worker, put it, 'once
you're a dancer, you never forget. You just need to hear the band
and that's enough.'[10]

Dancing is a group activity. Company is the other main attraction of going out. The last group of leisure activities which were
mentioned consisted of those which appealed above all as a way of
seeing other people. The need for this obviously differs. It is much
more important for the widowed than for couples. Half the married mentioned no regular social activity, but only two of the 15
single widowed. Less strongly, need is shaped by the availability of
other relatives. We shall look closely at grandparenting in the next
chapter. But there was altogether a great variety in the amount of
family contact. Twelve people saw a child daily, and these included
one couple whose son had not left home, and two retired men who
had moved back into their children's house. In all, 33 saw a child
or grandchild at least weekly. At the other extreme were 19 who
only saw them fortnightly or less. Quite often the problem was
distance, but attitudes were also crucial. One couple scarcely ever
spoke to a son who lived across the road from them, and another
couple had had too much of their nearby grandchildren. And a
professional couple who had moved to a beautiful village in the
south-west could clearly have encouraged their children to come
down to visit them, but had given their own activities priority:
their children came rarely 'because I haven't really got the room.
I've only got one spare room now because my husband has the

other as his little den.' It is noticeable that two-thirds of those who saw their children only fortnightly or less had some kind of social leisure, compared with half of those who saw them weekly or more (see Table 5.)[11]

Zest for human company does not diminish with age. The under-seventies were the least socially active, partly because more of them saw people through work: over half had no social leisure. Of those over seventy, by contrast, three-quarters were socially active (see Table 6). Some continued against severe odds. The most remarkable of all is Sadie King, an eighty-year-old Lancashire widow who had worked in the tailoring trade with her husband. He died when they were on holiday together, nearly twenty years ago. 'People say I coped very well, but what consoled me . . . he'd said, "Oh well, I hope I go quick" . . . He hadn't suffered . . . He was so fond of his work, he would have gone mad if he couldn't have done it. That's why he wouldn't retire.'

Left on her own, Sadie created a new social life for herself. For holidays she travelled to Singapore and Australia to see sons who were working there, or she went away with a single sister-in-law, or more recently her younger separated daughter. But her regular social life has centred around clubs. Until recently she went to an Old People's Club on Tuesday afternoons and a Bingo Club on Thursday afternoons: 'not that I'm interested in bingo really, but it was just an afternoon meeting people.' And she also became more active in a church, for similar reasons: 'I did become a member, but I'm not what you would call a very religious person. I mean, I'm not deep in it . . . but I think I've got a lot of friends in the church.' She went to the Women's Fellowship on Monday evenings, to the Ladies' Class on Wednesday afternoons, and on Sunday evenings she went to church with her sister-in-law, who comes to stay each Saturday night.

In the last two years her life has become much more difficult, since she has become crippled with arthritis, and needs a wheelchair to go any distance on her own. Yet she fights on with extraordinary spirit. Her typical day now begins with the struggle to get up:

Well it's usually about quarter past nine when I pull myself together to get out of bed. It takes me about twenty minutes or so to get dressed, and I crawl down the stairs, just like that, I

come down backward. I come down backwards, because I feel
safer that way than coming down frontwards. I crawl up the
stairs when I'm going up, although I've had a handrail up, they
have put me a handrail up. But I feel a lot safer going up with
me hand on until I get next to the top, and then I grab hold of
that at the top, and grab the side of the bannister, and pull
meself up the last two steps. It's getting up the last two steps is
worst . . .

More often than not, I'm ready for stopping in bed when I
should be getting up . . . I try to get my breakfast for the ten
o'clock news . . . And then I start knitting, and I'm more or less
knitting and watching television . . . I read my newspaper when
that comes. I just have an evening paper, sit and read that, and
enjoy it, and watch any programme that I'm interested in.

Sadie knits for a purpose, for others: she knits creative toys for
the church sale, with patterns she gets from Oxfam. She feels
herself 'not very often' lonely: 'if I hadn't my knitting to do, I
would do, I think.' If she gets fed up with knitting, she plays
patience. What she misses most is 'not being able to go out.' She
still does get to the occasional game of whist or Donkey Derby—'I
can enjoy myself'—but the difficulty is that she can no longer use a
bus. 'It's just a case of somebody being there to take me to these
places, you see.'

Although she now has a home help for cleaning, Sadie keeps to a
weekly routine. 'I can't sit still and do nothing.' On *Mondays* she
washes and on *Tuesdays* she irons. One of her four sons, who lives
next door but one, comes in with her pension and also shops for
her twice a week. On *Wednesdays* the home help comes in the
morning, and in the afternoon she goes with her next-door neighbour to the church Ladies' Class. The neighbour is a recent
widow, and they also go out to whist together now and then. 'We
sing about three hymns, and we have a cup of tea and a biscuit
afterwards.' They have regular speakers, and an occasional bring-
and-buy sale: 'that's when all me knitting comes out . . . I've got a
pile there for this June effort.' On *Thursdays* she may go across the
road to another neighbour, who does her hair. On *Friday* her
elder daughter calls, either in the afternoon to take her for a run in
the car, or in the evening. On *Saturdays* she spends the day
preparing for her sister-in-law, who comes to spend the night.

They sit down to high tea, and afterwards 'we watch television till about ten o'clock, then we start playing cards.' Unfortunately, Sadie complains, 'she's a bad loser.' On *Sundays* she can no longer get to church, but at least fortnightly another son and his wife, who looks after her garden, come with the grandchildren for tea.

Sadie likes cooking. Her main meal is high tea. She still bakes, making sure she has a home-made cake for visitors. 'Oh I do enjoy me food! I always have done, I've always enjoyed food.' She stays up quite late, sometimes watching late television. When she was younger with six children at home she used to treasure the quiet of that time of the day—'Thank goodness I've got an hour to myself'—and she keeps the rhythm. 'I'm a long while getting to sleep, because I read when I go to bed . . . Once I've got that first sleep, I can get to sleep again . . . But that first sleep I can't grab hold of.'

Many might be disheartened by a life curtailed by pain. 'I feel I could still travel if it wasn't that me legs wouldn't go. Yes, I miss being able to please myself, and go on holiday, go on coach.' Nevertheless, for Sadie old age is a bonus. 'We've had our three-score years and ten, we're living on borrowed time . . . I don't feel me age, it's just that me legs feel that old, but not me head.' Summing up the most significant feature of ageing, she says: 'contentment.'[12]

Clubs are not the only way of keeping in touch with people. A handful of people mainly visit each other at home. Rudi Fine, a businessman, whose wife is 'a great cook,' has retired to a manor. A highly political man, when in London he and his wife 'kept an open house' regularly once a week, talking into the small hours with 'people in the movement, people who were interesting—artists, lawyers, solicitors, sculptors—people like that . . . Tremend-ous discussions went on all the time.' One of the things he misses in the country is a good political argument: 'I like dialecticing . . . I swear at the government all the time.' But they still have their neighbours, also ex-Londoners, to dinner every Friday evening, and they are invited back on Saturdays: 'they're very interesting people and we have a lot in common.' A former factory supervisor cannot hear well enough to go to larger groups, 'so I'm rather restricted . . . I'm a great talker, love conversation, and a good listener . . . I love people.' But he can see friends privately: 'I've got a lot of friends who I can—on the spur of the moment—I can

either ring or I can just go.' Two women—both with other regular
social activities—keep in touch with people in other ways. One
feels it is an advantage of growing older that 'I make friends quite
easily ... When you're young, you're maybe more shy to make
friends.' She sees former work colleagues at the hospital Retirement Fellowship—'oh yes, good friends, you meet a lot o' folks'—
but she also makes a point of regular letter-writing. And Mary
Wesley, a widow who belongs to a variety of societies, makes
exceptionally heavy use of her phone.

> I phone friends ... I phone my sister in Paisley—she's an awful
> blether, you can be on half an hour and longer sometimes ...
> My niece just to see how they're keeping ... And a cousin of
> my husband's wife. After Dick died, he phoned me regularly,
> just to say, "How are you? How are things?" And I thought
> so much of him, such a nice man. So when he died, I did the
> same to his wife.[13]

Several of those who are keen club-goers belong to more than
one society. A civil servant retired to the home counties, now 78,
was active in politics, the churches, voluntary work, the British
Legion, amateur theatre, photography, educational societies, and
scouting. A London architect and his wife, Desmond and Julia
Churchill, had moved into a Devon village where they already had
a niece who had married a local farmer, and found it

> a very friendly village too ... We have quite a good social life. I
> belong to the WI: I'm on the committee. We belong to the
> church: my husband's the churchwarden. We entertain. We
> belong to the National Trust and my husband's on the commit-
> tee of that, so he does a lot with the local branch. He organizes
> outings and walks ... He's always doing something for somebody
> as he's always done—all the old widows and there are plenty of
> them ... There's always something going on in the village....
> We're very busy: we never seem to have time for anything.

But the less privileged could be very busy, too. Edna Rourke, a
retired London nurse from Northern Ireland, a clerk's widow, says
modestly:

> I have joined a few things. I go to the Methodist Ladies Guild
> on a *Monday* afternoon. I go to the prayer group meeting on

Tuesday afternoon—it's sort of mixed Christian . . . I go to the Grannies' Club on *Wednesday* afternoon . . . Cuppa tea and a chat, and we do our knitting. The others play bingo. But it passes a couple of hours . . . The 'Darby and Joan,' you know; but we've only got one old man. And *Thursday*, toymaking . . . *Friday*, I usually have a couple of cronies in for an afternoon cup of tea. Sometimes Terry comes home with the children on *Saturday* afternoons. *Sunday* we serve coffee after mass, in the hall. And that's about it.[14]

The variety of clubs and societies already mentioned is typical. They mostly fall into five groups, each with six to eight supporters among our interviewees. One group is connected with public causes—for example, charitable societies or political clubs; a second consists of professional and ex-service clubs; and a third comprises old people's clubs. The two largest groups are church associations, and clubs for games and sports: mostly games of chance like cards and bingo, but also some sports, like snooker, golf, cricket, or rugby—as a keen ex-mining rugby follower put it, 'that's my weakness that, I'm going tonight, they have a match tonight.'[15]

Although the old people's clubs had some keen followers, it is very striking how much they were disliked by most of the people whom we recorded. Altogether only seven out of the fifty-two attended them, and unlike other clubs, they were viewed with marked hostility by very many who would have nothing to do with them. 'Sounds like a real insult;' 'I wouldn't consider it;' 'no way;' 'I wouldn't be seen dead in them;' 'you might as well go and get in the grave straight away.' As Bill Duncan sums up the typical view: 'never had any intentions o'going to it, nut . . . There's some o'them that goes up there are a heck of a lot younger than what I am, and they'll just die on their feet.' The reason why so many older men and women are so hostile to old people's clubs is quite clear. They see them as places where they would be herded together in a passive group, disparagingly categorized as old, provided for and patronized by club organizers regarding themselves as unquestionably their social superiors. But they do not feel old and they do not want to be scornfully labelled as such. 'We're travellers under our own steam;' 'they patronize you.' The lonely bank manager's widow who would not think of joining such a

club—'I'm not being snobbish, but I don't feel . . .'—has just the
same view as the ex-pitman who feels at home in the rugby crowd,
but shudders away from a pensioner's group: 'I like to be select—I
like one or two.'[16]

Nor is this just an outsider's view. A retired woman factory
worker tried an old people's club, but 'it made me feel old . . . Old
ladies and bickering who was doing this and who was doing
that . . . I give it up.' A Midland car-worker's widow still goes
weekly, but is scarcely more satisfied: 'don't get much entertainment at all . . . Couple of games of bingo, that's all. Tuppence a
game—bloomin' heck! I thought to myself, last Tuesday . . . it's a
waste of time getting washed and changed to go down . . . it's a
waste of time!' Others who never went, conjured up similar pictures. A retired foreman asked, 'Can you imagine me? They've got
quite a few o' them round this way. Go in there, you sit with the
old dears and have a cup of tea, and they talk abut their aches and
pains.' And a 74-year-old former milliner responded—

> Oh my God no. I'm not old enough for that. God—no. Ooh no.
> If anybody asked me to do that, I'd die. I would think I'd had
> it . . . Me ideas aren't that old, love.
> . . . I like to be out and about with young people and do things
> with young people. It keeps you young yourself. Oh, God,
> no—I'd die of fright![17]

These men and women do not want to be brought together for
negative reasons: whatever their age, they need to be valued for
what they are. Their past is part of it, and some enjoy gathering
with former workmates or war veterans. A Cypriot elder values the
community centre where he can 'sit with my other friends there
and we chat and play backgammon.' He used to do the same thing
at the local café in Cyprus: 'one good thing we got in Cyprus is the
weather. We can sit outside—some of our relations they come to
visit ours to make us some coffee—just we do that.' Others gather
to have fun in their own chosen way—'I'm a great singer;' or just
'having a game of cards and a drink.'[18] Their sense of themselves,
of their individuality, of their past experience and present skills, is
bolstered rather than undermined.

While most of these associations have a predominantly older
membership, it is an essential merit of them that they do not
exclude somewhat younger men and women. Old people's clubs

are the only exception. And where older people gather for less precise purposes, the mixed age group may be an important attraction. A few enthusiastic women were active members of a rural Women's Institute or a Townswomen's Guild. Two men—and another three husbands of wives we recorded—were regular pubgoers.

A regular visit to the pub may boost morale, but unfortunately has less happy long-term effects: regular heavy drinking tends to shorten life, and encourage bad temper and moroseness. Four out of these five men were under seventy—presumably the older drinking husbands had already died; two were depressed, and none had companionable marriages. But there is one widower, in his seventies, who has succeeded in constructing a 'mellowed' later life around evenings in the pubs.

Dick Tiverton lives under the same roof as his daughter and grandchildren, but quite independently. He sees them for a brief chat each day, but looks after his own cooking and cleaning. On a typical day,

> I'll probably get up between ten and half-past, and feed my cat, and make some tea and perhaps a piece of toast and marmalade ... In the morning, I have set times (to go next door). I go in somewhere about eleven o'clock to pick up the *Guardian* and bring it back here. I don't get up very early in the morning these days, especially in winter. There's not much point ... I sit down with the *Guardian* and read it until it's finished, round about 12.30, and perhaps make myself a light lunch.
>
> If the weather's fine, I might go out and have a little bit of a walk, but if the weather's like this, I read or listen to the radio. Do the odd bit of dusting now and then, and maybe some dab washing ... I can always find something to do, if it is only sitting reading or listening to the radio, or pottering in the garden. I don't get bored at all ... And then make myself another meal at tea-time, usually round about 6.30, all the washing up, putting away. Go up the village to do a little bit of shopping and chat with anybody I meet on the street until about nine. And then I'm out, gossiping in pubs.

The time home varies; it might be around midnight, it might be two o'clock in the morning.

Dick's week also includes meeting regularly with a retired businessman for 'a slap-up lunch.' They always 'go to the same place because it's very pleasant. The girls know us; the management know us.' But he sees most of his friends in the evenings, in a regular weekly rhythm.

On *Monday* evenings, 'I go up to the "Old Dog" up there—it's about five minutes away—and I meet some friends'—an ex-teaching colleague and other regulars. On *Tuesday* evenings he goes to a canalside pub, 'The Navigation', where 'I meet another great friend of mine, an ex-colleague, and there are usually several others I've taught with, or their husbands.' On *Wednesday* night he finds some of the same 'crowd' at the 'Old Dog.' *Thursday* is the turn of 'The Britannia' up at the top of the hill. 'There are one or two friends up there... *Friday* we're back at "The Navigation."' *Saturday* night is an outing to the 'Eagle and Child' in the next village; and on *Sunday* he is at home again in the 'Old Dog.'

The crowd arrange transport between them. 'It's a costly business, but very pleasant.' Usually Dick is only there for the last hour and a half, 'but sometimes I stay on longer because we have a very good sing-song and a good laugh.' Here he can exchange fun with a younger generation. 'The crowd in "The Navigation," especially in the summer when there might be ten or twelve there, they range from me down to young people of twenty. And we all get on very well together.'[19]

It is part of the freedom and fun of later years to feel that if the body is ageing, the spirit is still young. 'I have intentions of stopping as young as I feel,' as one woman put it. 'I like people of all ages,' said another. Many of the old reach out for contact with young people. It is most likely to be grandchildren who 'kept us young,' but others also prefer young friends: 'oh well, they keep ye younger.' A few even deliberately turn their backs on their own age group. 'I love children,' said one dissatisfied housewife; 'I wouldn't enjoy old company.' More remarkably, a 78-year-old Scots wife, once a cleaner, with a husband who has long been chronically sick, could spare no sympathy for the old. 'I hate old people! [Laughs.] Isn't that terrible? No, I can't stand people that's always moaning, moaning, moaning. It really gets to ye.'[20]

She is right that some get more fun from later life than others: and they put more in, too. Contrast this 'moaning' with Annie Mimms, 78-year-old Green Belt seamstress, now diabetic, but as eager as ever to get on with life, with her friends, her family, and her clothes-making: 'I want to live till I'm a hundred you know, that's what I've always told the children. And they said, "Whatever for?" And I said, "I've got a lot of things I want to do." '[21]

9

Grandparenthood

To My Grandchildren
Come to yet grandad—and dance on his knee
Once he wor little an'helpless like ye
Yor th'second cletch at's some trailing along
Makin' th'owd homestead both happy an'throng.
                    Ben Turner, 1930[1]

IN the past and in the present, as we have already seen, family relationships vary greatly in both frequency and intensity. No relationship brings out more clearly than grandparenting the mutuality of later family life, both in the opportunities it offers, and also in the obstacles to their realization. What are the expectations and the realities of contemporary grandparenting? What influences shape relationships between grandparents and their grandchildren? This chapter is exceptional in that we are able to bring together experiences and opinions from all three generations in our families: grandparents, parents, and grandchildren. They emphasize both the pleasures and the problems of being a grandparent or a grandchild. Their stories suggest a complex relationship in which parents play an important role, and in which there is—for grandparents—a measure of tension and reluctant acceptance as well as involvement and joy.

Some American sociologists have suggested that the grandparenting role is an empty one with no clear rights and responsibilities. They argue that this enables grandparents to have more control over their relationships with their grandchildren, more personal choice in their behaviour, than parents can have in their relationships with their own children.[2] Our evidence suggests, on the contrary, that the grandparents' role is no more free from cultural shaping than any other familial role. Though it does lack clear rights and responsibilities, this is in itself a restriction on what grandparents can or should do.

We live in a society that assumes the nuclear family as the ideal and values men above women, younger adults and even children above the old. All this pushes grandparents to the edges of family life and implies different rights and expectations for men and women, old and young. Patterns formed in this way are modified by individual character and by family tradition. Grandparents do not simply follow the stereotypes, but they cannot help but be influenced by them.

Grandfather sitting by the fire smoking his pipe; granny in her rocking-chair, knitting; both white-haired and elderly. This remains the popular image of the grandparent both past and present—despite the fact that most people including the grandparents here, have typically first become grandparents well before old age. The belief nevertheless persists that earlier middle age is 'too young' to be a grandparent, and in the same spirit, that grandparents ought to play little part in everyday family life, except to give a helping hand now and then or, more importantly, to treat and even 'spoil' their grandchildren. But their lives are also supposed to revolve around their grandchildren and children: as if they should live vicariously through them, having little life of their own, accepting the attentions offered and never expecting or demanding more. As Cathy, a grandchild of 18, put it: 'I think grandmothers are always close to grandchildren, they like giving them sweets and taking them to the shops and things!' And another, Lorna, aged thirty, whose grandmother had died eight years earlier, said, 'She was your typical grandma, you know, sort of old with a pinny on and what have you. She was lovely. Open fires . . . things like that.' Whilst Sue Keeler remarked of her father-in-law, who lived with them and took a primary role in his grandchildren's care, 'He hasn't interfered—which is a good thing.'[3]

When Mary Vorse writes in her autobiography, published in 1911, of this passive ideal, her anger is never far from the surface. She recalls hearing a young woman named Eleanor bemoan the decline of the 'real grandmother': a women always there whenever her grandchildren should want or need her.

When an older woman is 'always there', depend upon it, there is some deeper reason and a sadder one than that she was waiting for her little grandchildren. . . . Each generation permits a different type of young girl, but the older woman must not change.... She must be like Eleanor's grandmother, 'always there'—waiting, waiting, with a smiling face through the long, quiet, empty hours, for her grandchildren to come home.... I hope I shall fall short of this ideal in all respects. I do not wish to become a mere ornamental nonentity about whom people shall say, 'what a sweet old lady'... [4]

The same image of the grandmother as a sweet old lady still appears to be thriving among grandchildren today. But the reality is that many grandparents do not fit this ideal. Even within the same family, where one grandparent may be your 'typical grandmother', the other might be quite different. The young woman whose paternal grandmother wore a 'pinny,' for example, also had a maternal grandmother who died last year. This other grandmother still worked in a mill in her seventies. She was a widow and had remarried a man much younger than herself. Far from living for her grandchildren, as Lorna pointed out 'she was very much wrapped up in herself.' And Sue Keeler said of her parents, in comparison with her father-in-law:

> My own parents have tried to interfere. Like if I'm buying them something ... my own dad would say, 'Huh, the money you've wasted on that,' and 'Why didn't you get a second hand one? ... A second hand bike is good enough for him.'

Cathy's mother confirmed that her parents do not fulfil the grandparents' ideal for her, though this is what she would like:

> My parents tend to think that they are a disciplining figure, and they tend to dictate a little to them at times—'You should do this and you should help your mother more'—and it aggravates me because I tend to think that they should spoil them. Grandparents are supposed to spoil the children and not worry about that side of it. [5]

As we shall see, spoiling them is indeed what a lot of grandparents enjoyed about having grandchildren. Interestingly, Cathy's parents are divorced. The grandparents' behaviour in her family may well result from their feeling more protective and believing that their daughter, a single mother, will have more disciplinary problems with her children than would a married couple.

Many grandparents who did not fit the usual image were considered rather odd by their grandchildren:

> My grandmother wasn't a close sort of person really. She was more a freak, she liked enjoying herself and . . . she . . . was a little unusual! I remember taking her out on a bus and people . . . they used to sort of stare, the lady with the makeup on.

On the other hand a number of grandchildren disagreed with the idea that grandparents should be elderly. But this change in attitude from old to young as the ideal has its price: the negative stereotype of old age. 'Old' generally signifies negative characteristics to these young of today: past-it, boring, slow, out of touch—stereotypes nurtured by wider social attitudes towards the elderly. Barbara, aged 19, discusses her grandparents. She has a good relationship with her maternal grandparents and a poor one with her paternal grandfather, now a widow. She explains that the former are willing and able to join in her life, whilst the latter remains aloof from it:

> I had my eighteenth birthday party up here and my grandmother was there in the middle, that's Grannie and Poppa (maternal)—they were all here—and my friends just loved them, because they can join in with anything. They were super. They were really great. I'm never embarrassed with them. You know, you sit there and cringe and think, 'Oh no, why did they say that.' But they're never like that. They're very good. I'm very impressed with them.

In comparison she remarks of her paternal grandfather, 'I've always thought of [him] as old—he always complains. . . .'[6]

Referring to her teenage granddaughter, Meg Jacks from Wigan, aged 62, also brings out this point. Above all else, her granddaughter wants her to stay young:

> We're having a little bit of a thing at present about my hair . . . Because of course my hair should be white [naturally]. Well, she's not having a nan with white hair. So, 'No nan, don't have it white.' So I have to put a little tiny bit, take that whiteness off. She says 'Because you're not a grandma grandma!'
> And the same as when I'm buying anything, you know. She'll say, 'Now don't buy a grandma one.' You know. Like she agrees

that I shouldn't buy them young like she has or anything like
that. But I mustn't go too, you know how you see some as they
dress very old all time. I'm not to do that. I mustn't.[7]

Thus, the stereotype not only coloured but also confused people's
views of grandparents. They were to be young, to be old; to be
active, but not interfering; to 'spoil', but not discipline; to be
interested, but not influential. Though the stereotype suggests
gentleness, warmth, and generosity, all positive characteristics, on
closer inspection the image is also strongly negative, serving largely to constrain and restrict the grandparent.

There were nevertheless pleasures to be sought and found in being
a grandparent and in having grandchildren; many felt, 'We've had
a lot of pleasure out of them.' There were particular pleasures
about becoming and being a grandparent which were quite distinct
from those of being a parent. Many expressed a feeling of biological renewal. Some earlier research has concluded that only
grandmothers view grandparenthood in this way, but we certainly
found grandfathers who feel like this too. As Jim White, retired
caretaker, put it, 'You just look back and you say there's a part of
me. A new generation, another branch of the tree.' Another grandfather, Sam Pinkney, an electrical engineer, said:

> Oh I thought it was great. I think it's another achievement on
> life's way, that. A lot of people say 'Oh, I couldn't stand being a
> grandparent, I'd feel old!' And you don't. It's another lease of
> life, it is. You've got something to look forward to. They show
> their faces in this place and the place lights up. . .[8]

These quotations suggest not only a feeling of biological renewal,
but also a sense of one's own life having renewed purpose after a
settled period—though obviously this is not the case for all—
between children leaving home and the arrival of grandchildren,
when family roles and responsibilities are few; something also
suggested by Ben Turner's verse at the beginning of the chapter.
Grandchildren gave grandparents something to *do* as well as *be*.

Another pleasurable aspect of grandparenting, as distinct from
parenting, was the relative freedom which grandparents had simply to enjoy their grandchildren: something they did not think open
to parents. In this sense grandparenting could be seen as a less
responsible role. As one parent put it, 'Grandparents spoil the

children while the parents get lumbered with making them do
what they ought to do'; and another, 'When you're young you
don't have time for your children like grandparents do.' One
grandparent put it similarly: 'You can spoil them and then send
them home to mum and dad when they want disciplining . . . you
get the best of both worlds.'[9]

These pleasures, however, were sometimes marred by a reluctant (on the grandparents' side) understanding between grandparents and parents that it was not the former's place to 'interfere' in
the upbringing of their grandchildren. Like Mary Vorse they discovered 'a whole set of rules and regulations . . . that are not self
imposed but imposed by custom and enforced by the younger
generation', which greeted them on becoming a grandparent.
Even those grandparents who spent a lot of time with their grandchildren were regarded by themselves, their children, and their
grandchildren as being one step, one relationship, and one generation removed from an explicit role in childrearing. When they did
intervene, this was usually resented and labelled as 'interference'.
Mary Barrington comments of her mother-in-law: 'She tries to tell
Teresa what to do and I mean, I can't tell Teresa what to do these
days, so certainly Grandma can't . . . I think she resents Grandma
interfering a bit.' Whilst Mary Ridings, a grandmother, remarked:
'We've only watched and seen what's been going on . . . It was
usually presents, but no, not as far as saying that they ought
. . . We do at times . . . I know they resent it.'[10] This norm of
non-interference was also found both by Cherlin and Furstenberg
in a North American, non-immigrant community, and by Sarah
Cunningham-Burley in her study of Aberdeen. It appears to be the
predominant norm of white Anglo-American society today.[11]

Although there were exceptions among our families, that grandparents should not interfere with the rearing of their children's
children was both the most common view, and the most common
practice. One grandmother, aged sixty, remarked:

No, I never interfere with them. . . . They're their children. . . .
If they get a smack while they're here off their mother or father
for doing something, I never say 'You shouldn't do that', you
know, they're their children.[12]

This belief that the grandparents should take very much a secon-
dary role is well illustrated in the Tiverton family. The Tivertons
are one of the few among our families where three generations are

living together. Mr Tiverton senior, Dick, lives as a widower in a
cottage next door to the 'big house'—which was once his—
connected by a sliding door in the dividing wall. In the big house
live his oldest daughter, her husband, and their three children
aged eleven, seven, and three. Dick Tiverton, a retired school-
teacher, is very conscious of not 'intruding', as he sees it, on his
daughter's territory. Referring to the grandchildren he said: 'I see
this lot practically every day. But I don't purposely go in and see
them when they are there as a family because I don't want to be
bobbing in and interrupting their conversations or anything.' Dick
has two other children and three more grandchildren. Referring to
them all generally, he commented: 'They've got their families and
its no good poking your nose in too often. They like to be on their
own for a bit. I'm quite sure of that. I know we did when we were
young.'[13] Our nuclear family culture pushes grandparents outside
its perimeter—even where the three generations are practically
living together. And the belief that this is right and proper goes
back, at least in the Tiverton family, to when Dick was a young
man.

A second example where three generations also live together is
the Keeler household, where a widowed grandfather lives with his
son, daughter-in-law, and two grandchildren. It was Sue Keeler,
the daughter-in-law, who said that her father-in-law had not interfered with the upbringing of her children—even though he had
spent much time caring for them. Later in the interview she also
remarked that 'sometimes it doesn't feel like your house', again
suggesting that the extended family was no more than a household
arrangement. It did not affect significantly people's views of 'the
family'. The grandparent remained an 'extra', even though they
had bought the house together, and the grandfather had retired
early in order to be able to look after his grandchildren when their
mother was out at work.[14]

Some grandparents will go to great lengths to ensure that there
can be no suggestion that they are 'interfering'. Last year David
Roberts decided at the age of 14 that he wanted to stay at his
grandmother's house every Wednesday night. He asked her and
she replied:

> Yes, but you must get your mum and your dad's permission
> first. . . . Tell your mother to give me a ring to let me know that

it's alright and then you can come and stop any time you want, providing it's OK with your mother and father.

She said to David's mother when she called:

Are you sure it's alright? It's not me you know that's asked him . . . I don't want to take him away from you or do anything that you don't want him to do.

Dawn Roberts, the grandmother cited here, is housebound, a widow, and lives alone. John and his parents live about half a mile away. She has one good friend whom she sees every week. She is heavily dependent on her family for emotional and physical support and her sensitivity to her grandson's request is possibly connected with this dependency. But even if she is unusual in this degree of dependency, her reaction is typical.

In another sense, however, Dawn Roberts is an exceptional grandmother. Despite her lack of confidence in her role, her warm relationship with her grandson has ensured that she has some definite influence over him. Thus she did in fact tread where many other grandparents feared to do so; giving her grandson advice and disciplining him herself. For example, it was recently discovered by David's parents that their son was smoking. Dawn Roberts was asked what she would do if she found he was still doing so after being disciplined by his parents.

I wouldn't give him away. I wouldn't go and tell his mother and father if I caught him smoking. I'd give him a lecture myself, and I'd tell him how disappointed and upset I am about it. Now you see David hates to see me upset. I can do more good by telling him how upset I am, how surprised I am and I didn't think he'd do it again and things like this—I can get more out of John by going on at him than telling tales on him. I don't believe in going telling tales about him. I deal with him in my own way.[15]

This was the closest among our families to the children with 'two homes', free to choose between sleeping at their mother's or their grandmother's, whom Peter Townsend and Madeline Kerr describe in poor working-class districts of London and Liverpool in the 1950s. Nevertheless, despite the norm of non-interference, there were indeed families where the grandparents were closely involved with their grandchildren and were more influential with them—just as we found in earlier accounts from the nineteenth and early twentieth centuries. As then, this occurred most often when a grandparent had become a substitute parent. Looking back to the interwar years, one woman recalled:

> My great grandmother had brought my mother up, more than her own mother, because the father died. They lived first of all with the grandmother. . . . So my mother had a much closer relationship with her grandmother than her own mother. She was much more like a mother to her.

Another woman in her mid-fifties recalled how her grandmother had played quite a large part in her upbringing, 'because my mother went to work and so my grandmother was in charge of me really such a lot'. A man whose parents had separated recalled his grandmother's role in his upbringing:

> In the short period which must have been about a year or so after my parents broke up, she played a fairly active part. She acted as a mother in a sense, although of course my sister and I were always at boarding school so we weren't totally dependent in that sense. She was always a typical grandparent. Always ready to help or offer advice when she felt she was needed.[16]

Significantly it is grandmothers rather than grandfathers who figure in these stories. When these experiences are compared with those of the Keeler and Tiverton families—where grandfathers and not grandmothers lived with their grandchildren—the more influential role of grandmothers is further emphasized. There are no equivalently important substitute fathers to be found among these contemporary grandfathers. Meg Jacks's situation strengthens this impression. Meg's daughter Olga came to live with Meg and her husband when her marriage broke up. Her two children—Meg and her husband's grandchildren—came too. They lived together for six years until Olga remarried eight years ago. The result of these six years is a very strong bond between Meg and her grandchildren. The grandfather's relationship with his grandchildren, on the other hand, was not particularly close. Meg's description of their departure illustrates the ongoing importance of her own role in the family:

Oh it was terrible. It was like losing them you know. Anyway . . . Andy [the stepfather], he's very good . . . and he was
very understanding, and we did it, we phased it over. And they
said they would look and get a house as near as they could in
walking distance as I could walk over there as I felt with them,
and they could walk over here you see . . . [17]

Grandmothers are more easily brought into the family than are
grandfathers because of their traditional childcaring role. This
makes them both practically valuable to the family—particularly if
mothers go out to work—and actively involved in it. But if a
grandfather is willing and able to take on this role and if parents
will allow it—if they have the confidence to discard male-female
stereotypes—he too can be more firmly embraced by the family,
despite an earlier more passive role. Ted Keeler, the ex-fisherman,
has two grandsons, aged 15 and 17. When they were much younger Ted's wife Ann used to look after them quite often, so that he
saw them regularly. Ten years ago Ann died, and soon afterwards
he came to live with his two grandsons and their parents, his son
and daughter-in-law. They still live together. One of the main
reasons for this move was that it would enable his daughter-in-law
Sue to go out to work full-time, if Ted was to take over some of her
responsibilities for housework and childcare. In fact the maternal
grandparents are still both alive and live about ten miles away. The
grandmother now suffers from senility. But years ago she and her
husband would have been available, in theory, to look after their
grandsons. The reason they did not do so seems to be that they did
not get on very well with their daughter and did not support her
wish to go back to work.

An American research project of the 1960s found that only
grandmothers acted as surrogate parents to their grandchildren.
Despite exceptions such as the Keelers, this does appear to be
overwhelmingly the case in our families. There is no sign yet that
many grandfathers are taking up more active roles as carers, reflecting contemporary pressures on fathers to be more involved. [18]

Active caring usually brought grandmothers and grandchildren
closer together—at least for the years during which it occurred. 'I
looked after the baby and she [daughter-in-law] got a job . . . and I
minded Anita, and I thought the world of the kid,' one grand-

mother recalled. Most grandmothers who 'cared' for their grandchildren found it a fulfilling experience. However there were also
costs: fatigue and anxiety. Meg Jacks, for example, looks after
her son's 14-month-old twins for the whole day every Saturday, so
that he and his wife can go shopping and have some time to
themselves.

> Now that wants some doing I tell you. Because they want
> changing two . . . two at once. And giving 'em their dinner and
> they're trying with—just at that stage as they're trying with a
> spoon. Well you know, they turning it upside down and . . . I
> enjoy them but it's like this, they're better littler and
> oftener . . . Less hours and oftener, than all the full day. . . . But I
> think what it is too, is when you're older and they're not yours
> you tend to watch them a lot more. You know, they let them
> have a bit more freedom than I do . . . I think you make them
> harder work because . . . I'm behind them. If they go outside I'm
> behind them . . . Where they just let them have the run of the
> garden . . .[19]

Belinda Simonson had helped at the births of her first six grandchildren. But after the sixth she felt that it was becoming too much
for her. She had done all her two daughters' washing for a week
each time they had had a child, and in two cases, where the
daughter did not live locally, she had stayed with her daughter and
looked after her husband and other children while she was in
hospital. When her seventh grandchild was due she decided she
had had enough! Belinda does not see much of her oldest daughter's three children as she does not get on very well with them.
But she still takes a very active part in the lives of her other
daughter's children, of whom there are now nine. She does all
their mending and knits, sews, and bakes cakes for them, and at
least one of them stays at her house every weekend. Belinda
described how she entertains them:

> Well I read to the young ones. I take the others up to the town
> and we usually treat them to something. Take them in the
> market . . . My oldest grandson will go on his own and have a
> look round, but the others, I usually go up and take them
> around, or take them into a restaurant and have a cream cake
> and a cup of coffee . . . They go to the cinema sometimes. But of

course we've got a video now so we get lots of films or record things for them that we know they'll like and they watch that . . . They have had a television but she's got rid of it now . . .[20]

As in the past, an exceptionally close relationship between grandchild and grandparent was sometimes the result of a child having a poor relationship with a parent. Laura Creswell, now 43, was very close to her paternal grandmother. When Laura's younger sister was born she stayed with this grandmother for two weeks. She was then two years old. She recalls:

> Because I was the first grandchild you know, she absolutely ruined me, and I think that this bond was formed then and it never really went. . . . I miss her even now and she's been dead . . . it must be getting on for 15 years.

Laura had always felt that she did not receive the same love and attention from her mother as did her two sisters. Consequently she turned to her grandmother:

> I'm very fond of my mother, don't get me wrong, but as a child I think I tended to be pushed out for my younger sisters. Yes, it's true to say that . . . And I think that's where my Nanna stepped in . . . Yes, my Nanna did give me an awful lot of loving.

She also recalls of her grandmother:

> I think she helped a lot with my creative abilities, she used to encourage me to knit and sew, and that sort of thing, and my own mother didn't do any of that . . . I think really, if I think about it she did play quite a large part in my values of life . . . And as a child I was very insecure, . . . no self-confidence, and I think possibly she helped with the self-confidence I now have.

Laura's mother did not have a close relationship with her mother-in-law. Her daughter's closeness to the grandmother may have worsened the situation, causing jealousy of the attentions Laura gave her grandmother as well as of the attentions she received from her. Laura was asked how her mother felt about her closeness to her grandmother. She replied, 'I think she accepted it, she had my sister. . . .' Laura's mother, on the other hand, suggested that it had been a mistake to send Laura to her grandmother's when her sister was born as this had been the beginning of her own difficult relationship with Laura:

> It was the wrong thing, because his mother absolutely spoilt Laura while she was there. She never let her spend a minute on her own and consequently by the time she came back home I had terrible trouble, a terrible time with her...[21]

Fortunately there were other families who appeared less weighed down by such jockeying for position. Alice Kitchin remembers being scolded by her mother if she slapped her daughter, but shrugged this off without complaint; whilst Sam Pinkney, a grandfather, said he did not hesitate to say things to his daughter when he disagreed with his grandchildren's upbringing—again, this did not appear to sour relations in any way. On the contrary it could be seen to strengthen them, the grandfather being accepted as having a right to comment on matters regarding *his* family.

Nevertheless, such contentiously influential grandparents were unusual. More common were those who were seen as simply always being there, taken for granted, even where grandchildren expressly felt a close attachment to them. As the ex-fisherman's grandson put it, 'He's with us everyday so he's just like another parent as it were.' But even living together did not necessarily bring recognized influence. Pat Gladstone looks back on her grandmother as

> Somebody I remember greatly. As I say I lived with her for four years, 'til I was four years of age. Just somebody you wouldn't really forget... She was just your nan, she was there, type of thing and that was it...

She described her own children's relationship with her mother similarly:

> Well, she's just their nan. I wouldn't say she played any part, just the fact that they have a nan who they can go to and who'll play with them and all the rest of it.

Of her own grandmother she commented:

> I think she had a lot to do with shaping your childhood but not as you—not as an influence. I wouldn't say that, no. My mum is

very like her mum, yeh, so I think me mum's had more of an influence than me nan. Me nan was an influence as a kid, but not in shaping me life. Making me younger life a lot happier in having grandparents to go to and all the rest of it, you know, oh aye.[22]

Grandparents have to carve out a role for themselves within limits of expectation and custom. This is a sensitive task. Some found grandparenting a more tricky role than parenting: one could not do just as one liked, but had to abide by parents' wishes and ways. Disciplining and indulging could become equally treacherous. Jim and Gloria White loved their young grandchildren—aged nine and two—coming to see them, but found their parents' rules made their time with them less comfortable than it could have been. They were not allowed to give them sweets, nor did they feel comfortable about telling them off when their parents were present. 'You can handle your own [but] you've got to be careful with a grandchild' was a common view. Gloria White described what this meant for her:

> You see on Saturday they will come and Robert will say, 'Tweet gran!' He means sweet. Well, I can't give him one cos they only allow . . . You see I buy them sweets and then they pocket them and they don't give 'em them. Well if it was me he'd have the packet immediately . . . I know that it's wrong but that's how you are you see. You're a bit restricted aren't you with your grandchildren?

Jim agreed with his wife. He remarked:

> Yeh, you're a bit restricted. You're sorta cut off as far as some sort of things are concerned. They're your children while they are here, but you're still restricted in the fact that you can't give them what they or you want. The icecream van comes and you've got to crack on that it's not there . . .[23]

Although grandparents were usually regarded as the ones to 'spoil' grandchildren, there were also grandparents who thought parents far too lenient with their children. These feelings were largely kept to themselves. Sometimes differences of opinion nevertheless filtered through and resulted in friction between parents and grandparents and in turn between grandchildren and

grandparents. Dennis Young, a father in his forties, explains the
relationship between grandparents and grandchildren in his family:

> Well they see them rather seldom, and they have never been
> particularly close or friendly with them . . . I think they find the
> idea that the children don't eat everything put before them, I
> think they still find that a bit hard to take. Because [with Jane],
> my wife's oldest sister . . . it was the same sort of thing that had
> come right down through three generations. You must eat it all
> up—and rigid attitudes like that. OK, perhaps we've been a bit
> slack, just because we find it too wearing to beat down on them all
> the time . . .
>
> I seem to recall my mother saying that she had heard my
> wife's mother saying 'Oh well, I would just give him a good
> smack'. . . . My wife . . . obviously reacted against that kind of
> behaviour.

For her part his eighty-year-old mother-in-law comments:

> Jane's brought hers up more or less the same as me . . . Dennis's
> got different ideas. I think myself they let them rule them too
> much . . . cos according to him they mustn't be frustrated.[24]

There were other families where there was more continuity
across the generations and where grandparents felt much more
comfortable about seeing grandchildren on their own. Both disciplining and indulging could then be practised with greater confidence. The grandchildren were thought to behave better away from
their parents, as they knew their grandparents would not let them
get away with behaviour deemed unacceptable by their parents.
The grandchildren too liked to stay with grandparents without
their parents, as it made them feel more grown up, and this again
implied behaving well. One grandmother and grandfather remarked:

> GRANDMOTHER. I'd much rather have them here to stay without
> their parents.
> GRANDFATHER. Aye, it's strange that but it's true. They're less
> trouble. They don't try and take the same liberties, they know
> they won't get away with it.
> GRANDMOTHER. I suppose it's perhaps too many people telling
> them what to do, maybe that's it, I don't know, but I find it's
> easier to have them on their own.[25]

Paradoxically, when children enter adolescence, staying with grandparents typically becomes thought of as a childish rather than adult activity and usually peters out.

The persistence of differences between the roles of men and women from childhood through to grandparenthood makes women —both grandmothers and granddaughters—much more closely tied and involved in the family than are either grandfathers or grandsons. Grandmothers generally took much more part in the lives of their grandchildren than grandfathers. They helped at the time of their births, cared for them as young children, knitted and sewed for them. There was a hint among many grandchildren that only grandmothers were real grandparents. Grandfathers were much less prominent in their lives. As women tend to live longer than men, many grandchildren only had grandmothers. But even where both were still living, grandchildren tended only to talk of grandmothers when asked about grandparents.

American research suggests that the role of the grandmother and the grandfather differ in a number of respects. One project reported that grandfathers and grandmothers sought to influence their adolescent grandchildren in different ways. Grandfathers confined their influence to 'instrumental matters' such as jobs or finance, whereas grandmothers hoped to be influential in the realm of interpersonal as well as 'instrumental' concerns. Another suggested that male skills are often out of date by the time the grandfather is in a position to teach his grandson anything, and that this is far less true for women.[26] Many of the grandmothers in our families had indeed taught their granddaughters to knit and sew. No grandfather appeared to have passed comparable skills on to his grandson.

A shared interest was obviously one way of drawing grandparents and grandchildren together. This was, in turn, often linked to gender. Ellen, aged thirty, is an only granddaughter. Her grandmother who died recently also had three grandsons, none of whom were as close to her as was Ellen. Ellen felt that this was because she and her grandmother could share more as women. Her grandmother had taught her to knit and crochet: 'She could indulge in that with me, whereas she was that little bit more detached from the boys because they had interests that she didn't understand a lot of the time.' Other examples demonstrated how, though granddaughters and grandfathers could share interests, gender still proved a more powerful factor in shaping the relationships they developed. Indeed, the belief in its importance was in itself significant: for believing in a stereotype can lead to its fulfilment. Barbara, aged 19, shares more interests with her grandfather than her grandmother. As a result she feels closer to him: 'He's an accountant, and I've specialized in accountancy at college, so we've always got that to talk about . . . I tend to relate to my grandfather a bit more.' However, she also remarked that she felt her grandfather was closer to her younger brother than to herself, because her brother wanted to join the army and her grandfather had been a military man in his younger days, thus giving the two males a shared interest which overshadowed that between granddaughter and grandfather.[27]

Becky Werner, who is 18, feels her grandfather is closer to both her brother and her sister than he is to her. She thinks that this is partly a decision of her grandfather's to compensate for her grandmother's favouritism towards her. On top of this, her grandfather and her sister have a shared interest, whilst he and her brother have the male bond.

> He used to have a lot more to do with my sister, because he's really into—his main topic of conversation is education, and music . . . It was always my sister that he spent a lot of time with, mainly because I was with my gran as well . . . And now with my brother as well he's with him . . .

Becky was also aware at some level of a particular bond between her paternal grandfather and her brother, which had resulted in a change in her relationship with him: 'For a start there was my younger brother. I know that he was very pleased when mum and dad had a son.'[28]

As always, there were exceptions. Dick Tiverton, for example, feels much closer to his young granddaughters than to his grandsons: though he thinks 'that might change as the grandsons get older'. He says:

> I think little girls are far more intelligent, that's the point. Very often you can have what you might call a reasonable conversation with them whereas little lads are all action and rolling about and fighting . . . [29]

As men get older the tough image of masculinity softens. With this may come an opportunity to become more emotionally ex-

pressive and affectionate. Grandfathers—usually older men—
talked much more emotionally and lovingly about their grandchildren than they did about their own children. Many spoke with
delight of their relationships and their conversations with them:

> I'm very fond of Judith. We strike sparks off each other. Argue
> and that. That could be because she's the youngest. I get along
> very well with my granddaughter in London, Susie. I think
> that's because I'm her only grandfather . . . I think kids do like to
> have grandparents. Well we went to pick Susie up at playschool
> in London once when I was down there and she was busy saying
> to all these kids running about, 'That's my grandpa'. . .

A number of men and women suggested that their fathers had
mellowed with the years and were able to be far more loving with
their grandchildren than they had ever been with their own children. As Sonia Robinson put it:

> My father was very strict with us when we were little. You
> couldn't have said anything to him. Now I can say anything. And
> even with my children, how soft he is now, with my children to
> what he is with us . . . Oh they love me dad, they think he's a
> comedian . . . Jeremy, being only 15, . . . he idolises him . . .[30]

Masculine and feminine images thus exert a crucial influence on
relationships between grandparents and grandchildren. Attitudes
to ageing are also influential; they too are subject to change in the
course of the life cycle of each generation.

Despite Belinda Simonson's extensive involvement in the lives of
her grandchildren, as each one gets older she sees less and less
of them. This is something she seems to accept, with resignation:
'I don't have so much to do with them as they've got older now . . .
I expect I'll get one or two out of all that lot.'[31] Close involvement
with young grandchildren does not automatically lead to close
involvement later on. The most common pattern seems to be for
grandchildren to see their grandparents quite often and to feel
close to them when they are young, to become more distant
during teenage years, and sometimes to re-establish a close relationship in adulthood.

This third stage was largely the experience of granddaughters
and grandmothers. Sylvia Tandy spoke of the relationship between
her mother-in-law and the latter's grandson, who had lived

together for the first three years of the grandson's life and who now lived about a mile apart:

> She had quite a lot to do with his upbringing in the early years. But of course, as you grew up and that you tend, you don't want to go and see your grandmother, you'd rather go out with the lads and that, so they don't see so much of him now.

If grandparents lived long enough to see their great-grandchildren then this was often a time when they began to see more of their grandchildren too. Now in her late twenties with a child of her own, Sylvia recalls how often she used to see her grandmother, who died recently:

> Well, up until I left school, once or twice a week, I used to spend weekends. Go over there and stay Saturday night with her, you know, spend the weekend with her. Then when I started work [at 16] of course, you're too busy aren't you? All your family get forgotten. So I hardly saw her at all unless she came to visit us at weekends.
>
> But then I stopped work to have the baby, I started going over there again regularly. Once or twice a week I'd go over there with her [her own daughter, her grandmother's great-granddaughter] to see her. It was only really in the last year or so that we've become close again, really close. That's why it was a shame in a way she died so quickly after, sort of getting, well, really getting to know her again.[32]

There were some grandparents who believed it was inevitable that teenage grandchildren would drift away from them. Ben Bradgate, an ex-pitman now in his mid-seventies, used to see his grandchildren every week. Their visits are now more irregular. Although disappointed, he is understanding, and explains:

> You see they're getting their own lives sorted out, and their grandad's a bit in the background. I don't mind really... I can always go down to them and see them, it's only a bus ride for me. And so, I'm not blaming them for it—but it's always nice when they come.

Derek and Esme Hibblethwaite's grandchildren are all still very young and they believe they have a good relationship with them. Yet all the same they also expect their grandchildren to 'grow away' from them as they get older. Esme believes that this is 'bound to come' and Derek that 'you can't alter that'.[33]

This view was also held by some grandchildren. At 16, Philippa Barrington was in no doubt that her relationship with her grandmother was changing as she got older:

> Yeh, it's definitely changing because when I was much smaller, I used to go because I wanted sweeties and things like that. And I'd say we're growing further apart as I get older, mainly because I'm doing more things, and going out more, and away from home more.[34]

Paul Robinson, aged 21, is aware of a difference between the way he and his younger brother relate to their grandfather:

> I don't know if it's the age . . . He seems to get on a lot better, but then again, I think it's just the age. I think, he's only 15, and he's sort of all over his grandad, sort of thing, you know. . . . I think you grow out of that sort of thing, I don't know. He'll have a play fight with him or something, you know, something that I wouldn't do. But I'd rather sit and talk, you know. . .
>
> But [Jeremy], my brother, I just think it's with him being younger, you know, that he gets on with him maybe a bit better . . . He takes a lot more time to see my grandad when he is over than we maybe do. So yeh, I think my brother's the closest really.[35]

Many grandparents accepted the widespread idea that it is 'natural' for old and young not to be able to communicate. They believed in a 'generation gap'. One grandmother who saw her grandchildren about once a fortnight remarked:

> Generally they don't stay long. They just come and say, 'We've come to see you nana,' . . . They don't stay long because I don't think—I think they can get a bit bored with older people, can't they, the young ones . . . I think half an hour's enough talking with older people.

Another with grandchildren aged 16 and 21 said that she would not like to see them more than she does:

> No, there's a difference in the wavelength, children and grandmothers. I realize that, some people don't, do they? I thoroughly realize that they're two generations apart . . .

Leonard Seldon, speaking of his 21-year-old granddaughter who lives about twelve miles from him, said:

> She has been but not very often really. I mean it would be a bit boring wouldn't it? No, I don't expect that of youngsters really. Because it's a bit boring isn't it. I used to think so when I used to think of elders.[36]

These examples suggest a low sense of self-worth in terms of what older people feel they can offer the young. It also illustrates the strength of social prejudices about ageing, for it is assumed to be simply on the grounds of age and not of individual character that the young are rejecting the old, whilst the old themselves are using this criterion to measure their own value to the young. Some do not appear unhappy with this situation. It is accepted as an inevitable fact of life. Others, however, found this distancing difficult to accept. It was for some both painful and surprising:

> Our May was never away from me at one time, now she's got a boyfriend . . . No, I was a bit upset when she was 17, they had a big party but she didn't ask her grandma, and I was really upset. . .[37]

Though relationships undoubtedly changed as both grandchildren and grandparents grew older, they need not always weaken. Sometimes change was seen as something positive, whilst for others it meant relationships were different but no less strong. Barbara Seldon, aged 19, has a close relationship with her maternal grandparents who live over 200 miles away from her. When she was younger she used to stay with them every summer for two weeks. She still sees them regularly. They visit her and her parents twice a year, and she also visits them, though she no longer stays for two weeks. According to Barbara, her relationship with them has changed from one where they 'cared' for her to one of mutual friendship. She enjoys talking to them, and they discuss what is going on in each other's lives. She is no longer their 'little girl' but their 'equal': they are friends first before they are grandparents.

Mary Drysdale, whose grandchildren were all under nine years old, remarked that she thought her relationship with them was good now, but was bound to change as they got older. Again this was seen as potentially positive:

I think as they are now, they love you, but they love you in some ways, it's like cupboard love. Because when you go to nanny's you get this, you get that, and you get the other. But as they grow older they love you for your person, because they understand it better. They understand the love better. You know, I mean they come here and they sit on your knee and they get a cuddle, and they tell you about school, and you listen to them and everything else. And then they'll go off, you'll be forgotten...

But I think as they grow older it's a different kind of love that comes along, you know, between you... I don't know, I've got to find out yet. You might get a clash of personalities as they grow older, or you might disagree with them... and they might say, 'Oh I'm not going to my nan's she always tells me off, you know.' So that has got to, you know, develop, I think as they get older, the love.[38]

There were also a few grandparents and grandchildren who remained 'close' throughout their lives. Sadie King, now in her eighties, is very close to Bie, her oldest grandchild out of fourteen. Bie is thirty and lives alone in Portsmouth. Her grandmother lives in Manchester, much nearer to many of her other grandchildren. Sadie was asked why she thought she was closer to Bie than to her other grandchildren. What comes across strongly is that Bie is the one who makes her grandmother feel welcome and needed— unlike the relations between many of the other grandchildren and grandparents quoted here. For the past several years Sadie King and her sister-in-law have spent two weeks a year at Bie's flat:

She's the eldest, and it's because I think we've gone on holiday to her flat and that, you know, because... she's always made us welcome, and she's always glad we go, you know, rather than being on her own, it's a bit of company for her. And usually when we've gone we've got a meal ready for her coming home from work, you know, and I think she likes that part of it, somebody there to get a meal ready for her, she's always been thankful. And we've always been thankful we've been able to go. I mean we don't pay digs, you know, we all put so much in the kitty, we all put the same amount for the shopping.[39]

Sadie King was also very close to both her own grandmothers as a child and as a young woman, and she remembers that when courting she would often walk with her boyfriend to her maternal grandmother's house. Another woman also recalls having a close relationship with her maternal grandmother as a teenager, the two of them even going on holiday together. A third example, this time cutting across both age and gender stereotypes, is provided by the Roberts family. Dawn Roberts, aged 75, recalled of her teenage sons' relationship with her mother that they 'absolutely idolized her. Mont, the eldest one that was in the Navy, many a time he came home and he'd say, "I think I'll go and stay, keep me gran company for a few days," and he'd go down there and stay with his gran, you know.' Her younger son, now 42, recalled how he used to stay the night and the weekends at his maternal grandmother's and how 'I thought a lot of my grandmother really.' This is a particularly interesting example as his son David, aged 14, is also at present very close to his grandmother, suggesting a family custom or tradition of close involvement between grandparents, particularly grandmothers, and grandsons, which has proved stronger than the dominant patterns of the wider culture.[40]

Change in the grandparent–grandchild relationship occurs not only through the ageing of the grandchild, but also through that of the grandparent. Frailty and infirmity can result in relationships once characterized by activity becoming much more passive. Louise Barrington used to have her grandchildren to stay and would take them out for picnics with her husband. Now a widow in her late eighties and very frail, she still sees them, but less often, and she does not *do* anything with them. Another example is that of the Keeler grandchildren, who used to spend quite a lot of time with their maternal grandparents. Their grandmother is now suffering from senile dementia and their grandfather is totally occupied in caring for her. The grandsons rarely visit, feeling uncomfortable around their grandmother. Consequently contact between them has sharply diminished. On the other hand, Dawn Roberts and her grandson David have become more closely involved over the last few years, both since Dawn has become more frail and since her grandson has become a teenager.

In contrast to age and gender, like Cherlin and Furstenberg we found that class does not appear strongly to influence the nature of grandparent–grandchild relationships. There are examples of close and of distant relationships to be found in both middle-class and working-class families. Only in relation to financial involvement does there seem to be a direct difference—although the geographic spread and separation of families also carried a class component which in turn affected relationships.

There were a number of middle-class grandparents who had a financial involvement with their grandchildren's lives which went beyond the giving of pocket money, a practice common in both middle and working-class families. Some were saving money for their grandchildren, whilst others were paying for their education. For some grandparents such financial support was their only way of expressing their interest in and love for their grandchildren. Hans Werner, a widower, lived in Germany. He paid for his eldest granddaughter Becky's education for many years. In return Becky sent him her school reports at the end of every term. This enabled a geographically distant grandparent to become involved in his grandchild's life, and gave them both a basis on which to build a relationship, though they saw each other rarely. This would not have been an option open to a working-class grandparent. Becky recalls:

> He paid for me, because when I was younger I didn't get on at school and I had a very bad year, I missed a lot of school . . . It was more like school phobia than anything else. So he paid for me to go to a private school to catch up, and I was only supposed to go for a few years . . . But I enjoyed it so much he continued paying and I had all my education there. And he, I had to send him the reports every term at the end of the year, and he took a big part in that.[41]

In another family a grandmother, also a widow, was paying for her youngest grandchild's education. She had a tense and strained relationship with her family, feeling she was a burden to them. The financial help she gave them, which also included pocket money, was her only means of retaining a sense of value and status within her family, and even a relationship with her now 16-year-old granddaughter, long after she had stopped being an 'active' grandparent. In the past she and her husband had often taken their grandchildren out, had had them to stay, and had babysat for them when their parents had wanted to go out. She is now too old, frail, and depressed to do any of these things, whilst her grandchildren have grown out of their need for this type of grandparenting.

I still give them pocket money now! The little one said the other
week, to her mother, 'I don't know what I'd do without grandma's handout.' Yes, and I pay for the education of the young
one. Did they not tell you that?[42]

Many working-class grandparents were also interested in their
grandchildren's education. Their means of supporting and encouraging them were quite different. It involved rewarding them
for good results: 'They gave me a watch for passing my O levels,
and it was ten bob for every O level I passed.'[43]

Middle-class grandparents and grandchildren from our families
were much more often living great distances apart than were
working-class grandparents and grandchildren—a result of different career opportunities and patterns. Obviously middle-class
grandparents and grandchildren were therefore likely to see far
less of each other than were working-class grandparents and grandchildren. But this did not necessarily mean that they had weaker
relationships. Becky Werner, a middle-class teenager, even feels
she had a more harmonious relationship with her grandmother
when they lived 200 miles apart than she does now they live in the
same town. She explains:

> My grandma reckons I don't spend as much time with her now
> she lives here as I did when I was in London, because when I
> was in London I'd gone to see *her*, and so I had no other friends
> to see or something to do. Whereas if she comes here, I'm
> either just going out, working, or got something else to do.

The Hibblethwaite family provides another example of closeness
between geographically far-flung grandparents and grandchildren.
Andrew (a policeman), Joyce, and their children live in Manchester, as does his wife's mother, a widow. Andrew's parents are
retired farmers living in Scotland. But the Hibblethwaite children
are far closer to their distant paternal grandparents than to their
nearby maternal grandmother. Joyce Hibblethwaite remarks of
this:

> I don't know how to explain it—maybe because she [her mother]
> sees them more often than Andrew's mum does. You know, I
> mean she thinks the world of them and things like that, but they
> don't actually stay at my mother's. Whereas every year the
> children go up and stay with Andrew's mum and dad for maybe

two weeks in the summer holidays. And when I had Tina,
Denise went up to stay with his mum for three weeks . . . His
mum and dad are always . . . —if there's an emergency, it would
be his mum and dad we would phone if we wanted helping out.
Where we needed somebody here, then, yes, we would phone
his mum and dad.[44]

The widespread assumption of many sociologists and social historians that physical nearness can almost be equated with emotional
closeness evidently does not apply to the relationships in our
families. Individual character and family culture oust many of our
common-sense assumptions. There are stronger and weaker personalities in all our families and the stronger will be significant
influences wherever they happen to live.

What about the equally common assumption of community and
family sociologists that the bonds on the mother's side are normally
stronger? Certainly a common pattern appears to be that parents
and children lean more towards and are more involved with one
side of the family than the other, in relation to grandparents.
Those who were equally involved with both maternal and paternal
grandparents were unusual. But we did not find a tendency to
stronger involvement on the maternal side, a tendency towards the
'matrifocal tilt', in our families—despite the fact that a myth ex-
isted amongst many to that effect. Some cited the old maxim about
gaining a son and losing a daughter when a daughter married.
Several, usually women, argued that their family unit—parents
and children—were closer to the wife and mother's family than
they were to the husband and father's just for this reason:

> They visited my mother more than they did their [paternal]
> grandmother, because they were closer to my mother you know.
> I think that happens with all girls really. I think the children
> seem to be closer to the girl's mother than the boy's mother,
> unless the girl hasn't got a mother . . . But I think with—where
> there's girls, the mother of the girl, of the daughter always
> seems to be that much closer to the grandchildren. I think It's
> because the girl automatically turns to her mother, you know.

What May Drysdale fails to mention here—though it emerges in
her daughter's interview—is that she is a Catholic and her mother-
in-law a Protestant, something which very much affected the

family relationships. Pat Gladstone, May's daughter, recalls how, when visiting,

> I used to be aware of getting inspected when we used to go. Our clothes inspected to see where the labels were and this type of thing, you know. Always got dressed up to give no reason to talk about what you'd got on.

Asked about her other grandparents, she replied:

> Well... me nan, it was completely different. You just went, your tea was there, drinks, biscuits... Icecream. Just like going from one home to another. No sort of like segregation or anything like that.

In another family, Pat Sims says that her sister-in-law Ann is much closer to her mother-in-law, Ann's mother, than she is herself—

> Because Ann is the daughter, right... She was always looking after Ann and Ann's children, and now they've grown up very close and the kids go there every day. I mean [my son] Luke goes about twice a week, just calls to see his nana. He thinks a lot about her, but he's not as close as Ann's children. Because they were virtually brought up with their nana... Ann had to work with her sewing so [my husband] Joe's mum brought the children up. In Ann's house, but Joe's mum was always there.

It could well be argued from this, however, that Ann and her children are closer to their maternal grandmother than her children are to their paternal grandmother because the former were brought up by her, and not simply because they are the children of a daughter rather than a son. Pat Sims and her children, it should be added, are not particularly involved with or closer to her mother, their maternal grandmother. They are in fact closest to a paternal great-aunt.[45]

Which set of grandparents were more involved with their grandchildren often depended more on the parent–child relationship of the older two generations than on any 'matrifocal tilt'. For example, Sue Keeler did not get on well with her parents, and consequently, when she had children of her own, they spent much more time with her husband's parents with whom Sue had a good relationship. Here, as sometimes elsewhere, this resulted in rivalry between paternal and maternal grandparents, particularly grandmothers. Sue recalls how when her children were born:

> We were always friendly more with me in-laws, as a group, as a unit, than me own parents. But oh yes, I mean, deciding who was going to buy the pram, and who was going to push him out, you know, oh yes, they were in there. But it was a competition.

But by no means all maternal grandmothers felt displaced by not taking priority. When Dennis and Elsie Young's first child was born, only Dennis's mother came to help. This was to be her first grandchild. The maternal grandmother had already had several, and as she relates, immediately gave way:

> Dennis's mother was with her, with Alex, and I wanted to go up. And she said Dennis's mother, 'So I won't put her off.' So I said, 'No that's alright.' Because you see she only had Dennis...[46]

Such 'selective investment' could be seen from each of the three generations. In the Keeler family it was the parents who were in control. In other families the grandparents made the choice. In others it was the grandchildren. Often combinations of all three are involved. Belinda Simonson plays an active part in the day-to-day lives of the children of her youngest daughter, Deborah. But she sees the children of her eldest daughter, Marion, rarely. The latter do not live close by, though they did for some of their childhood years. The former live near their grandmother. Belinda was equally involved with both sets of grandchildren when they were babies—helping her daughters extensively during the first few weeks of each new arrival. Belinda and Sid Simonson do not see eye to eye with Marion and her husband about childrearing, and over the years this has led to a distancing in their involvement with each other. But it has been mutually instigated by all three generations. Marion comments of her parents and of her children's contact with them:

> They're quite straight-laced in their outlook in a lot of things ... and I do not think that they were always fair ... They are not very worldly-wise ... They see them occasionally, that is all ... They do not tolerate them very easily now. My mother

and father did not have much to do with them when they were young. So I think somehow the children have grown up with the knowledge that they do not have a lot to do with their grandma or grandad...

Marion's eldest daughter, now 18, remarks: 'She just thinks we are rude and things like that.' And Belinda Simonson feels that Marion allows her children too much free reign. She comments, 'They have far too much television... She allows them to stay up later than we agree to. Still, that's her business, we don't interfere.' To compensate, she has put all her energy into Deborah's children, of whom there are nine, and with whom she has no such conflict. Deborah, the impression is given, is simply grateful for her mother's help! On the other hand, Marion has made up for the distancing between herself and her parents by forming a close relationship with her mother-in-law:

> Yes, we saw more of her [the mother-in-law). We used to see her every week... She used to come down more frequently at Berkhamsted. She used to come home with him on a Friday and stay the weekend. We used to see a lot more of her... She looked after me once when I was ill... rather than my mum.[47]

Grandparenthood today, like parenthood itself, has been increasingly affected by the increase in marital break-up through divorce. Some of our grandparents had themselves divorced. As after widowhood in the past, it is the second marriage of a grandparent which can change relationships,—and here the impact was wholly adverse. In every case it resulted in a weakening of relationships. Either new partners were not accepted by the existing family, or they themselves did not want to become part of it and pulled the natural grandparent away. Grandparents who remarried were also likely to be more preoccupied with their own lives— enjoying a new relationship—than grandparents settled in a long standing relationship. Rudi Fine, for example, who had two children from his first marriage and two from his second, sees little of his grandchildren from the first marriage. It seems that children and grandchildren are closer to 'intact' grandparents than to separated ones.

The Seldon family's experiences bear this out too. They also illustrate the problematic role of step-grandparenthood. Leonard

Seldon divorced when his own children were eleven and 13, and neither they nor he himself have seen his ex-wife since. Leonard remarried several years later. As a consequence, his grandchildren have never met their natural grandmother, though they have known a step-grandmother. Barbara, one of the grandchildren, had always wanted to meet her 'real' grandmother. Her grandfather has been very against this. Three years ago she went behind his back and found her. Though they have only known each other for three years, she claims that they are closer than she and her step-grandmother—who recently died—ever were. There seems here to be a mixture of influences at work: the excitement of discovering a new relative, the powerful myth of the 'blood tie', and the fact that Barbara's step-grandmother, understandably— possibly pre-empting rejection—put more of her energy into her relationship with her new husband than into that with her step-grandchildren. Barbara's maternal grandparents, on the other hand, have always shown great interest in their grandchildren. This is very important to Barbara, now 19, and helps her to explain the stronger relationships she has with her maternal grandparents: 'that's come from them originally, and then it has been passed on to us: you know, who cares. Children's instincts.'[48]

Another example of a poor relationship between step-grand-children and step-grandparents is provided by Lorna Hampton. Since her grandmother died a year ago, she has only seen her step-grandfather, her grandmother's second husband, twice. Her feelings for him are not strong. She has never thought of him as a grandfather—even though her 'real' grandfather had died and her grandmother remarried before she was born. It seems likely that all contact between them, apart from the occasional Christmas card, will peter out. She explains:

When I went to visit my grandma, before, he was always work-ing, so I've never had a lot to do with Ronnie. Like my grandma always used to buy for the kids for their birthdays and Christ-mas, but he's never bothered, you know, which really, I sup-pose, you couldn't expect him to, but he's never bothered since she died. You soon lose family ties, don't you, but he's not really my family, is he?

You know what I mean? I've nothing against the bloke, but he's not really related to me in any way, is he? I suppose it's not like having—I've always called him Ronnie, I've never called him grandad or anything like that. So really, without sounding rotten, I suppose if he were to die tomorrow, it wouldn't leave me with any gaping wounds or anything like that. I'd be sorry of course, but the bonding's not there, because you're not related, you know.[49]

A third example came from the Werner family, where the paternal grandfather, who lived in Germany, had remarried. His second wife did not seem interested in his family—his son, daughter-in-law, and their three children—since she had her own. The result was that the grandfather's visits became less frequent, whilst his family were not made to feel welcome when they visited him and his wife. His daughter-in-law recalled:

> He always visited us and he was always interested in the children, in his grandchildren, because my husband's an only son. And we felt as though she didn't really like him, you know, she didn't allow him to come, in the end. She came with him every two years and he came on his own on the year in between . . . But we would have preferred him to come more. And if we went there she wasn't exactly welcoming . . .
>
> We felt that as they were not her children . . . We did feel as if it wasn't the same as if it had been their real grandmother. And obviously his contact lessened considerable after. I mean he'd always come for Christmas, and he never came once he'd remarried . . . It's as though he just didn't like to push it . . . So that was really just the disadvantage to us, we had less contact, me and the children. He sent them money for birthdays and things, but not any real outgoing contact.

One granddaughter, bitter yet also understanding, said of her step-grandmother:

> She stopped him coming over here . . . She didn't like coming. Well it wasn't her family for a start. But she was definitely— she's got her own son from her first marriage, and we went there once and she near enough ignored us, . . . and told us off for coming too early when they were in the middle of tea. And then her son arrived unexpectedly and she dropped everything and got him sandwiches and beer, and she didn't even offer Dad or anybody anything. But I suppose it was her son and we weren't her real family.[50]

When the second marriage was in the parent's generation, the effect on the grandparent–grandchild relationship could be similar: a weakening of ties. On the other hand, it could also bring grandchildren and at least one set of grandparents closer together. In Cathy Webster's experience it resulted in a weakening of her relationship with her paternal grandparents. Cathy's mother describes her children's relationship with her ex-parents-in-law:

> It used to be closer but my ex-husband's wife has two children and I think they may feel that they've had their noses pushed out of joint a little, so they feel more comfortable going to my mother's...

Cathy herself said:

> If we go round they'll say, 'We don't see very much of you.' But we always felt left out, because my dad's wife's ... children, took over the place. So we didn't really have much to do with them.

The new grandchildren—the children of Cathy's father's second wife—both Cathy and her mother felt, had usurped Cathy and her brother's position in the lives of their paternal grandparents.[51] Behind their feelings lies the ideal of the 'intact' family unit: a family group not complicated by separation and remarriage, a unit which does not involve membership of more than two sets of relations—the mother's and the father's. The paternal grandparents in this example found it easier to build a new relationship with their step-grandchildren, who lived with their son and new daughter-in-law, than to maintain a relationship with their 'real' grandchildren who live with their ex-daughter-in-law. The grandchildren in this situation became ex-grandchildren, no longer living with a mother and father to whom the grandparents could relate as a couple.

By contrast, two of Meg Jacks's grandchildren and their mother lived with her for six years when their parents split up. This strengthened the grandchildren's relationship with Meg, whilst that with their paternal grandparents became non-existent. The mother has now remarried and the children live with her and their stepfather. He comments that his mother has never treated his stepchildren as her grandchildren. This again suggests that grandchildren are more likely to retain a relationship with the parents of the parent they stay with, whilst step-grandparents and step-grandchildren seem less likely to form close relationships.

Yet there are once more exceptions. One is the Creswell family. Laura, now aged forty, married in 1964. After nine years and having had three children, the youngest of whom was then three, she divorced. The children have never seen their father since and their mother has married again. But they have remained involved with their paternal grandmother Hannah Lawson—even though they now have a step-paternal grandmother as well as maternal grandparents. Hannah has continued to visit them and take an interest in their lives, sees them more than their other grandparents, and appears to have a good rapport with both her ex-daughter-in-law and her grandchildren. Laura speaks very highly of her: 'We've got a very good relationship. We've got a superb relationship now . . . She was wonderful, she really was. I can't speak highly enough of her.'[52]

There is another way besides remarriage which can provide new grandparenting relationships. In three of our families nieces and nephews and eventually great-nieces and great-nephews adopted their childless aunts and great-aunts, uncles and great-uncles, as substitute or additional grandparents. The Sims grandchildren, for example, do not have a close association with either of their grandmothers. Both their grandfathers are dead. They have one step-grandfather. Their paternal grandmother is closer to their cousins, and their maternal grandmother has remarried within the last ten years and has a very passive relationship with her grandchildren. But their paternal grandmother's sister, Phoebe, and her husband Ben, who have no children of their own, took the place of the two 'symbolic' grandmothers and have been actively involved with the Sims family all their lives. Phoebe and Ben fulfil the 'active' grandparenting role to such an extent that Pat, the mother, refers to them as like grandparents, though the grandchildren have always called them by their forenames. For both young and old it was in some ways a compensation. It gave the grandchildren 'active grandparents', and it gave Phoebe and Ben a chance to be involved with children otherwise denied to them. 'That is just how it seemed to balance out really, and of course, Phoebe had no children of her own,' as Pat puts it. The Sims children's association with their natural grandmothers has always been limited to brief weekly visits. With Phoebe and Ben it was entirely different:

My children are probably closer to Auntie Phoebe than anybody. When Uncle Ben was alive they used to do a lot. He was very intelligent as well and they used to all go, every Friday, straight from school. That was a ritual, they always went for tea on a Friday. And they had this bungalow in Wales and they used to take them off... They used to do such good things with them. They'd make things. They were like grandparents with them really. But Uncle Ben especially. He'd sit at the table here with them, building models and they thoroughly enjoyed his company. When you're young you don't really have time for your children like grandparents do. But they spent the time well with them. They just didn't spoil them. They did things with them.[53]

In another family an unmarried woman has lived with her married sister for many years, and has become involved with her sister's children and also grandchildren. The married sister, Agnes Dunbar, now in her sixties, was asked whether her sister played any part at her grandchildren's births:

Yes, oh yes... She would go up and perhaps a couple of weeks before, and stay a week with them. She'd go to the hospital with them if I couldn't go, you know, she'd take the time, when she was working. She'd take the time off work to go and stay with them, if I couldn't go or, you know, if they weren't well. And the children, after they'd had one of the children, the children come here. She would mind the children while I went there to look after them... It's really her family as well as ours.... They look to her as a second mother really.... On Mother's Day they always give her a card to 'our second Mother', oh yes. She's been very good to them... and even the children, like, my family has become her family.[54]

The belief that grandparents fulfil an important need within family life is strong enough to make both older and younger generations seek out substitutes and feel that those children who do not have them 'miss out' when the conventional nuclear family has failed to provide such relationships. One father whose children do not have a lot to do with their grandparents makes this point:

I suppose they are missing something really, yes. Partly by seeing them so seldom and partly by not having much of a relationship with them. Because they really need some other adults who understand their little ways and deal with them differently than us, which is what they don't have at the moment. They really only have us and people who are not in the family.[55]

There are on the other hand adults who do not believe fulfilment in later life comes from closeness to grandchildren. They prefer the company of their own age group. Leonard Seldon takes pleasure in being 'the head' of his family, but prefers his friends at the golf club to his granddaughter a dozen miles away. He thinks the 'generation gap' makes this natural. There were others too, particularly those who had married a second time, whose relationships with their grandchildren appeared superficial. Even for the majority, being a grandparent was only part of their identity. But they saw grandparenthood as an important aspect of their lives, and a fulfilling one: it was a desired state. One grandmother can speak for many in this:

> There was only ever one child born—over the moon, over the moon. We'd waited five years for her. Over the moon, absolutely![56]

We have seen ample instances of the help which so many grandmothers give to their adult children, today as in the past, especially after the grandchildren's arrival. But what about the other side of the coin? Is caring mutual? Who cares for grandparents themselves? It is commonly said that families no longer care for their elders in the way they did in the past. But our findings suggest that patterns of family care have not changed significantly over the past fifty years. Both then and now many children look after their elderly parents; and today, as in the past, the work which this care involves falls largely to women. We have already seen how heavy a burden it can be. The availability of services such as home helps and meals on wheels has undoubtedly eased the burden for some women and enabled some old people to continue to live independently in their own homes. However, their impact can be exaggerated. Nationally, fewer than one old person in ten has a home help, for example. Among our families a similarly small minority had used such services. In the present climate of social service cut-backs it seems more likely that the caring role for women will grow than diminish. Experiences varied, depending on the health of the elderly person, how long they lived, where they lived in relation to their sons and daughters, and the kind of relationship they had with the latter. There was, in some families, a clear expectation that adult children, particularly daughters, would care for the elderly parents when the time came. We have already encountered the Stephens family where the father, who had deserted his wife and children when they were young, turned up years later and expected his daughters to care for him in his later life. Bitter and reluctant, they nevertheless took him in and he lived with them—one after the other—until he died. Among the older generation a common experience had also been for their last living parent or in-law to come and live with them for the last few years of their lives. For working-class families this sometimes meant sharing a bedroom, as in Sadie King's case, or sleeping in the front room, as happened in Sally Peel's family.

Though direct comparisons between the middle and older generations are difficult to make, because our older generation are by and large still fit and active and not in need of family support, there are examples which illustrate how little things have changed since the early part of this century. Gillian Brill gave up her job when in her forties so she could devote more of her time to looking after her mother, who died recently. Kathleen Peel's mother came to live with them for six months when her husband died, sleeping on a 'z bed' in the front room. She then got a sheltered flat of her own, but in fact is hardly there, instead staying with her daughters one after the other for several weeks or just a few days at a time. Gracie and Ed Field, a couple in their early fifties, do all Gracie's mother's shopping and regularly take her to their house to stay for the weekend. When Ed's mother died he would have liked his father to come and live with them but, as Ed explains, he would not do so:

> That wasn't because he didn't want to. I think it was physically impossible for him to do so because we lived near the sea and the salt air used to affect him. He used to get bronchial asthma and had to go back home...[57]

It must also be remembered that many older people, unlike Ed's father, choose to continue to live independently rather than go to live with their married children. It is not that the latter are refusing to take them in. Rather, the elderly cherish their independence. Sally Peel, for example, says of her sons:

Charles wants me to go, he's had a room built for me. Our
Norman has had a room built for me. but I'm not giving my little
home up, and that's what upsets them. They think I shouldn't
be on my own now. But I'm not giving up my home for
nobody.[58]

It is not always possible for children to look after their parents
when they want to. This was the case in the Robinson family. The
Robinsons are a close-knit family, and when David Robinson's
father became ill they very much wanted to take care of him. He
was 61 when he developed a cancer which soon affected his mental state. He was living in Manchester. As his son David and
daughter-in-law Sonia, who were living in Yorkshire, explain, they
first arranged for a home help and for David's sister, who lived
close by, to take him a meal every day.

> DAVID. My sister used to go down every day and see to things
> but he was getting mixed up and confused and I used to go
> over...
> SONIA. He [David] used to pick him up on Friday night, and
> bring him over to us for the weekend, in Yorkshire. But he
> was getting worse and I said he hadn't to come again, because
> he was frightening the kids, you see, because he was shouting
> 'Kathy' all night.
> DAVID. I mean it was affecting his mind.

In the end, David managed to convince the doctor that his
father was not safe living on his own, as he had begun to leave the
gas on. His sister, who became ill with the worry of it, was also at
the end of her tether, so it was arranged for the father to go into a
hospice where he died a month later:

> DAVID. I said, 'I'm sorry but we're not prepared to take respon-
> sibility for him now...He's going to set fire to his
> house...' It was just one of those unfortunate things where
> we couldn't cope with him. It would have been nice to be able
> to look after him, but we couldn't do it really.
> SONIA. You can't when you've young children.[59]

In our families, however, the older generation were more often
still fit and active—offering support to their children and grandchildren rather than the other way around. Carol Werner's
mother, now in her seventies, pops into her daughter's two or

three times a week to help with the ironing and often takes some mending home with her. Belinda Simonson at 65, as we have seen, does all her youngest daughter's mending and often has her grand-children to stay—giving her daughter a break. Gloria White, in her sixties, still looks after her youngest son who lives with her and her husband, whilst the Hibblethwaites drive regularly from Scotland to London to stay with their divorced son in order to help look after his son—their grandchild.

Caring, in short, like grandparenting in general, is built out of mutual needs, but needs fulfilled in many varying forms: patterns shaped both by the expectations of the wider society, and by particular family traditions, and by personality and circumstance. How do these influences weigh against each other?

Our material suggests that expectations of grandparenthood are moulded by wider cultural norms. But there were nevertheless clear patterns within some families which suggest family cultures could also be significant. There were, for example, families in which, quite contrary to the usual expectations, for two genera-tions or more grandsons and grandmothers had been particularly close. And there were others in which, equally unexpectedly, for two or more generations granddaughters talked of being specifical-ly influenced by their grandfathers. Equally clearly, a pivotal in-fluence in shaping the relationships between many grandchildren and their grandparents are the particular attitudes of the parent. Undoubtedly individual character, the likes and dislikes, of grand-child and grandparent are also crucial. But given the reality of the norm of non-interference and of a dominant parental influence over their children, a grandchild is less likely to form a close relationship with a grandparent if the parent and grandparent do not get on well.

Grandparents, in short, stand at the perimeters of the nuclear family, seeking an entry which is largely controlled by parents. As Sarah Cunningham-Burley has written, we too found this meant grandparents had to act with great care and tact, to put their children's needs and wishes before their own, and to wait to be asked rather than assume any involvement by right:

> My grandma's played quite a large part I think . . . She'd have played a much larger part if she'd have been given the chance. I know she doesn't agree with certain things mum and dad agree

with . . . She thinks my dad's too fussy . . . Little things, because they've never really got on that well.[60]

How much is lost through similar exclusions we can only guess; but our families show abundantly how grandparenting can be both a precious fulfilment in later life, and a valued emotional and practical gain for younger generations.

10
Companionship, Loneliness, and Love

DESPITE the importance of the wider family as a source of mutual support and meaning in later life, very few even among the most involved grandparents built their lives around it. Only the widowed ex-fisherman caring for his grandchildren stands out as an indisputable exception. Less than one in five saw a child or grandchild daily. Most of them looked elsewhere to meet their need for human intimacy: in marriage, but also in widowhood.

Living together into later life had brought new challenges which had reshaped some marriages significantly. A man's retirement in particular was a turning-point which could precipitate a crisis. 'I was dreading the retirement,' a roofer's wife confided. A retired cleaner has 'a brother and he's retiring this year and his wife's having a fit. She doesn't know how they are going to get on.' 'Once he does retire, he'll have to find something to do,' a working wood-machinist's wife prophesied gloomily. 'He's a creature of habit. I don't think I'll alter him now.'[1] How did they fare when they retired?

The short answer is that while a fair proportion of couples did manage to adjust, it was mostly too late. Let us look for a moment only at those who were still married. Of these 24 couples, only eight described close, happy marriages; the other 16 were either not close, or at least one of the pair was seriously discontented or depressed (see Tables 7–10).

This was not due to lack of material resources, although they could perhaps have helped to mitigate troubles: for none of the close couples still in a first marriage were middle class. Nor were any of the unhappiest couples, although the only two divorcees were middle class. One described his first marriage as 'a disaster'; another commented, 'I think the worst thing in my life was my first marriage. I've never understood it. Why?'[2]

Certainly the least contented group was those couples who

had long led very separate lives, and had changed little in this with retirement. These 'traditional' marriages were as common with middle-class as with working-class couples. Here husband and wife had always had clearly demarcated roles, with the man undertaking little or no domestic responsibility: 'You tend to wait on them'; 'He's never been one as'd do any housework. Not unless there was something wrong'—and even then he would underline his own incompetence, 'make the bed and it'll be all hanging.' While both partners had enough to preoccupy them, with jobs or family to care for, they usually got along without too much mutual discomfort. A working docker's wife described evenings with 'Fred asleep in that chair and me asleep in this chair.' In the closest of these marriages, the couple used their different interests positively as a way of letting off steam: 'we don't get into hassles like we did . . . I don't think we ever quarrel . . . When he's fed up he goes in the greenhouse. When I'm fed up I go in the boxroom and sew . . . Just to say, "Yes dear," and walk out. Rather than blow up.' Once they retire the men all make some symbolic gesture towards regular help in the house, but these gestures are strictly limited. One man helps to shop; two make a morning cup of tea and sometimes hoover; one just washes up—'she cooks it and I do the washing up'; another 'has his little jobbies that he does—he sees to the logs and cleans the fire out.' Several also do repair work and garden. But their continuing sense of male and female roles being quite distinct is accepted: 'that's not a man's thing, is it, going round markets? he doesn't really like it, he doesn't like trailing behind'; 'I like to do a thing myself, I canna be daeing wi' anybody in my road.'[3]

These couples also carry on managing their finances in exactly the way they always have done. Typically the woman continues to take all the responsibility: a Lancashire husband, for example, who always tipped up his wage, 'tips his pension up now. We get the notes and there's 15p over that's his spends . . . I know every ha'penny what he's got, and he knows mine.' One husband controls the entire budget in a truly patriarchal style: 'If she needed money for any reason, he would give her some. But he would do all the spending, pay all the bills and the food—they go shopping together and he pays.' One wife describes a joint arrangement which involves considerable badgering: 'usually I go moan moan moan.'[4]

These couples succeed in living together above all through their own different interests. Only one such couple spoke of themselves as close. The others at best got on reasonably. One wife felt that now 'the pressures are off, I suppose maybe we get on better than we used to do,' and her husband concurred: 'I don't think we argue quite as much.' When a professional husband retired to fulfil his dream of a rural retreat, his wife had the sadness of 'leaving my lovely house' and 'moving away from the children,' on top of having her regular daily routine upset. In retirement 'I think you're got a lot of adjusting . . . I did find it difficult having him at home all the time. I think the basic thing is that I've always had the day to myself, he's gone off to work . . .' But now 'we both go our own ways and do our own thing and we're quite happy.' But three other wives were acutely discontented. One could scarcely tolerate a man who was now a chronic invalid. Jean Macpherson resented her ex-labouring husband's weekend drinking at a club, but had little more time for him in the week: 'he's always under my feet son, except for weekends, then I don't see him.' She had grudgingly concluded that being together was a good thing, 'in a sense, because when you get older, you realize more or less that you do need each other. Whereas when you're young . . . I had my work, he had his work, he had his recreation, I sat in the house; which pleased me.' And Meg Jacks was equally disapproving of the money her woodworker husband Tom spent at the pub:

You see, he's one of those school, followed on from his dad, and he likes going for a pint . . . I like other things. So we go our separate ways. We do and we don't—there was never any trouble or anything. But he doesn't like the same things as I do.

So he doesn't bother if I go and do anything, and I don't bother—I know where he go. I can put me hand on him at any time . . . We don't fall out much really. He's quite easy really. I mean, if I went out at morning and didn't come back till late at night, he wouldn't bother—as long as I left him a bit of something as he could eat.

What I mean is he's not interested in things but he doesn't stop me from doing anything . . . We always rubbed along like. Had our ups and downs . . . I would like if he would be a little bit more outgoing . . . I'm easy really, as long as I'm out—if it's looking at a market, little ride and a mooch here and there and

I'm satisfied . . . Oh he makes me sick! . . . There's nothing *to*
getting old, we'll say that . . . There's not a lot to like about it.[5]

These couples also had the most negative attitudes to sex. At the
most positive, they said that their sexual feelings were 'diminished,' but still important to them; 'It's not strong, but it's there';
'okay, not the be all and end all, no.' But five women clearly felt
that sex had always been more a husband's privilege than a pleasure of their own, and had never been much interested themselves. 'I think it's more for a man than a woman'; 'no, not to me
particularly, but to a man it is right.' As one wife put it, 'I think if
you want to keep your husband, if he's interested in sex, well,
you've got to be as well—I don't see any difference in the age you
are.' One was glad this phase was past: 'I think it's a thing that you
serve your time at, when you're younger, and then when you get
older it doesn't appeal to you so much.' But the most disparaging
image came from a man.

A young fellow, he's chasing it all he can, in't he? It's like a dog
chasing after a bitch, and she's coming in season, you'll see five
or six of them fighting with each other, who's going with her.
But when you get older it doesn't bother you same. When we
are away next week, where we are going they'll be walking
about topless, won't they? You just don't bother.[6]

A second group of eleven couples had by contrast more of a joint
approach to both the pleasures and the responsibilities of their
lives. Half said they had moved substantially in this direction since
retirement. There seems therefore to have been a remarkable
shift in attitudes among them. Their memory of pre-retirement
patterns seems convincing, because it fits closely with the recollections of the widowed, some of whose spouses had already retired
before they died. It looks as if four out of five marriages in our
whole sample were 'traditional' in their earlier years, but of those
surviving in couples when we recorded them, half had moved to
sharing, joint roles (see Table 10).

Yet it was only for a few that this shift was the making of a close
marriage in these later years. It is true that the group as a whole
were markedly more often happy than the still 'traditional' marriages, and none were openly hostile, but for several couples the

change had evidently come too late to bring a fundamental change in mutual feeling. Fred Kitchin had taken on more work in the home to allow his wife Meg to go back to work: 'housework, he does windows, kitchen, bathroom . . . He's at home, so he's going through the house every day like normal . . . Oh yes, that was one of the bargains, that was one of the things we did say when I said I was getting a job.' but although retirement had drawn the Kitchins together, it was only in a rather limited way: 'we're probably closer, we're more pally, we've more time for each other you see. We can sit for hours and not say anything, but it's pals in a way.' A Scots couple where the husband now did more housework than the wife obviously felt better than the wife's sister, who complained of her own husband, 'It's murder . . . See that man o' mine, he's a lazy sod . . . Put doon fir a meal, and never gives a remark.' The sharing husband felt that he and his wife were 'a lot closer than we were,' and they certainly had a lively relationship—'aye, we argue mair, ha ha ha!,' she chipped in—but she was nevertheless a deeply unhappy woman. Two other couples now shared the housework—'we do it between us: I would say Albert does a bit more than me at the moment'—but in one couple both are depressed, while in the other the husband is depressed, and the wife calls herself a 'sour old married woman' who is glad to see the back of him down to the pub. 'It's a bit of a relief for the two of us. Cause it's a bit of a strain on a marriage being together 24 hours a day . . . We do get on each other's nerves sometimes.' Another husband 'helps now of course he's retired,' and the wife feels retirement 'if anything it draws you closer, mh mn: I suppose it would be because you're constantly together.' but although 'we get out more,' their regular interests still seem very separate, and he gets very fidgety 'when there's no bit of gardening to do, he gets—the wintertime's the worst.'[7]

These couples may have changed their approach to housework, but there is little sign of a shift in attitudes to money, or to sex. The wives still handle the cash; and none of them is interested any more in sex. One woman, whose wedding night had been a deep shock because she had thought sleeping with a husband would be like sleeping with her sister, now thought sex unimportant; another agreed that sex 'makes no difference to your relationship . . . Ye've had yer family.' A third wife is also 'not very interested . . . Anyone

over the age of thirty shouldn't be.' And one woman openly relished
her husband's declining powers:

> SHE. Quite correct, we are not interested in sex. I jist ken that
> he's a man and I'm a woman . . . This load of rubbish aboot the
> older the fiddle the better the tune, it's utter rubbish.
> And as for snow being on the roof-top and fire underneath,
> that is tripe.
> HE. I wouldn't say ye're not interested, the point is ye're not
> able.
> SHE. We've had enough, let's face it . . . I wouldna gie ye a bit o'
> steak and chips fir all the sex that wis ever thingmy. Let's face
> it, sex is no necessary if ye love a person.
> HE. No, that's true.
> SHE. Sex isna—it's an overrated pastime. I think it's mair attrac-
> tion fir the men than what it is fir the women . . .
> Ye ken I often torment ye aboot sex—
> HE. Oh I ken—
> SHE. It would be a dull day if I didna. I've seen me saying,
> 'Come on, lock all the doors an' we'll stay in bed all day.' But
> he never takes it.[8]

Fortunately not all the accounts of the later years of married life
are so gloomy. We shall come to a different story with the remarried. And among those still in their first marriages, too, there is
a small group of distinctly close couples. Two have changed their
practical division of roles markedly, and one of these wives found it
quite difficult adjusting at first to her husband's continual presence
in the home. 'I'd been used to being on my own and doing things
as I wanted to do them. But it changed when he was home all day.
Sometimes I'd wish he'd go out so that I could be on my own and I
could do little jobs that I want to do, that he says to me, "Leave
it."' But both couples have become closely companionable. 'We're
thoroughly enjoying ourselves . . . We go out every day, somewhere'; 'we made up for lost time.' One husband, a gardener's son,
finds it especially apt to be back at gardening after years running
the village post office; but for both these couples the garden is like
an outdoor room whose pleasures they share, spending their time
when they are at home 'in the garden mostly.'[9] More important,
they give the sense of a happiness which goes back *before* retirement, and has simply been more fully realized since.

The two happy couples who have always shared their responsibilities at home are similar in this. None of the four partners show the inflexible attitudes to money or hostility to sex of so many other marriages, and sex remains positively important to some of them—as one of them enthusiastically exclaimed: 'oh yes, yes—oh yes.' Both men help cook as well as clean. They are also openly affectionate—'very much, very much so'; or as the other wife describes, 'yes, oh yes, we are close. Oh yes: he still tells me he loves me as much as he did when he first met me. And then he gets told not to be so soft and sloppy.' Both of these wives have strongly developed interests of their own, and one (as is one wife of the previous two couples) is still at work. They combine independence and mutuality in what one wife calls 'more of a companionship.' The other—Annie Mimms, the Green Belt seamstress—describes how her marriage works:

> He went outside [Walter is another passionate gardener] and I had my little things to do, and I went to my meetings, and I had different fields . . . It just worked . . . I had a lot of things to talk about when I came home—'Have you seen anyone today?,' 'Oh no,' he'd say, 'I haven't seen a soul,' and I said, 'I'll tell you about all the people I've seen'. . .
>
> We're pleased with each other, and we like to have each other—you see, I suddenly think of something and I run down the garden, and have my little say, and then we'll have a walk round. . .
>
> We've got a very good relationship . . . oh yes, yes, very good, yes, very good, very good . . . We've had a really nice time, the last fourteen years.

Just turning eighty, they think their present age the best time of life.[10]

Even a bad marriage will often seem better than none. Some of the married look over their shoulders: 'Can you imagine it? Being a sour old spinster now instead of sour old married woman. Yes, I've been exceptionally lucky.' And the widowed still more agree. It does not look as if in retrospect they reinterpret their daily patterns and predominantly traditional roles in marriage very much, for these match well with the accounts of the still married. But they do appear to revalue the meaning of their marriages. While only a quarter of those still married to their first spouse say they feel close to them, of the widowed, two-thirds now recollect happy marriages (see Table 10).[11] This reconstruction of the past is a consolation in their time of loss.

All older people face death regularly at close quarters, and not only by being widowed. They also lose friends and family. Oliver Ridings kept a flat in Heptonstall for a while to keep in touch with old friends, but 'I packed it in . . . You see, when you leave a town at my age, before you know where you are, you haven't any friends left. You see, there's nobody gets to eighty-odd, is there? It's all gone.' It was similar for a woman in her late seventies: 'I used to go, you see, to visit friends, but I'm afraid my friends have died off.' Meg Jacks, just in her sixties, who still worked part-time in the family chipshop, had lost her two sisters, and the brother to whom she was close who had lived across the road, and his wife, all of heart failure, within five years.

> It was bad really because it all came at one time. I had a family, then I had none, You know it was—well I'm not over it yet really to tell you the truth . . . I sort of broke down . . . I had so much trouble and so much upsetting . . . I had a big family and I was very close, I went everywhere with these two sisters . . . You have a big family and then I had just nobody. It was very hard . . . It suddenly crashed on me . . . I seem to have jumped from young to old . . . Suddenly—I went old over them, that period like. Felt old, felt old after. I look old.[12]

Loss of loved ones is not only difficult in itself. It forces those who survive to confront their own mortality. None, not even the religious, welcomed death in itself. One widow had found her religion a comfort, but a widower had had the opposite reaction. 'I've lost a lot of faith since I lost my wife. I thought, "How could they take a person like that?" . . . She loved people . . . She lived for people.' But the nearest to a religious sense of death as a gateway to rebirth in paradise came from Bill Duncan, militant atheist: 'as far as I'm concerned, I've no time for the churches. No, no. My father was buried withoot a minister. I had t'dae the service at kirkyard.' Bill has not much more time for politicians, but he keeps a secret longing for a New Jerusalem on earth which he must have imbibed from his socialist grandparents. 'I tell you what would make a big difference to my future, if by some means I could be informed that the world was coming to peace, right through from end to end, I would die happy.'[13]

Most people had more modest hopes. They had quietly accepted the limit to their own lifespan and were more concerned to go painlessly and with dignity. Some couples talked openly between themselves of death. But in wider circles, especially with younger people, the bereaved may encounter a pervasive evasion of public discussion. This often leaves the widowed with no intimate to talk to just when their need is greatest, isolation heightening their risk of depression. One widow tried to talk with her daughter-in-law and granddaughters, but found herself rebuffed: 'I talk to Mary and the girls, and they say, "Oh, she's off again." So I've given up trying.' And even some of those older people who are still married deliberately turn their backs on mortality, defying death by never speaking of it to their most intimate companion. Brenda Steel kept the unspeakable secret right to the end of her husband's slow death from leukaemia, through which she nursed him:

it wasn't so bad as it sounds, for the simple reason I've been in nursing all the time, you see, and I know what's gonna happen. But it also helped that Les didn't know anything about it. Right to the end, Les wasn't aware of it . . . He once said to me, 'I don't know why they tell people they're gonna die.' He said, 'I think that's the most distressing thing.'[14]

Forewarned or not, the sting of death when it came was scarcely muffled. To the survivors, only the loss of a child—which some had also suffered—could cause equal pain. Again and again they named it as the worst thing in their whole lives.

Some were still deep in its shadow. 'I've only one thing—he didn't suffer long,' said a new widow. 'Takes some getting over, it does. No. I haven't . . . It just broke everything up. It's totally different . . . I haven't a goal now.' Nor did time alone mend things. A carpenter's widow, who with her husband had been a keen cyclist and dancer before he was killed in a motorcycle accident 34 years ago, still lived her meagre life in his memory. 'I've never gone with anybody else. I never met anybody else. I never even thought about it.' Louise Barrington began to cry as she described her husband's sudden death, self-reproachfully:

I suppose I'm silly getting upset . . . Mind you, it's nine years ago, I should be over that by now. It's a lonely life, and it is, when you've been close together, and we were very close. I used to say to him before he died, 'I hope we both go together'. . . . I never wanted to grow old, I never wanted to live this long.

She likes 'nothing' about her present age. 'I think my grandchildren think I'm grand, but they don't know how often I sit here depressed and lonely.'[15]

Most of those who had recovered from the depths of their despair still remembered it all too vividly. A foreman who had nursed his wife for seven years became a 'drifter' after her death. 'I just had no interest and I felt lousy . . . I couldn't rouse myself. I just stayed and sat.' An engineer reacted similarly. 'It nearly killed me. I was quite a while before I could go back to work because I had a responsible job and I'd lost confidence. I was under treatment from the doctor.' Mary Wesley, a former maid, had had 'a lovely life together' with a scientific instrument-maker, 'a right gentleman. He would open the door for you and took off his hat to you in the street . . . He was very kindly . . . just like my father I thought.' When he died suddenly on his way to fetch the daily paper, none of Mary's friends or relatives could understand her despair. 'It takes another widow to know what ye're suffering. Ordinary married folk, they don't realize what it's like . . . I wasna here. And that was nature's way of letting you heal, I can see that now.[16]

Within a year, or two, or three, the depression would begin to lift, sometimes miraculously. Mary Wesley continued, 'I can see that now, because it came back exactly for three years . . . I was sitting watching the television and I shouted out something and fae that—that was *me*! It was over and I was by.' She had found that in the worst time, the church helped 'greatly, that's when my faith really came to my need.' More often one of the family, or a friend, provided a lifeline. For ex-fisherman Ted Keeler it was his younger brother: 'I never saw a lot of him before my wife died, and I think he helped me at the time—he made me more or less, made me get up. "Come on out," and so on.' For Dick Tiverton, 'it took me maybe the best part of a year to come to terms with it. My friends were very good and they would come and pick me up and take me out and make sure that I go out and have a drink and a chat.' Like five others, he also stayed with his children. 'Gradually I've adjusted fairly well, but you never really get over it. But if you don't make an effort, you're not going to do yourself much good.'[17]

These last comments applied to nearly all of those who, to some degree or other, built new lives for themselves after bereavement. 'You carry on and you do ... but it never does go and it gets worse,' remarked one of the best-adjusted widows. 'All I can say, "It's you that can pull yourself together" ... It doesn't go. I don't know how to get rid of it. I don't and I'm not a miserable person ... I miss Dave's way of going on.' But most found a way to adjust. Two of the six men threw themselves into work. One was Bill Duncan, unstoppable worker; another a younger widower, John Bridges, then a factory under-manager, who deliberately decided to make himself available for demanding overseas commissions. 'You see I became a workaholic when my wife died. That's all I thought about was work, work, work.' John still fills his hours with unpaid jobs.

> My lifestyle now is what it is because of the loss of my wife. Yes. It's as simple as that. I do things now, not because I really like doing—it's because I've got to do something. I've got to utilize my time. I can't just sit here. I've either got to be working, if I'm not I've got to be out and talking to people.[18]

Four widows continued work as professional nurses. Like the men, they were recovering by using inner resources and skills which they had developed earlier. Dawn Roberts, the floral champion, was helped by the remarkable new interest which she had already developed since retirement. And all of them set about creating a new social life for themselves.

This was not easy. At the beginning most had felt like a car-worker's widow: 'I didn't want to go out and meet people.' As a nurse put it, 'You get indrawn. You can't hold a conversation.' And although this feeling lessened, with many it was still there inside. John Bridges now has 'many very good friends,' but 'although I socialize ... it doesn't matter where you go, what you do—you're always on your own. If you lose your partner, you're never—I always feel as though I belong to nothing. I'm a nobody.' A London Irish widow with an active round of clubs still felt 'loneliness' as the main feature of her age. Two Scots widows emphasized the special social difficulties which older women on their own have to face. 'I find it difficult now, you're always single and you find it difficult when there's couples. It's very difficult,' a nurse put it: 'you don't want to be gooseberry when there's couples.' The other, Mary Wesley, explained,

there's one thing I miss in life, it's the only thing, is company. If
I'd a friend or somebody that I could go around with, I would go
to the dancing. I love dancing . . . And I can't go out now on my
own . . . See when your husband dies, that's you—they all cut
you off—your friends. Because there's no man. They love entertaining a man, but no wife, no one woman without a man.
Friends I speak to and they say, 'Yes we've found the very
same'. . . . You've to try and make friends that you can, if they
havena a husband maybe. People like that are a widow.[19]

Certainly the friendship patterns of the widowed men and
women did differ. The widows depended almost wholly on family
or on women friends: only one widow stood out for her friendships
with men. Much more typical were two nurses, each with a feminine social circle. One had become especially close to a widowed
lollipop lady, while the other had two special nursing friends,
unmarried or widowed. On the other hand all but one of the men
had both men and women friends. They were able both to start
new one-to-one friendships with women, and also to get to know
younger couples. Bill Duncan's closest friends, for example, are a
much younger couple whom he met at work. He began by taking
them for day outings, but now they take him out. They also
holiday together, and the wife each week makes him enough soup
for the whole week. 'It's always a big pot.' Big enough, indeed, for
him to share it with 'an old blind man' who lives by him,
'doonstairs.'[20]

It is easy enough for men in later life to find the chances for new
friendships with women as well as with men. The demographic
balance favours them in the first place: there are more
older women than men, and many more widows than widowers.
They can easily find workplaces or homes, or pubs or societies,
where they can meet both sexes. This is far less true for women,
for social habits exacerbate the demographic imbalance. They cannot confortably go alone to the sports or professional clubs or the
pubs where most widowers, including most of those we recorded,
are to be found. None of the widows was anticipating remarriage,
partly from marital loyalty, but also because there simply did not
seem to be any chance for them. As one of the Scots widows put it,
'No, I had a good husband and I don't think I could get the same
again.' The carworker's widow was blunter: 'They [men] don't

interest me. We haven't got many men down there, anyway.' And indeed, of those we recorded, only seven attended old people's clubs: two married women, five widows, and no men.[21]

This does not mean, however, that women have more difficulty in fully recovering from widowhood than men. If we contrast those who found a new fulfilment, either still widowed or in remarriage, with those who could only patch up a routine to conceal a still empty heart, it emerges that the men who do well are those widowed early, before they are sixty. Middle-aged men had good chances, primarily because they could still relatively easily remarry. Older widowers, who were more likely to have to make a new life on their own, were markedly less successful in this than older widows (see Tables 11 and 12).

The two men and six women who succeeded in creating fulfilling lives without remarrying were all remarkable people. Bill Duncan is already familiar as the unstoppable worker. Even more contented was ex-fisherman Ted Keeler who had made himself into a househusband for his son's family. Around this new home base he had also organized a regular social life, and exercise. He was thoroughly enjoying his retirement, taking every day as a gift of fortune. 'That's supposed to be your allotted span, isn't it, severty? So every day acts as a bonus.' His attitude to sex was typical of the six: it had its place, but 'to be companions and friends is more than sex, in my opinion.'[22]

With the women there was more than this: each of them conveys a powerful sense of new fulfilment in the discovery of previously stifled independence and energy. All see themselves as much better off now than if they were to be locked in marriage again. Glenys Howells, a retired factory nurse, who is a keen walker and has an abundant social life with old friends as well as children and grandchildren, turned down a chance of remarriage for just this reason. Sometimes she regrets it: 'I think maybe I did the wrong thing, because I wouldn't be here on my own now. I'd have someone in the night-times to talk to.' Remarriage looked positive in principle. but when confronted by the reality of it, she had immediately decided against it. She had been friends with the proposer when they were both married.

The person I knew, his wife was a—how shall I say? She was a person that you couldn't get out of the chair before she'd got a duster and pumping up the cushions, sort o' thing. And he'd got so used to it, that I knew that he would go on doing that. And that would grate on my teeth. That would make me agitated. That would cause trouble.[23]

Marjorie Dickens is sustained by her close relationship with the best friend of her early childhood. Although kept apart during their married years in different towns, 'since they've both died we've got together properly': 'we can be as rude as we like to each other, and nobody takes offence.' At eighty they still share a common enthusiasm for sport—golf and tennis—and go on walking holidays together. Two other widowed women are still working as private nurses, each with their work and women friends, and both were quite clear that, however painful the loss of their husband, they had gained something new. Brenda Steel works in the home counties, and uses weekends for trips with friends to London markets, or the theatre, or a lunch at the seaside.

I know lots of ladies who would be very glad to be in my shoes ... with the opportunities that I get. I meet lots of gentlemen like that and I've had lots of opportunities to get married, if I wanted to. But I don't want to ... Well, I should find it very difficult to adjust because I really rather like the fact that I haven't got any time margin and—I can do exactly as I like ... I haven't got anyone to get the tea for or to get home for and—I really quite enjoy that.

The Scots nurse, Verity Hampshire, felt very much the same way:

Since I've been a widow, I'm more active. Because I have to get out and do things now, you see there's nobody there. I'm no tied down to the house either. So I find that it's good to get out ... I found that was the best thing I could've done, to go into the community and get involved ... Being my age now, I feel that there's a whole lot of responsibility of family and all that is taken off me now. So I'm really free to lead my own life and make my own ways.[24]

Dawn Roberts is, like Bill Duncan, already familiar to us, as the floral champion. Life is also simpler for her without a husband. She had a lively, even tempestuous marriage. Walter was a tailor, fanatically involved in his work.

He never got a meal ready nor nothing. He used to come in and expect to sit down to everything. He didn't demand it, it was just his way. To come in, sit down and wait for his tea stuck in front of him and he'd eat it. Then he'd leave the table and I'd go and clear the table: he'd never think of going in and washing up.

They had different tastes in many ways. He 'always liked some noise going on around him' and would use the television as background; she turns it off unless there is something worth watching. Dawn enjoyed being cosseted in bed, but Walter would 'never go to bed once he was up.' 'He didn't like change, Walter, he liked everything where it was; and I was a devil for change.' They seem to have agreed about sex:

> I never liked it. I think it's an over-rated pastime, myself. No, I was never fond of it—ever. And Walter never forced anything on you. He used to joke about it. He'd say, 'Oh, I might get me leg over tonight.' But he never did. Never bothered. No, as soon as I could get rid of it, I did.

They were also both great talkers. Walter was amusing—'he had you in stitches'—but relentless: 'he followed you around everywhere yapping at your ear' ole.' Dawn is also abundantly articulate. Looking back, she thinks the worst thing about her life was their quarrels: 'We'd torment each other a bit too far sometimes.'

Once Walter had finally retired, their marriage improved. 'We didn't torment each other as much . . . mellowed . . . and we had more time together.' He started to wash up the dishes and to help her in the garden, mowing the lawns; and more imaginatively, taking a positive interest in her hobby.

> When we went up the country, he was all the time looking in the hedges to see if there was anything that would be useful to me for flower arranging. Such as that piece of wood round that vase—he found that—'Is this any use to you, Dawn?'

Then when she was seriously ill,

> he looked after me like nobody's business. He went out and he bought all the special foods to tempt me to eat that he could think about. He was running up and down the stairs in attendance the whole time—as a matter of fact, he used to drive me mad—'Do I want this?'—'Do I want that?'—'Do I want the

other?'—all the time. And I used to say, 'Just let me go to sleep.'

Then—to her astonishment—it was Walter who collapsed. Her return to caring for him in that last week brought a deathbed reconciliation between them. 'I don't think I'd have the strength to do a lot now, although when Walter was ill that week, I never even thought about myself, I did everything for him.' He died holding her hand. 'I'll never forget his last words . . . "You're looking after me, aren't you, Dawn?"'

After Walter died, Dawn Roberts went on flower arranging, but she also bought new furniture. 'I turned this house upside down. I started to decorate. I decorated it from top to bottom.'

She misses him. 'I used to blame him for everything that went wrong and he used to blame me for everything that went wrong. But now there's nobody you see . . . I wish he was sat in that chair and I could have a go-go at him.' All the same, for Dawn, 'life's very sweet in a way.'[25]

The last of the four has much more time for men. Sally Peel is also a woman of exceptional resource. She is the 'venturing widow.' Once a cleaner, she has turned to nursing. Now 76, a loving woman with a talent for caring, she is also very shrewd in her handling both of money and of human relationships.

Sally had a tough start to life. Her father, a travelling Scots steel erector, had to give up work after he got a piece of steel in his eye. Her mother 'had a terrible struggle' bringing up 13 children in stark poverty in Salford. Neither parent could work, and they depended on church charity for coal and blankets. Both her mother and her father cracked up and died in their early forties. Her mother suffered from severe bronchitis, and her father developed throat cancer. After that, 'my eldest brother brought us all up'. As soon as she could, Sally was sent to the mill to earn her keep. Later on she was a bus conductress, and then a cleaner. In the meantime she had met and married Les, a baker's van driver.

They had two sons, but not content with this, Sally took in three teenage foster-children voluntarily. The last one she just found on the beach, having fled from a home. She looked after all of them for over six years until they married, and is still in touch with them. And she would have gone on accumulating strays, but her husband then said, 'We're having no more.' She describes herself as a no-nonsense, even tough mother: 'one word and it were a clout with me.' But she conveys a special pleasure in children.

Some time after the war, the couple decided to move to Blackpool and buy a house there, where Sally Peel now lives. She had got to know the town working on the buses during the war: 'I always loved Blackpool.' She raised the money ingeniously, helped by her sons, by buying an unfinished house and selling it at a profit—'so method in me madness.' But Les, who had been badly injured in the war, was already unable to work. He was developing an incurable, debilitating disease, a wasting of the nervous system, from which he finally died twelve years ago. For the last eight years she nursed him.

Far from being deterred, Sally built on her harrowing experience. She taught herself to drive, and took up private nursing. She specializes in caring for invalid ladies, washing and cleaning and nursing. 'Oh, I love cooking and I love washing.' She is fearless in the face of death. 'I found about seven dead. I'm not frightened of the dead, it's the living you've got to be frightened of. I'm expecting this one [to die] any day.' And they have been grateful too: 'They all left me £200 . . . all these ladies I've looked after.' She has spent the money on trips across the world to see her foster-children and on seaside holidays with friends.

After Les died, she radically reconstructed her house to make a new base for herself, socially and economically. She kept the downstairs for herself, with two rooms, a kitchen, and a bathroom, but converted the upstairs into two bed-sitters with a joint bathroom. She then took in two elderly men as lodgers. This gave her an income—and also company. Sally Peel has both women and men friends, and she describes her best friend now as Martha, a married, retired civil servant with whom she goes bowling. She has a regular social life, fitted in between visits to 'the sick people I'm looking after,' and seeing both her sons and her grandchidren. She and Martha go bowling twice a week 'with the men.' She goes to a parish church on Sundays—not the local one, where she quarrelled with the vicar years ago over the altar flowers. And four afternoons or evenings a week, she goes to an old age pensioners' club to play whist. But it is her friendships with men which are most exceptional.

'I took it very hard after Les died, because I'd looked after him so long. And I prayed for him to die. But when he went, it hit me . . . It changed me. I was very—I used to cry and cry and cry.'

After a time she had reshaped the house and the two lodgers had moved in. One was Tim. He too had been recently widowed, and they came together in their grief.

He used to cry about his wife, and then he had a son died at fifty, and they had a little girl eight-year-old that died—she got pricked with a pin. He was a very sad man, he was. A very sad man. He'd sit up there and he'd be crying. And I'd be crying . . . And he used to come down, and he said, 'Come on, get out. I'll take you out.'

Eventually, they fell in love. But it was never a full sexual relationship. 'I think when you've been married for about forty years, you've had enough.' Sally is decidedly not interested in sex: 'Oh I'm not, no, no, no, no.' And she does not like men who are.

I don't want no more sex, Oh no, I've got a fella now—he keeps phoning me up. But that's all he wants . . . This Tim that I went with for six years, he couldn't do it. He loved me, he loved me, but he couldn't do sex. That's what I liked, I liked that.

What they gave each other was companionship, and fun. Tim already had a woman friend of sorts, but he ditched her. 'He said to me, "Can I take you out?" . . . He told her he was going to Scotland fishing.' But it was really a honeymoon. 'So we set off for Scotland, and we had a marvellous holiday. I drove 2,000 miles.' They took in the sights, they played bowls together, and they had celebratory meals. One night they even slept out in the car. And they kept up the fun when they got back to Blackpool. They had regular suppers together, although he still slept upstairs. They went out bowling; and 'we used to go to the Cliff, on the front, dancing, a Saturday night.'

Tim was her friend for six years. He had been a building repairer, and helped her improve the house. But he was a heavy smoker, and he died of lung cancer. Sally nursed him, too, briefly: he fell ill when they were on holiday in Spain. He left her everything. 'He had lovely clothes. That's his gold watch.'

After Tim died Sally suffered, but less than the first time. 'I felt empty, but I didn't—no, I weren't upset, because we were just good pals. I missed him, nobody knows how I missed him, I did miss him. I missed him terrible. I felt empty after that. But we had a marvellous time together'.

Sally Peel was now over seventy. She decided it was the moment to go to Canada, to visit her foster-daughter, and also her foster-grandchildren, whom she had never seen. Almost at once, she was involved in other adventures:

> I went by boat to Canada, I went to Tilbury and I went by boat. It was fantastic, I was ten days on the boat . . . Oh, one or two o'clock we were dancing! And I got an old man on the boat, he came from Vancouver. And he wanted me to stay the night with him, and I thought, 'Oh no, no. That would be madness.' And I said, 'No, I can't.' And when we got off the boat, he says, 'I've booked a hotel for tonight. Will you stay with me?' We used to walk round the boat, and he said his wife was a Lesbian, and he'd never slept with his wife for 15 years. I says, 'They're not tampering with me, mate.' Anyway, we had a lovely time on the boat, and I left him at Montreal.

Having turned down this chance, she went on to Toronto to sleep off the journey. And when she woke in her foster-daughter's home, 'I heard these two kids shouting, "Grandma, grandma, wake up!"'

For Sally Peel, life is far from over. 'I don't think myself old . . . I've had an exciting life, and I wouldn't change it for the Queen.'[26]

None of the others who were still on their own had anything like Sally's confidence in handling sexual relationships on her own terms. The other widows had mostly ruled them out as impossible or undesirable. The men, on the other hand, at the very least still felt a positive interest in sex: 'it diminishes but it's still there.'[27] The difficulty of these older widowers was in coming to terms with these feelings, which were mingled with a deep need for close companionship and intimacy with another human being. They no doubt suffer from the social conventions, perhaps even stronger for their generation than today, which inhibit so many men from speaking of their deeper feelings to another man. Women, because they have been encouraged from much earlier in life to be emotionally expressive, can relate intimately to both women and men. In later years, especially if they have no strong sexual wants, they can therefore quite readily build an emotionally fulfilling life entirely with other women. Men, on the other hand, more often go on longing for the companionship of a woman. But their very sense of maleness is also much more bound up with sexuality—again because they have been encouraged to think in this way from boyhood. They assume that a full companionship with a woman should be sexual. Yet they also know, like the women, that to start a new marriage in their last years is not easy. It is hard for them to resolve this dilemma.

Three of them found some kind of intimacy and emotional warmth in a family context. One tellingly conveyed what he was lacking through sensing it in his granddaughter:

> Samantha can come over here and I can get hold of her and hold her in my arms and it's entirely different. The feeling is absolutely tremendous. Because it's just like holding my wife. It's the blood relationship, I suppose: she's *part* of you. I never thought that was possible.[28]

Still more moving is the confusion of a 74-year-old ex-pitman. Ben Bradgate has been a widower for five years. With his chidren around him—'I can touch them all by bus'—and his enthusiasms for rugby and cycling, he leads an active life. The one thing lacking is intimacy. 'I'm missing the—of having a lady to talk to . . . I don't like men friends really.'

Ironically, he felt much less like that when he was married. At weekends he used to be out every evening with a friend: 'he was a handsome chap, terrible, he could get a woman, where I wouldn't walk.' Ben himself used to sing in the pubs, getting new hits off Radio Luxembourg before other people had heard them. Although he thinks himself ugly, he is still a bit of a dandy. 'I've all kinds of suits'—blue, brown, or grey, and a red bow tie for weddings: 'I can dress for the occasion and I always do.' He drinks rarely now. He 'made a vow' to drop the club after he left the pit, because of the cursing, and he only goes to a pub once a week.

His wife Janey was a miner's daughter, herself a cleaner. Her family were Primitive Methodists, but Ben's were Catholics. They were undoubtedly strongly drawn to each other to get married at all in the religiously intolerant Lancashire of the 1930s. 'I fell in love with her and I liked her so much, I said, "I'm not letting my ideas—" and of course it upset my family. And nobody—my father and mother didn't come to the wedding.' He abandoned Catholicism.

The young lovers all too soon became a quarrelsome pair. Ben expected Janey to manage all the housework as well as bring up their four children. His only regular contribution was to turn the

handle of the washing machine. Janey never had a chance to join
Ben, who was off enjoying himself at the pub. 'I'm not saying it
was a perfect marriage . . . I think most marriages suffer a certain
amount . . . because it's the woman who has to do the chasing for
the family, in the main—the fella might say, "I'll go out for a
drink", and she'll have to look after the kids . . . And they would
get annoyed and fall out with you.' He thinks that if it had been
happening today, they might have split up. But they survived, and
she kept her sense of humour. She was 'one of the most jovial
people'—in later years, he was told, she was 'a scream at bingo'.
Things were better after they retired: he was drinking less then,
and helping more. Even so, he concedes, 'well, we got on each
other's nerves probably. Yes, she'd say, "Get out of road, go for
ride on bike or something!" You know! But by and large we didn't
do so badly.'

Probably throughout their marriage—though it too waxed and
waned—their sexual relationship was central to Ben's understanding of intimacy. It had drawn them together in the first place, and
perhaps both of them had enjoyed sex in the early days: 'she was
pretty good in the beginning.' At times it may have been the best
part of their relationship. Later on, when Janey did not want 'to be
bothered', he took her acceptance of his more eager sexuality as a
sign of loving. 'I was always on the sexual side, and she understood
the position. Even if she weren't in fettle, she wouldn't worry if I
said, "Let's have a bit of fun, come on lass!"'

The most extraordinary moment of intimacy was their last night
in bed together. Janey was about to go into hospital and was in
pain from the cancer which was to kill her. 'She must have had this
idea in her head that she would never see me no more . . . We had
a cuddle that night . . . "Come on Ben, there might not be many
more times in your life" . . . to her eternal credit she did do
that . . . and it's never left me that, it's never left me.' That last
intimate physical moment is a symbol of their mutual love which
he holds on to. For Ben, the worst thing in his life has been 'losing
me friend, me pal, and me bed partner'.

Ben would definitely like a close relationship with another
woman, and he would like it to be partly physical. 'I'd like a lady
friend, let's put it that way, if it's only for somebody to talk to,
have a little cuddle now and again, even if nothing else happened.
I think it brings some happiness to your mind.' But he has neither

the confidence in himself, nor the social skill, which he needs to
find one. He also suffers from deep, confusing guilt: partly perhaps
a legacy of the sexual puritanism of a Catholic upbringing. But Ben
is also very aware that an older man's sexuality is widely dis-
approved of. He risks being scorned as 'a dirty old man'. He
argues that this is a wrong view: 'well, I don't treat it that way.
There's no difference to me, older people doing what the younger
people do, you've got the same ingredients to make it.' But then,
he cannot bear to admit to his own family that he has these
longings. In the evening he plays music on his records, 'aye, aye,
and I'm thinking about women. There's something wrong with me
in't there—there must be, I shouldn't be thinking about women,
my age.' He poured out his feelings in the interview, a confession-
al refrain to which he returned again and again.

Putting his wishes into practice had so far failed dismally. He
has to be attracted by the woman, and 'there's one woman does.
And I daren't look at her!' Ben has 'broached it' with her, and
simply got the brush-off. ' "Oh," she said, "Ger off with ye!"—and
I don't blame her. I know we're old.'[29]

Two other widowers had thought of remarriage, but had themselves drawn back so far, though not quite ruling it out. They were
both middle-class men, who went about things more circumspect-
ly. One has a long-standing 'very close friend' in a widow, with
whom he regularly spends a day each week. They met soon after
his bereavement, and 'I've got a lot to thank her for, because her
house was an open invitation: I could go straight from work, she
would do me a meal. I regard her as a good friend, possibly my
best friend.'[30]

The other man, widowed at 79, did seriously think of remarriage
for a while.

> The Health Visitor said to me, 'You know, Mr Seldon, you don't
> want to worry. You're a marvellous man for your years and you
> look a lot younger. And for every man in your position, there are
> nine women.' And I said, 'I only want one!' Because there are
> stacks of them . . . I'm giving you my innermost thoughts
> through these years . . . So then it came down to a sort of
> shortlist.

But by chance he met somebody quite new. 'She had lost everybody; she'd reached a pitch of life where she had nobody. No

relations. No nothing. Very charming girl. And we have formed a sort of—usually I see her about once a week', for a coffee and a chat.

> Nothing at all, but it's very nice indeed, and it's one thing I look forward to. I don't suppose it would work . . . But otherwise I've given up all attachments. It only leads to a lot of trouble. And if I paid for a professional woman to come and housekeep for me as a companion, there's always a risk . . .

But for the risk, he would certainly prefer to live with somebody. 'I don't like this single life at all. I'm not kidding there. I hate it. I hate it . . .' He finds his days 'boring', and he is certainly lonely: 'oh yes, yes. I can't hide it. It's terrible. It's just pride that keeps me going, that's all . . . I'm a rather independent cuss.'[31]

Why is it that only two of these widowed men and women now share a roof with one of their children? One woman, still married, was quite cynical:

> they're no waiting to look efter their parents, let's be honest . . . They all want to go oot and work, to make money and get on in life, which I dinna blame them for . . . They don't plan for their parents. They would look after ye I suppose, they'd have ye if ye were able to potter aboot, and dae their work and tidy up and that fae them coming in fae their work. But if you've to be nursed—Well . . .

But this was a rarely gloomy view. Most of those who needed active support were in fact getting it from children. More than two-thirds of the widowed were being visited by them at least weekly. The truth is that the ideal of living independently in their own home, fat from being imposed by children, was deeply ingrained in the older generation too. The widow crippled by arthritis, for example, was determined to stay where she was. Ben Bradgate had moved when he was widowed, to a bed-sitter with a folding bed, because he felt more confident of keeping such a small space neat on his own. Others would have had a great deal to lose in moving: the floral champion would have lost her garden, for example. The same was true of the 'venturing widow' with her purposely adapted house. Each of her two sons had even built a special room for her and invited her to live with them, 'but I'm not giving my little home up for nobody.' All these men and women

held the firm cultural assumption which has been so long established in Britain. As Mary Wesley put it:

> Oh she's good, very good, Shirley, been awfully good to me.
> Her husband's very nice. Get on very well with the children.
> There's nothing against. But I wouldn't plant myself on them. I
> don't think it would work. I'd rather keep to my own wee place
> as long as I can.[32]

It was thus through remarriage alone that most could think of
sharing a home again, of fulfilling companionship: a bed as well as
a roof. Seven of those we recorded had remarried. Now had this
happened? And how had it worked out?

Although those who remarried are now older, the women on
average in their later sixties and the men in their seventies, with
three in their eighties, it turns out that in fact at remarriage none
were among the older widowed. The women had remarried at an
average age of 39, and the men at 48. And they had lost their
spouses a good deal earlier than that: on average, six years before.
So the marriages we see now are almost all the outcome of much
earlier misfortune and recovery. Even so, they seem strikingly
different from first marriages now that the couples have reached
retirement.

On the one hand they tend to be more traditional. One reason is
that the husbands are considerably older than their wives. The age
gap averages eight years, and rises to twenty. It also looks as if the
marriages were initiated by the men. Three men had married their
juniors at work; another man had been asked by a dying best
friend 'to look after me—his widow'; a fourth sent his sister-in-law
as an intermediary. Yet though traditional, these marriages were
also happier than the first marriages (see Table 9).[33]

The reason would seem to be that they were always seen in
contrast to the deep unhappiness that had gone before them.
These husbands and wives knew what it meant to lose a companion, and counted themselves fortunate to have one at all. This,
helped by the maturity of starting older too, made them more
tolerant. In this spirit, a widowed waitress could feel 'happy'
remarried to a second husband who was 'very possessive, very
jealous . . . I wasn't allowed to talk to anybody . . . He was good, but
he was so possessive.' She had always the time before to look back
on, when—'Oh God—I didn't have anything . . . I had no feeling at

all.' Her second marriage had rescued her: 'I was happy, I'd got him, and I'd got Kath [her daughter], so I was happy.' A manager said similarly of his second wife, 'She saved my sanity.'[34]

These couples especially stand out in their attitude to sex. Only one—she was one of two now widowed for the second time—had no interest in it. Four said that they had active sexual lives. One woman, asked if people over sixty had no interest in sex, said, 'Oh don't you believe that! That's getting a little bit too personal!' Her husband is in his late eighties. And another man replied: 'very much so. I'm still—at eighty—alert to sex and we have sex twice a week. Yes, very much alert to it.' These were both close marriages. Here, as in the first marriages, there was a very striking tie between a couple's general closeness and their continuing sexual activity. Age did not seem to be a significant influence at all (see Table 13).[35]

Of the close couples, two were of successful businessmen and their wives, at last now fully retired, with attractive and comfortable homes, active social lives, and a variety of leisure interests. But such resources were not necessary to contentment. Two other couples were working class, and in each case were enthusiastic dancers. One pair, who seem inseparable apart from his occasional outings 'on his bike in the country,' go dancing three nights every week. 'We're always together... We never fall out... We both like the same things.'[36] And the other couple live as if reborn on the dance floor.

Jackie Stephens is a Lancashire railwayman's daughter. Now seventy, she worked first as a factory machinist and later as a shop assistant, right through until she retired ten years ago. She still lives in the council flat which her parents occupied.

She met her first husband, Bert, a coach-trimmer, in a cinema. They were unable to have children. But she has taken other people's children to her heart instead, especially the daughter of a cousin, whom she first looked after for a fortnight at the age of five, and then kept close to. She is an active godmother in this family: 'I love them all so dearly... They're the next best thing to any family that anybody could have.' She has been almost equally involved with her brother's family, from childbirth on, 'knitting and doing and preparing.' As she says, she 'never had any children of me own, but oh boy, I've had a lot of fun with other folks'.

Jackie and Bert were a fond couple. He was a keen gardener,

competing for the chrysanthemum prizes in the local shows. Their
whole social life was together. 'Bert did like fishing, that was one
of his great enthusiasms, and he used to go fishing without me.'
But in the summer, he used to take her out sea-fishing. And they
danced, while he was fit. In his later years, he suffered from a
weak heart. When Jackie was 53, he died from it.

Jackie felt utterly lost without him. After Bert's death,

> When I went to church on Sundays I used to pray for a purpose
> in life, because there didn't seem to be any purpose in it at
> all...
>
>   I remember feeling extremely sorry for meself one night when
> I was coming home from work, and it was a dreadful night. It
> was cold and it was raining, and I was walking down by the Mill
> wall there, and feeling very sorry for myself: wondering what
> the heck it was all in aid of. And thinking, 'If I drop dead by this
> Mill wall here it wouldn't matter to anybody very much',...

It was a family crisis which finally spurred her into a new life of
her own. Her brother's wife fell ill with cancer. Jackie was already
close to their children. With their mother slowly dying, 'I was
necessary to them, and they relied on me a great deal. And it went
on of course for three years. And as Pat died in the June, Dennis
came into my life a month later.' She had rediscovered a life
purpose. 'Again I had somebody to look after.'

The initiative came—at least indirectly from Dennis, a factory
quality-controller, who was also widowed. Dennis's sister-in-law
was Jackie's next-door nieghbour on the council estate, although
they had never said more than hello. Nevertheless, 'It was his
sister-in-law approached me one day when I was in the garden.
And she said, "Did you know you've got a secret admirer?"' ... It
never, ever crossed me mind that there would ever be anybody
else. She said, "Well, think about it, and let me know."' Jackie
consulted her brother, who approved. 'Well, everybody egged me
on, encouraging me. And he [Dennis] was all bent for getting
married immediately.' But Jackie still hesitated. She insisted on
waiting for two years. Finally she took the plunge and Dennis
moved in with her. 'I've never regretted it.'

By this time Jackie was sixty and Dennis 56. He has a son, who
lives opposite to them, although they have only irregular contact.
Dennis is one of a family of eight, who are up to twenty years older

than him, but although several are nearby he has surprisingly little contact with them. 'I have never been what you call really involved with my family,' he says. 'We've mainly seen them by accident,' Jackie agrees. 'They live in one another's pockets, for they all live close. The reason we've seen them is mainly because of ill health.... Their mother was like a mother who kept her chicks all around her': her grown-up daughters were expected to call daily, and two never married. But Dennis had to go away to the war at 19. 'He was the one that got away. Where the others were kept close to the nest.' He kept more to himself when he came back, and seems to have passed on a similar attitude to his own son, young Dennis: an electrician with whom Jackie and Dennis get on very well in a jokey way.

Jackie's Dennis had been left a widower twenty years before with the sudden death of his wife, when his son was eight.

> Considering he comes from such a big family, he seems to have lived very much to himself, and I think losing his wife was such a terrible shock to him, it took him an awful long time to recover... He's rather self-contained actually. You see him now to the way he was ten years ago, he's not really the same person. I've brought him out of his shell. Very shy, very reserved.

Jackie gave up her main shop job on remarriage—although she still goes once a week to help on a market stall—because Dennis was keen that she should be at home. He had never been a domesticated widower. He relied on his sisters to clean and wash for him, and ate his main meals in the factory canteen. Jackie wanted to be the traditional wife he had missed through all those long years. 'I always felt he'd not had a wife for twenty years, and he'd come in from work at night to an empty house to getting his own tea ready, such as it was ... so I felt he deserved somebody to look after him.' Dennis is now retired himself, but Jackie continues to look after the money and do all the cooking and housework, although they now shop together.

Their lives are focused on their joint leisure activities.

> Dennis won't stray anywhere without me ... And for some reason ... we don't get on each other's nerves, even being together all the time. Repeatedly you will hear people saying, 'Oh I can't be doing with him under me feet all day long.' Well I'd never say that. We are just—amicable together.

They have a striking variety of interests. They go out walking, in the country or by the sea, watching birds; and in the summer they go on farm holidays. They swim together and they garden together. Dennis says: 'She grows chrysanths, but I mix the soil and fill all the pots for her. She doesn't do any real lifting.' Dennis writes poems and stories, and he also likes music. When they are inside, 'he might be there playing the organ or typing. I might be in here sewing or reading. We do crosswords together . . . or sometimes we'll have a game of scrabble.' Most important of all to them is their dancing. Altogether, it makes for a full week.

Dennis is not a churchgoer, but after their marriage Jackie continued to go to church fortnightly on *Sundays*, alternating this with a visit to her brother in the days before his recent death. From then on, there is a complete sequence throughout the week:

Monday is rent day and pension day, so Dennis invariably does that, while I do some work in the house, preparing and doing.

If it's nice we might go out for a walk on Monday afternoons. Monday evenings we go swimming.

Tuesdays I always go shopping. We always go to Bolton, Tuesday mornings early, nine o'clock, we go off in the car . . . Marks and Spencers and the market principally. We usually come home and I pick up my pension on the way and then call and have my hair done.

Tuesday afternoons we may go out [to a dancing class] or just dabble around here, especially in the winter, doing whatever we feel like doing. Dennis doing his typing and I do some sewing or whatever.

Wednesdays we don't have any real commitments, we can please ourselves. I'll be busy round the house in the morning. [If the afternoon is fine, they like to take her cousin's children out.] If it's a poor afternoon we go dancing. And then we go again Wednesday evening: the Monaco. We go to the big ballroom at Hindley. 2.30 to 4.30—40 pence. It's a beautiful ballroom . . . It is sequence dancing on Wednesday afternoon, and a little bit of modern quickstep and waltz maybe.

Thursday, up till now we've always gone shopping for Dennis's sisters [who have been unwell]. We also have gone round there to them each day and made a shopping list out—and done the shopping. And taken it and laid it away. And had an hour with them, to chat with them . . . That more or less takes care of Thursdays.

Then *Friday* I go off to the market [to Wigan, to work on the fruit stall]. So I'm off at eight o'clock in the morning. I don't come back home till quarter past one.

Saturday I usually put me washing in—bung it in the washing machine. I peg it out if the weather's suitable. Iron it and make the bed up if I've stripped the bed . . .

If there's rugby on television, Dennis watches that.

Sometimes we have a lazy Saturday afternoon—if I'm not cooking dinner. Ready for dancing at night.

That is the week's highlight.

Jackie and Dennis are both fit themselves, but last year was made difficult by the illnesses of two of his sisters, his brother-in-law, and Jackie's brother. In later years, Jackie thinks, 'the major stumbling block seems to me—health. When you don't feel well, then you feel old . . . You feel it in many ways—we've just had a series of invalids, who have needed us to go to look to their needs, which restricts your own freedom. Now, hopefully we feel that we can lead our own lives.'

Jackie took her time in deciding to remarry, but in Dennis she has found new love in later life. Ten years later, they live like a honeymoon couple.

I've never regretted it. We've had a marvellous ten years, both of us. I wouldn't undo it . . .

We seemed to have so many things in common. We both liked to dance for one thing . . . So away we were, and we've been going ever since; and it's great.[37]

11

What has Changed and What Matters

STANDING at our own particular moment in time, we can trace back changes in later life into the past, and we can also try to project some of them into the future. In both contexts two great transformations stand out.

The first and most fundamental is the lengthening of life itself. There are simply many more of the older generation alive, and many more of them in better health. But the demographic changes have been uneven. Women's lives have lengthened much more rapidly than men's. At the same time couples have had much smaller families of children. So in today's older generation women predominate; and they are much more often alone than in the past, not because families care less, but simply because more of them are widowed, and many fewer of them have living brothers or sisters or children. Much more today than ever before, later life means living alone.

Looking ahead, as medicine continues to focus on the diseases which kill middle-aged men, and as more recent generations of women have become more exposed to the occupational and dietary risks which men used to monopolize, the gap may begin to narrow. And we may be sure—short of global ecological catastrophe or world war—that a study of this kind a generation ahead would be giving much more space to men and women in their nineties and above: both to how they too find fulfilment, and also to the increasing numbers of those in their seventies caring for them. And many slightly younger women, if high remarriage rates continue, will still be caring for their youngest children at the same time.

The demographic trends thus warn of a growing crisis of caring, not only for the older people without living children who are unrepresented here, but more generally. Nevertheless, the constancy of family support in the past suggests that ways of providing it are likely to be found. It is not true, as so often supposed, that families today are less willing to look after older relatives, take them into their homes, or give them financial support. On the contrary, they give them more financial help than they did in the past and remain their mainstay as regards caring. As for sharing homes, the reluctance to do this goes back at least four hundred years. Families would share in a crisis, or at transitional moments, and to an extent which has surprised us they still do so today. But reluctance to share is the other side to a long standing ideal of each generation's independence.

Longer life has also brought a new strangeness to death itself, which is no longer a common experience right through life. Today many people only have to come to terms with close loss through death, and the imminence of their own mortality, in later life. Whether they confront or evade it, this will be one of the most difficult tasks they ever face.

The second great change has been the rise of retirement on a pension. Victorian grandfathers were with few exceptions still men at work. Since then, a completely new stereotype has been imposed of later life as a time of obligatory idleness and leisure. Many older men and women, as we have discovered, find ways of overcoming this restriction, because work brings meaning and company into their lives, but most do so only by sneaking into unregulated trades with poor conditions and poor returns. It is of course absolutely right that after forty years workers should have the choice of retirement on a reasonable pension. But present policies have divided the retired between, on the one hand, growing numbers assisted by occupational pensions and, on the other, a full third caught on the poverty line, relying on money benefits which, in relation to average wages, are less generous than the community support given to the old in need two hundred years ago, and prevented by welfare regulations from effective earning through work.

It seems difficult to believe that these policies can persist into the future in their present rigid form. On present trends the proportion of the population at work will continue to shrink, thrusting a growing burden of taxation on them if pensions and benefits are not to be significantly reduced. This looming intergenerational conflict could be eased by the reinvolvement of more older people in the workforce. Their wish to continue in some kind of useful work after the usual age for retirement needs to be recognized as perfectly normal and valid, rather than stifled by a mythical new ideal. Until the very recent past, older people have always been a valued resource for the community, and they ought to be welcomed again.

The rise of retirement and the introduction of state pensions have thus not removed the inequality which is one of the fundamental continuities of later life. Incomes remain sharply divergent. We still find that a retired businessman lives in a manor house furnished with antiques, while an ex-collier sleeps on a camp bed in his bed-sitter. Above all, death and illness continue to strike unequally in class terms. Working-class men and women bear the toll of harsher lives, and not only die earlier, but suffer from more disabilities.[1] The shadow of class follows them right through later life.

It follows them, nevertheless, in a way which makes its effects much less obvious than earlier in life. This is not only because the structure imposed by work has gone, so that all share in principle a degree of new freedom and choice. It is also because survival seems to be associated with an ability to use that freedom positively. Certainly that is only possible when basic needs are met: a functioning mind; a body without too many pains; adequate shelter; and reasonable income—and the amount of income will be a crucial constraint. Certainly too there are some who survive against their will—who have not succeeded in dying: and one of the most widespread fears of old age is of becoming totally dependent, vegetative and senile. But it is a myth that old age is typically a time of passivity. The truth is closer to the opposite: since later life is a time of sharp changes, it demands a special responsiveness and imaginative adaptability. Those who make or seize their new chances are most likely to flourish on their purposefulness; those who cannot find meaning to their lives, to fade altogether. Consequently the longer they live, the more survivors are likely to have this resourcefulness in common.

The patterns of class thus become in many ways less easy to discern. The men and women whom we interviewed are by definition survivors of their generation. There are many reasons why some have lived longer than others. Women survive men. Differences in income, housing, occupational hazards, diseases and stress, drinking and smoking, and possibly diet, help to load the class dice. But the ability to maintain a meaningful like focus may be equally crucial. Recent British medical research by Elaine Murphy has brought striking evidence that among the elderly, depression can precipitate a fatal illness, and may even bring a doubling of death rates. Similarly Aaron Antonovsky, through a long series of studies in Israel of how people who had suffered intense stress managed to stay reasonably healthy, has concluded that 'the sense of coherence' is their key defence. In her study' of ageing in Australia, Cherry Russell pinpoints 'the need to maintain psychological integrity' as the central task of those she interviewed: 'the experience of being old is often a lonely and relentless struggle for meaning.' Recent work by British psychologists and sociologists has begun to explore more particular sources of meaning: Andrew Sixsmith, for example, the importance of house and home, Helen Evers that of daily routines, and anthropologist Sharon Kaufman has picked out a wider variety of thematic sources of meaning in later life in *The Ageless Self*—an exploration of the life stories of sixty older Californians, strongly influenced by the emphasis of psychological work on the importance of a sense of personal continuity over the whole life span. She identifies the key to later life in how 'individuals symbolically connect meaningful past experiences with current circumstances'.[2] There are, in short, an increasing number of indications, from a variety of perspectives, that ability to find a continuingly meaningful personal way of life is crucial. And this certainly fits our own evidence.

To a greater or lesser extent all the stories we recorded convey this search for meaning. But the older those who spoke, and the more difficulties they had had to overcome, the more they needed the vital resilience of the survivor—and so, in that sense, the more they had in common. Those who had survived from the most disadvantaged backgrounds had needed the strongest qualities simply to do so. Later life can indeed be seen as the most challenging stage of all, 'a constant struggle to maintain cherished lifestyles against the threatening impact of both external events and internal changes'. More than at any other age men and women need the strength and adaptability to meet loss: loss of paid work, loss of full physical energy, loss of loved companions. Some have the ability to fill these gaps; others cannot.[3] These life stories offer us a precious insight into that vital resilience.

'Don't give in,' writes one widow of 80 to another of 76. 'This getting old is very trying isn't it.' But the worst thing would be to become like the inmates of a home she has just visited, where 'the poor old things don't seem to have any inclination to *do* anything, they all sit around doing nothing.... I am sure it is better to struggle on, than to give up your home, and have to submit to all sorts of rules and regulations.... The most important thing for us is to keep one's brain active ... Now what could you find to do?' And she lists all sorts of volunteer work for the handicapped, and craft classes, and mending church hymn-books or doing the altar flowers, and inter-continental travel. Others would no doubt have produced different ideas, but the underlying message would have been the same: 'Don't feel that because you are 76 you can't start something new!'[4] And most of our survivors do feel they can.

Because inevitably it is only survivors whose stories we can hear, it is much easier to show the strategies through which they manage, and the kinds of meaning they find, than to disentangle the factors in earlier as well as present life which influence why some succeed while others do not. Nevertheless, some factors do stand out clearly. We have already remarked on many instances of the importance of the culture of particular families: some encouraging relationships or traditions which contrast positively with narrower general conventions, others transmitting disaster down the generations. Religious beliefs or political ideology, by contrast, only very rarely seem to have an important influence on outcome: those who frequent churches or political clubs see themselves as sustained by the company rather than by the doctrine they offer. The influence of education is a more problematic issue, since educational advantage is impossible to distinguish over a lifetime from the undoubtedly crucial force of class background and later occupation. It may be more important to note the significance for some who came from a working-class background of quite modest opportunities through adult education classes later in their lives. And this leads to a more general and fundamental point relating to public policy in the widest sense. The ability to make the choices which construct individual meaning can only be fully realized where the means and opportunities for them are open to all. The current shift away from universal pension benefits and services in health, education, and transport, towards a narrower support targeting only those in need, threatens to have a much wider effect in fostering dependency: for it will undermine the material basis for making choices which is essential if individual resilience is to flourish. So far from encouraging individual responsibility, it will restrict opportunity for older men and women as a whole, and in terms of what we have learnt here of the vitality and variety of later life its impact will be seriously retrogressive. We should be aiming, on the contrary, for the broadening of support on the basis of universal rights and opportunities which could provide real freedom of individual choice in later life for all.

Our evidence shows four basic ways in which older men and women find their fulfilment today. First, we have already spoken of the importance of work for many of them, and the need for this to be recognized through a change in public attitudes to older workers. This is one area in which the powerlessness of older men and women to make their own decisions is particularly painful. Even minor changes could help here. We found, for example, that choosing the precise time of their retirement, the month, or just the day of the week, made people feel better about leaving a lifetime's job. It would be even more of an improvement if there were an organized range of new jobs open after retirement. And for those who genuinely wish to cease paid work, there is no doubt that 'extensive retirement preparation schemes should be provided as a right',[5] to help stimulate the transformation of an empty anticipation of freedom into positive dreams.

The second sphere is that of leisure. Here we found at one extreme that a quarter of those who described their lives to us had very few leisure pursuits. None of them were very happy, and they included some of the most discontented. At the other extreme were those who had developed special new leisure skills in later life, such as toymaking and flower arranging and sequence dancing: activities which brought intense pleasure and meaning into their lives. But it was particularly striking how few out of the whole group belonged to old people's clubs, or had anything but scorn for them. They do not like the patronizing atmosphere of these clubs, typically run by middle-class organizers who assume the passivity of the working-class members. They do not feel old themselves. The assumption that people want to be associated just because they have reached a certain age is fundamentally mistaken, and an unfortunate basis for public policies. It has the result that old people's clubs lack the very people with determination and inventiveness who ought to be models to their contemporaries. In later life, as at any age, people like to get together because they share common interests. What is needed is not ghettos for the old, but specialized support, including both educational programmes and meeting-places for particular activities enjoyed by older people, open to their control like the newly-founded University of the Third Age, but preferably in a context which allows younger adults to join in too. For the same reasons, in terms of housing, while the need for good sheltered accommodation for older people whose health is vulnerable is undeniable, there should be more caution at proposals like those of Help the Aged for self-contained 'continuing care communities', new villages built 'for elderly people, complete with hobby rooms, restaurants, shops and hairdressers'.[6]

The third sphere of fulfilment is grandparenting. We have traced this back as experienced within families for over a hundred years. There are important continuities of pattern in, for example, the mutuality of support and the salience of grandmothers. More strikingly, our material does not support the suggestions by recent American researchers of a major shift from typically 'stiff, formal grandparenting' in the past, to 'informal, affectionate, warm relations' today.[7] On the contrary, although more grandparents survive to make closeness a possibility, in practice in every generation it is the variety in relationships which is most significant. If the joy in becoming a grandparent seems almost universal, the relationship which follows is one which needs to be positively created by winning a child's affection. Those who succeed feel that their role is easier and more pleasurable than parenthood, but in another way it is more difficult, because it cannot be taken for granted: grandparents cannot count on natural loyalty. Grandparenting, like so much else in later life, also builds on the choices of earlier years: those who give more of themselves to their children when younger are more likely to stay closer to them, and to be given the chance to become active grandparents—just as they are likely to be especially well cared for if they find themselves in need later in their lives. Whatever their views on family obligations, people make individual distinctions among their own kin which reinforce or deny relationships. So in retrospect, there were some grandparents who left no significant memories at all with their grandchildren; some who were hated as insensitive and disciplinarian; while others were remembered with tenderness and admiration. Meaningful grandparenthood, in short, is not automatic, but has to be achieved.

The last sphere is intimate relationships between adults. Later life is a time when these relationships need to be continually rebuilt. In this it is more like youth than the middle years of life. Those who remain married must adjust to retirement and to children leaving home. The most vulnerable appear to be those who have focused through their adulthood on a single sphere of activity: typically men on work, or women on childrearing. When deprived of this central life meaning, they had developed few other resources. Even if they tried to shift their day-to-day roles at home, it seemed too late to create either new fulfilments in outside activities, or a truly nurturing mutual relationship. Those who had married slightly later seemed to fare better; but most strikingly, some of those in second marriages seemed the happiest of all: like honeymoon couples. They had experienced unhappiness and loneliness, and had now seized a new chance of life.

The greatest challenge of all in later life is the loss of intimates: husbands, wives, and also friends. Little can take away the pain and suffering which this brings. But the resilient are those who can fill the empty spaces. Women especially seemed able to recreate fulfilling social relationships through networks of other widows. Again, determination and skill were essential.

Even living alone can be turned into a positive source of opportunity. As Glenys Howells, pitman's widow, who at 73 spends her days with family or friends or out walking on the hills on her own, puts it, 'I think the freedom I've got now is something I enjoy, because I get up in the morning and if I wanna go out for the day there's nothing to stop me. I've got no one to think about. So I can just pack up me bag and go.' If she doesn't meet somebody to talk to, she just listens to the trees, and dreams of trips to Shanghai and the Grand Canyon.

Similarly Marjorie Dickens, banker's widow of eighty, still active in the golf club, is off next year to Tunisia with an older brother. She has the financial means to fulfil this particular dream. But the way she thinks about her day-to-day life is just the same: 'I like it that I can do as I please, go where I want to, and if I can afford it, buy what I want to, and eat what I want. . . . I would never have dreamt of marrying again. I think if you've had one good man, you don't want to try again! . . . I don't like the loneliness sometimes, but you can't always be with people.' Her aim for the future is to 'just enjoy myself'.[8]

Later life is a time of constant reconstruction. We have seen

something of the variety with which older men and women de-
scirbe how they build, how they find meaning. But their accounts
need to be held within a frame of two kinds of constraint. These
are first, the need for material means for opportunity, and second,
the constraints imposed by public attitudes to older people.

In some ways the stereotypes of ageing have changed remarkably little over the centuries. The unflattering picture of second
childhood, helpless dependence, and degeneration was taken by
Shakespeare from the traditional cycle of the stages of life. Even at
that time there was a distinction between healthy later life and
senility, but then, as today, the image of old age which struck
deepest, just because it was pathetic and frightening and strange,
was that of senility.

We seize on myths because they help to make sense of life, to
justify the cruelties of mutual conflict, to excuse failures, to
explain senseless misfortune and pain. But we seize on myths at a
price. The myths of ageing which we are fed in youth and middle
age simply do not fit the typical experience of older men and
women. To them these stereotypes are degrading images, which
may apply to some of their age group, but which they un-
hesitatingly—sometimes indignantly or with acknowledged appre-
hension—reject for themselves now. 'I don't feel old' is a cry of
protest against a myth which causes both pain and fear: a call for
the recognition of human individuality and resourcefulness at any
age.

From childhood onwards most of us watch our bodies change
with age. For the first twenty years we may watch with eagerness,
even pride; from then onwards with regret, or at best acceptance.
We all know this is happening. But feeling old inside is quite a
different matter. You can feel old at any point in adulthood. Men
and women in their twenties or thirties or forties can feel they
have failed to find the right person to marry, or have made the
wrong career choice, and that they are 'too old' to start again.
Feeling old is feeling exhausted in spirit, lacking the energy to find
new responses as life changes. It is giving up. Feeling ourselves
means feeling the inner energy which has carried us thus far in
life. It means accepting our own pasts as part of our present. It
means feeling a whole person.

In later life this remains essentially the same. You may be
categorized as an 'old person' with a pension and cheap travel

concessions at 65, or according to medical and sociological special-
ists you may cross from the 'young old' to the 'old old' at 75, but
there is no reason why you should not still feel the same person
inside. The real turning-points are in your own life: giving up work
or starting a hobby, losing a loved one or finding a new friend. And
what matters, in later life just as earlier, is how you can respond to
the challenge of change. The fact is that you are by now a survivor.
So long as you feel yourself, you can still make the best of your life.

Feeling yourself and feeling old thus remain essentially different
at any age. Nor is this surprising given the image of old age which
is constantly thrust at us: an image of later life which is in fact
completely misleading. Thus the standard warning-sign for old
people crossing the road is of a grotesquely hunched old couple
leaning on a stick, evidently both suffering from osteoporosis, ill
as much as old. An actor will typically portray an old person with
the exaggerated shakiness of Parkinson's disease, a special affliction
which is not unique to the elderly. Television and newspapers
constantly present the old as pathetic victims of criminal attack,
even though the typical victim is really a young adult. Heart-
rending charity appeals and critics of inadequate social welfare
depict the old as helplessly needy, social isolates, fed by 'Meals on
Wheels', patronizingly entertained by OAP clubs, or abandoned
by their families into institutional homes. It is certainly true that
present pension levels leave many old people with insufficient
financial resources. But the vast majority look after themselves in
their own homes with no more than occasional help from their
family. Only one in twenty live in a hospital or institutional home.
Although physical disabilities do grow with age, two-thirds of those
over 75 have no physical difficulties with ordinary household activities like having a bath or putting on shoes. Loneliness is a real
danger, particularly for the widowed; but even among those over
75, four-fifths do *not* feel lonely: and only one in eight belongs to an
old person's club.[9]

The image of old age which we absorb is therefore a seriously
unbalanced version of the realities of later life. No wonder the
grandparents of this book do not recognize themselves in it. For
them, as for most adults, old people are *different* from themselves:
typically, less well, and needier. On the contrary, several are on
the other side of the fence, working as volunteers or nurses among
the needy of their own age group—for clients whom by contrast

they do see as 'old'. It is always easier to spot ageing in others. For oneself, feeling old is a danger of later life, but not its essence.

Later life from the inside—like life at any age—is a story with its dark side, its pain and suffering. But the message which comes most strongly from these accounts is of resilience in the face of the twists of fate; of adaptability; and in some of these lives, of a powerfully continuing ability to seize or create chances for fulfilment, whether in work, leisure, or love. To convey this message is the most important purpose of our book.

Notes

Four-figure reference numbers refer to our sample families: A indicates older generation, B middle, and C younger; F a woman and M a man. References to autobiographies (see Bibliography, Section 1) are given by author's name only (e.g. Lansbury, p. 178); other references (see Bibliography Section 2) by author's name plus date of publication (e.g. Townsend 1957:126).

Chapter 1

1. Malcolm Johnson, 'A Throng at Twilight', *Guardian*, 6 Dec 1988.

2. Fennell, Phillipson, and Evers 1988:6–7.

3. Townsend 1957 and 1964—in which he found that only half the old entering institutional care had a surviving child, in contrast to three-quarters of those living independently (pp. 152–4); cf. Tunstall 1966 and, in a more journalistic vein, Seabrook 1980 and 'Old in a Cold Season', *New Society*, 8 Jan 1988. A recent exception, on older women, is Ford and Sinclair 1987.

4. For oral history in general, Thompson 1978 and 1988; on reminiscence, Coleman 1986.

5. Elizabeth Roberts is the only oral historian who has examined family relationships with the older generation by means of oral sources. Blythe 1979 situates his speakers in the present and offers interesting material, but is marred by a tendentious perspective, mostly derived from Simone de Beauvoir.

6. Laslett 1977:174. Pioneering historical overviews include Stearns 1977 on France; Mitterauer and Sieder 1983 on central Europe; and on the United States, Haber 1983 and Achenbaum 1978.

7. Clark and Anderson 1967:67, 389–90, 425. For the same approach transferred to history, Hareven and Adams (eds.) 1982.

8. M. Johnson 1976:106, 109–11; Rapoport and Rapoport 1975:315; Rosenmayer 1981. The third edition of Bromley (1988) opens with a table describing the life cycle, which ends with the 'Old-old: Dependency; full disengagement; physical and mental inadequacy' (p. 19).

9. Examples include Young and Willmott 1957; Rosser and Harris 1965; Roberts 1984; Townsend 1965; and in the United States, Frazier 1939:146–59 and Komarovsky 1962:246–51; 268–70.

10. Matthews 1979; Sontag 1978; Itzin 1986*a*; Gibson 1984; cf. J.A. Pitt-Rivers, *The People of the Sierra*, 1954, p. 89.

11. Townsend 1957:137–53; Fennell, Phillipson, and Evers 1988:97–113; Szinovacz 1982; Cribier 1968 and 1981; Crawford 1971; Markson (ed.) 1983; S. Johnson 1971; Cunningham-Burley 1984; Cavan 1962.

12. Pulling 1987:11—a response to caring for her own mother. See also Finch and Groves 1983; Sheila Pace, 'The Forgotten Female: Social Policy and Older Women', in Phillipson and Walker 1986; Green 1985; Ungerson 1987; Sara Arber and Nigel Gilbert, 'Transitions in Caring', in Bytheway, Keil, Allatt, and Brynan 1989.

13. See Stearns 1980; Jerrome 1981; Myerhoff 1979:19, 267–8—her research centred on a life story class, through which her whole view was changed: 'I *see* old people now in a new way, as part of me, not "they"' (p. 19).

14. S. Johnson 1971; Jacobs 1974. The only comparable British study is Karn 1977.

15. Phillipson 1982:42–4 and 1978:135, 272–3. The thesis focuses much more on community differences than the book.

16. Foner 1984; de Beauvoir 1972.

17. Taylor and Ford 1981:331–3; Maas and Juyper 1974; Williams and Wirths 1965. We did not however wish to follow the wholly quantitative analysis of life-styles subsequently developed by Taylor and Ford.

18. In particular through the influence of Natasha Burchardt, Gill Gorell Barnes who organized joint workshops with us at the Institute of Family Therapy, and a workshop on 'Family Therapy with the Older Age Group' given by Dr Jeremy Holmes at the John Radcliffe Hospital, Oxford, 26 Nov 1984.

19. Plummer 1983; Mishler 1986; Thompson 1978 and 1988.

20. Thompson 1988:101–65.

21. The sample basis for our middle generation were informants interviewed for the Economic and Social Research Council study of 'Economic Stagflation and Social Change' directed by Professor Howard Newby, Dr Gordon Marshall, and Dr David Rose of the University of Essex. Informants for this study had been randomly selected from 200 polling districts throughout the country chosen in terms of region, political voting (as a proxy for social class), and population density, and the overall response rate was 62%. Our informants were chosen from a parallel sub-sample of polling districts concentrated in Scotland, the north-west, South Wales, and the south-east. With these middle-generation informants we encountered a high rate of removals

especially in the cities, and also of refusals, especially in the middle
social ranges, for reasons of privacy or lack of time. In order to ensure
a satisfactory social balance, we therefore added occupational class
quotas.

All of these 115 middle-generation informants were asked if we
could interview a grandparent in the family. In 34% of families a
grandparent was interviewed; 42% had no grandparents living in this
country; in 24% there was a living grandparent but an interview
was not obtained—either because it was refused (12%), or because
the grandparent was out of contact (3%) or insufficiently well for
interviewing (9%). These last three figures are at a reasonable and
expected level. The most substantial recent American sociological
study of grandparents used a similar method of finding informants,
and reported a refusal rate of 22% (Cherlin and Furstenberg, jun.
1986).

The 55 individuals on whom our analysis is based include 11
households where we were able to interview both grandparents. We
also interviewed three other older-generation members of the sample
families, of whom two were also grandparents, and one a god-
grandparent and stepmother: all three are included here. On the
other hand we decided to exclude from this analysis two younger
grandparents in their mid-fifties.

22. Herbert Blumer, *Critiques of Research in the Social Sciences*, revised
    edition, New Brunswick, 1979, p. xxxiv. In the population of Britain
    as a whole, 59% of those over 60 are women and 41% men: in our
    sample there are 64% women and 36% men. Of our women, 60%
    were married and of our men, 70%: this compares with 42% of women
    and 79% of men among those ever-married in the general population.
    This slight over-representation of the married is due to our interview-
    ing both partners in 11 instances.

    In terms of occupation, 63% of our women and 58% of our men
    had been manual workers. Abrams's survey (Abrams 1978 and 1980) of
    1,646 people over 65 reports a similar figure of 60% with working-class
    backgrounds. It is difficult to relate these figures to the national
    census, which recorded the proportion of the occupied population in
    manual work as falling steadily from 78% in 1911—the decade in
    which the oldest of our informants were entering the workforce—to
    54% in 1981. The tendency of those in later life to have risen to higher
    occupational groups thus has to be balanced against the fact that a
    higher proportion of the older generation started as manual workers,
    and also the effects of differential mortality. Certainly our figure is
    within the range expected.

    The lower proportion of former manual workers in our sample

reflects the higher mortality of working-class men. This bias is clearly illustrated by examining the 1981 census on a regional basis. Thus at age 55–9, the number of men in the population is 96% of the number of women in Oxfordshire, and 92% in Lancashire. But by the age 70–4, while there are still 78% men to women in Oxfordshire, in Lancashire the proportion has fallen to 69%. And at 80–4 there are 49% men to women in Oxfordshire, and 41% in Lancashire.

In terms of income, Abrams found that 84% described the state pension as their main source of income, but 30% also had income from savings and 19% had pensions from employers. Our questions were differently worded, but of our households at least 73% depended mainly on the state pension, 23% mentioned savings and 31% employer's pensions as significant (26% of individuals). The results are again similar.

In terms of health, *Social Trends* 16 (1986) reports that of men and women over 65, 15% are seriously incapacitated, bedridden, or housebound and 5% suffering from psychiatric abnormality (Bromley 1988:123–4). In terms of incapacity in daily living, Abrams reported that two-thirds of those over 75 have no physical difficulties with ordinary household activities like having a bath or putting on shoes (1978:55). Our sample does not include any of the 5% of the age group in hospitals or other institutions, or any of the mentally ill, or those who were physically acutely unwell. Out of the living grandparents of our middle-generation informants, 10% were not interviewed because they were in a hospital or a home. Of those we did interview, 2% were severely incapacitated and at least 20% suffering from a serious illness. Thus the sample is by its nature focused on the healthier 90% of the population, but there is no evidence that it is otherwise unrepresentative in terms of fitness, health, and capacity.

Finally, it does not appear that finding our grandparents through their families resulted in a sample who were more than usually in touch with them. Of our households, 64% were visited weekly by a child of the principal informant; while Abrams reported that of 75 year-olds with living children, 73% saw them weekly, whereas 65 year-olds saw their children 'a little less often' (1980:36, 43). Earlier community studies had typically reported figures of around three-quarters in working-class families and between a third and two-thirds in middle-class families (see Colin Bell, *Middle class Families*, 1968, p. 84).

Chapter 2

1. K. Thomas 1976:5, 7.
2. K. Thomas 1976:43–5.

Notes   257

3. S. R. Smith 1976:128–30; the French Protestant theologian Simon Goulart, whose *The Wise Veillard, or Old Man* (1621) was translated into English, also argued for a triple division.

4. Laslett 1977:181–96; Stearns 1977:15; E. A. Wrigley and R. S. Schofield, *The Population History of England*, 1982, p. 216.

5. Thus the Social History Society's annual conference in 1987 was entirely devoted to the history of death; see also Ruth Richardson, *Death, Dissection and the Destitute*, 1987.

6. Laslett 1976:103; Wall 1984:44. The European figures are very similar.

7. K. Thomas 1976:42.

8. 1638 translation of the original Latin, Published by Humphrey Mosley, pp. 27, 108–10, 125, 169–70.

9. Stearns 1977:30; Haber 1983:71–6.

10. Gaunt 1983; Goody, Thirsk, and Thompson (eds.) 1976 (esp. pp. 30, 117, 141, 350–5); Houlbrooke 1984:209–10; Spufford 1974:85–7; 106–18; 159–63; Howell 1983:257–69; Julian Harber, conference paper, History Workshop, Leeds, Nov. 1985—who in partiuclar pointed out to me the unwritten asumption in Halifax wills.

11. Townsend 1957:36–8; Gaunt 1983:257–9; Goody, Thirsk, and Thompson (eds.) 1976:22–3; Houlbrooke 1984:190; K. Thomas 1976:36–7.

12. Gaunt 1983; Arensberg and Kimball 1940:55–6, 115, 123–8, 131.

13. Macfarlane 1986:115–16; Goody, Thirsk, and Thompson 1976:29.

14. Gerard 1982:33; Adam Badeau, *Aristocracy in England*, 1886, pp. 43–4.

15. Davidoff and Hall 1987:206–14, 276–7, 284.

16. On three-generation households, see Laslett 1977:23; Anderson 1988:426; Davies *et al.* 1987. I am grateful to Richard Wall for help with household figures. Phythian Adams found a mere six three-generation households out of 1,274 in Coventry in 1523 (*Desolation of a City*, 1979, p. 95). No general European figures are available for the 19th cent., although Stearns 1977 claims that only 3–4% of French old people lived with their grandchildren. The contemporary British figure of 1% is markedly lower even than those for the United States, Germany, or France (4%, 5%, and 6%; Davies *et al.* 1987 and Wall 1989.

On the living arrangements of the older generation in relation to their children, see Shanas *et al.* 1968:211; Laslett 1977:201, 209–11; Laslett 1976:105–14. Hareven suggests that one-third of the older men and women in 19th-cent. Massachusetts lived in extended households. (Hareven and Adams (eds.) 1982:237); D. S. Smith 1979 shows from the 1900 US census that a fifth of men and a third of women over 65 lived in the households of other kin. There are again no general European figures for the 19th cent. For contemporary figures see Davies *et al.* 1987.

17. On living alone, Laslett (1976:110; Anderson 1988:436; Davies *et al* 1987; Wall 1984. Wall shows that the British proportion of solitaries is equalled in Scandinavia, and exceeded in West Germany; in France the proportion is only slightly lower. By contrast the Irish figure is half that for Britain, and the Netherlands, Portugal, and Hungary are close to this (Wall 1989:47).

18. Macfarlane 1986:92–3; Houlbrooke 1984:114, 189–91.

19. Laslett 1977:201. The proportion co-residing with married children in early modern England rises significantly with age in rural communities (though not in towns), reaching a third at 85 (Wall and Grundy, forthcoming).

20. Thus of the widowed, over 85% were living with relatives in Preston in 1851, and 72% in the Potteries; while in the market town of Ampthill, only 61%; Anderson 1971:55; Marguerite Dupree, 'Family Structure in the Staffordshire Potteries, 1840–1880', Oxford D. Phil., 1981; Thomson 1980:118.

21. Davidoff and Hall 1987:225–7.

22. K. Thomas 1976:38; Thane 1987:12; D. S. Smith 1979; Achenbaum 1978:96; Haber 1983:32–4; Hareven and Adams (eds.) 1982:228–9; Stearns 1977:53; M. E. Loane, *Neighbours and Friends*, 1910, p. 275; Lawrence Wylie, *Village in the Vaucluse*, Cambridge Mass., 1957. pp. 311–13. Townsend found that in early post-war Bethnal Green the commonest reason for men's retirement was still ill-health (1957:164)

23. B. S. Rowntree, *Poverty and Progress*, 1941:114; Tunstall 1966:59. However, G. Thomas says that 7% of 60 year-olds had income from boarders and lodgers, and 10% of retired women (1947:22).

24. K. Thomas 1976:38–40; Hannah 1986:6–11, 18, 26, 31–40.

25. Haber 1983:110–23; Achenbaum 1978:48–9; interview 47, p. 37.

26. Macfarlane 1986:109–11; M. Kendall and B. S. Rowntree, *How the Labourer Lives*, 1913, p. 64. Six of their 42 budgets mention gifts by the older generation to the labouring family.

27. Macfarlane 1986:105–8.

28. Thomson 1984.

29. Quadagno 1983:135; Booth 1894:226; G. Thomas 1947:22. Llewellyn Smith's analysis of 358 aged London applicants for relief in 1930

showed that 18% of sons gave some financial support, but a re-analysis by Gordon of *all* the elderly in his survey found only 7% receiving any financial help from their family (Gordon 1986). Two instances of earlier financial support remembered within the family are quoted in John Burnett, *Destiny Obscure: Autobiographies of Childhood, Education and Family from the 1820s to the 1920s*, 1982, pp. 293, 319. For a slightly later period, but for Bethnal Green only, Townsend gives a surprisingly higher figure, with over half the elderly receiving some cash help, including boarding money, from children (1957:76). Abrams reports a current national figure of 6% receiving some income from children (1980:49, 54).

30. R. Rider Haggard, *A Farmer's Year*, 1899, pp. 426–32; Lansbury, pp. 135–6.

31. J. W. Horsley, *I Remember*, 1911, pp. 203–4; Llewellyn Smith 1930–5:3. 199; Albert Funnel of Brighton, born 1989, interviewed by Andrew Durr.

32. Walter Greenwood, *How the Other Man Lives*, c. 1935:180; Llewellyn Smith 1930–5:3. 208; Rowntree 1901 (1910 ed): 38–51, 443; B. S. Rowntree, *Poverty and Progress*, 1941, p. 156; B. S. Rowntree and G. R. Lavers, *Poverty and the Welfare State*, 1951, p. 34.

33. Robert Roberts, *A Ragged Schooling*, 1976, p. 87; D. Caradog Jones, *A Social Survey of Merseyside*, 1934, pp. 122–7.

34. Rowntree 1901 (1910 ed): 38–51.

35. Llewellyn Smith 1930–5:3. 457–67.

36. St Philip's Settlement 1919:164–5, 216–25, 295–7, 315–17, 332–4.

Chapter 3

1. David Vaisey (ed.), *The Diary of Thomas Turner*, 1984, p. 129.

2. John Bright (ed. R. Walling), *Diaries*, 1930 (22 Oct. 1880).

3. The sample consisted of 25 upper-class autobiographies and 31 middle-class autobiographies (21 upper-middle class and 10 lower-middle class), all by authors born between 1830 and 1869, in selecting which I am particularly indebted to Leonore Davidoff; and 89 taken from John Burnett, David Vincent and David Mayall, *The Autobiography of the Working Class: An Annotated, Critical Bibliography*, 1, *1790–1900*, 1984, from which all autobiographers born between 1830 and 1869 who gave some detail on their family were included, to which were added, in order to raise the number of working-class women represented, all women autobiographers born to

1879. This list includes some unpublished autobiographies. In fact five of these 'working-class' autobiographies were by lower-middle-class authors. Although skilled workers' families are over-represented, some of the autobiographers came from very poor backgrounds, including the families of unskilled labourers. The sample titles are listed in full in the bibliography.

4. Lee, p. 82; Jermy, p. 185; Nevill, p. 301; Mumford, p. 95; Lockwood, p. 250; Pointer, p. 37.

5. MacLellan, p. 6; Edwards, p. 23; Carnegie, pp. 194–6.

6. Marsh, p. 22; L. R. Haggard (ed.), p. 4.

7. Sexton, pp. 232–3.

8. Vorse, pp. 10–11, 14, 17–18, 120, 222. The nearest contemporary British equivalent is Mary Stott's chapter 'Growing Old' in *Before I Go . . .* (1985)

9. Suffield, pp. 357–9; Layton, pp. 54–5.

10. Hardy, pp. 15–16; Roberts, pp. 13, 15, 117–18.

11. Roberts, pp. 117–18; Shaw, p. 88; Compton-Rickett, p. 31.

12. Turnbull, pp. 3–8.

13. Lax, p. 27; E. Hughes, p. 3; Harvey, p. 75; Mabey, p. 7.

14. Mackenzie, pp. 1–10.

15. Mackenzie, pp. 1–8.

16. Fraser, pp. 20–1; L. R. Haggard (ed.), p. 45; Warwick, pp. 15–17.

17. Balfour, p. 46; Barnes, p. 2; Watson, p. 51; Haddow, p. 10; Carbery, p. 22; Hare, p. 33.

18. Frisby, p. 8; Mallock, pp. 7–8.

19. Ross, p. 21; Pollock, p. 59; Lax, p. 30; Waugh, p. 58; Kendall, p. 33; Stirling, p. 20.

20. Bondfield, p. 20; Saunders, pp. 12. 20; B. Turner, p. 18.

21. L. R. Haggard (ed.), pp. 5, 8, 45; Thompson, p. 80; Jones, p. 19; Fraser, p. 9; Gosling, p. 6; Burt, p. 26.

22. Lonsdale, p. 4; Fletcher, p. 22; Gell, p. 34; Jersey, p. 16; Compton-Rickett, p. 22.

23. Ribbesdale, p. 12; Haldane, p. 31; Willoughby de Broke; Meynell, pp. 7–8, 114–15.

24. Raglan, pp. 16, 93–4.

25. Murison, p. 16; Gosse, p. 8; Bell, pp. 72–3, 84–5; Swan, p. 17 (cf. Benson; Hardy; Farningham; Roberts).

26. Airlie, pp. 13, 22; Turnbull, p. 27; Elson, p. 14; Johnston, p. 6; Clarke, 24 Feb. 1934; Desart, p. 80; Gower, pp. 2–3.

27. Birch, p. 20; St Helier, p. 11; Clarke, 24 Feb 1934; J. Taylor, p. 4; Meek, p. 128; Fox, pp. 17–19.

28. Willoughby de Broke, p. 21; Lansbury, p. 18; Farningham, p. 14; Carnegie, p. 3; H. Mitchell, p. 46.

29. L. R. Haggard (ed.), pp. 4, 8; J. H. Wilson, pp. 1, 4.

30. Stanley, pp. 29, 219, 40.

Chapter 4

1. The 444 interviews were collected on the basis of a quota sample designed to represent the British population in 1911 in terms of occupational groups, sex, city or town or rural community, and region. The quota was filled by deliberately varied means, including doctors and social service lists, old people's day centres, press and radio appeals, friendship networks and casual contacts (see Paul Thompson, *The Edwardians*, 1975, pp. 5–8 and Thompson 1988:126–7). These interviews have up to three figure numbers.

   For the second set of interviews, see Chapter 1, note 22: memories for these do not go beyond 1939 unless stated. These have four-figure numbers.

2. 191, p. 42; 141, p. 15; 151, p. 67.

3. 99, p. 2; 5207AF, pp. 5–6 (b. 1918); 151, p. 39; 5507AF, p. 10 (b. 1917).

4. 5507AF, p. 10 (b. 1917). 5413AM, p. 1; 5401AF2, p. 21.

5. 370, p. 7; 313, p. 32; 5503AM, p. 19; 6001AF, p. 14; 5201AF, p. 5; 6902AF, pp. 10–11; 6502AM, pp. 14–15; 6501AM, p. 16; 6904AF, p. 2 (he died in 1924).

6. Occupations: working class 20, professional 6, farmers 5, self-employed 26. 81, p. 1; 154, p. 4; 186, p. 1; 408, p. 1.

7. 396, p. 7; 6802AF, p. 15. An Oxfordshire painter inherited a house, but this only brought him £4 a year, about 3% of his income (23); and a South Welsh mining family lived in a house owned by the grandfather (452).

8. 141, p. 68; refusals of help, 19, p. 16 and 344, p. 5—'out you go and fight for your living'; 329, p. 6; 132, p. 18.

9. 263, p. 5; 6702AF, pp. 3–4; 2, p.5; 273, p. 20; 141, pp. 5–6; 230, p. 10.

10. 423, p. 36; 315, p. 11; 344, p. 95; 151, p. 56.

11. 164, pp. 2, 4, 15; 211, p. 20.

12. 424, p. 8; 387, p. 28; 6303AF, p. 8; 6702AF, p. 4; 6001AF, p. 20; 73, p. 90.

13. 19, p.7.

14. 6102AF, p. 5; 363, p. 119; 202, p. 15; 455, pp. 26–7, 65.

15. 3, p.16, 436, p. 28; 5404AF, p. 3; 5614AF, p. 15.

16. 129, p. 9; 282, pp. 24–5; 81, pp. 15–16.

17. 266, p. 25; 5401AM, pp. 5, 20; 5405AF, p. 27; 5406AF, p. 7; 5506AF, p. 11; 398, p. 2.

18. 183, p. 35; 236, p. 16.

19. 5206AM, p. 8; 266, pp. 25–6.

20. 5603AF, pp. 15–16; 286, pp. 3, 11; 141, p. 68; 38, p.31; 5201AF2, p. 19; 6904AF, pp. 5, 9, 12.

21. 5501AF, pp. 5–6; 6501AM, pp. 12–17, 61.

22. 5101AM, p. 22; 5507AF, pp. 20–1; 329, p. 19; 6702AF, pp. 8–9; 230, pp. 18–19.

23. 195, pp. 7, 15; 100, p. 20; 250, p. 22; 92, pp. 6, 18–19, 38, 41.

24. 315, p. 3; 409, p. 6; 442, pp. 5, 29, 73–4; 441, pp. 1, 5–6, 8, 24–5.

25. 23, p. 3; 134, p. 18; 392, p. 16; 287, p. 27; 5404AF, pp. 3–5.

26. 407, pp. 21–2; 366, p. 42.

27. 422, p. 19. In cases of co-residence up to 1918 the reasons, as remembered by the grandchild, were as follows: moving in with grandparent as a child or when grown up, in order to help them, 4; sharing for convenience of housing, 10; elderly or widowed grandparent moves into family household, 26; grandparent takes grandchild during family crisis, 21.

28. 344, p. 106.

29. 5302AF, p. 3; 5405AF, pp. 27–8, 81–3; 5401AF2, p. 3.

30. 290. p. 5; 262, p. 2; 33, p. 3; 6502AF, p. 34.

31. 5605AF, p. 12; 406, p. 8 (parental deaths, 126, p. 28; 273, p.6); 79, p. 3; 130, p. 5; 192, p. 11; 299, p. 8.

32. 13, p. 17.

33. 5401AF2, pp. 20, 66; 330, pp. 9–10.

34. 296, p. 10; 273, p. 36.

35. 5208AF, pp. 9–10; 221, pp. 8, 13–14; 5207AF, pp. 30–3.

36. The reasons in the 30 cases were as follows: death of a parent, 11;

housing space, 8; father deserts, 6; father unemployed, 1; mother ill, 2; illegitimacy or abandonment, 4.

37. 157, p. 6; 234, p. 6; 210, p. 18.

38. 87, p. 4; 222, p. 1; 89, p. 12; 299, p. 12.

39. 111, p. 11; 202, p. 15; 136, pp. 37–8; 18, pp. 1–2, 76–7; 178, p. 25; 114, p. 6.

40. 6802AF, pp. 1–2, 7–9, 17.

41. 6502AF, pp. 27–32, 36–7, 57–8.

42. 299, pp. 11–15, 17, 23, 42, 47.

Chapter 5

1. 5410AF, pp. 44–5, 5006AF, pp. 45–6.

2. 5408AF, pp. 28–32.

3. 5504AF, p. 60; 5605AF, p. 106.

4. 5405AF, pp. 77–9.

5. 6802AF, pp. 49–53, 57, 65.

6. 5605AF, p. 138; 6502AM, p. 130.

7. Townsend 1957:168; Phillipson 1978:250.

8. 5001AM, p. 28.

9. 5603AF, p. 52.

10. 5507AF, pp. 55, 63.

11. 5401AF2, pp. 141–3; 6502AF, pp. 82, 89.

12. Mason 1987:97–8.

13. 5405AF, pp. 3–5, 57, 74.

Chapter 6

1. 5204AM, p. 31; 5401AF2, p. 149.

2. R. N. Butler and M. I. Lewis (1975), quoted in J. Bornat, C. Phillipson, and S. Ward, *A Manifesto for Old Age*, 1985, p. 1; Levin and Levin 1980:393; Itzin 1986*a*:115.

3. Butler 1975:122.

4. Comfort 1977:20; Levin and Levin 1980:393.

5. Hendricks and Hendricks 1977:5; Butler and Lewis 1975.

6. Comfort 1977:13, 35.

7. Of the 55 older-generation informants, only 43 answered these questions.

8. 5614AF, p. 85.

9. 5410AF, p. 68.

10. 5204AM, p. 43; 5505AF, p. 107; 5208AF, p. 75; 5504AF, p. 62.

11. 5407AF, p. 64; 5201AF2, p. 116; 5201AM, p. 92; 5302AM/F, p. 81; 5207AF, p. 76.

12. 5502AF, p. 41; 5507AF, p. 64; 5101AM, p. 56; 5007AF, p. 51; 5412AM, p. 137; 5408AF, p. 37; 5506AF, p. 129 and 6802AF, p. 64; 5003AM, p. 69.

13. 5406AF, p. 87; 5503AM, p. 92.

14. 5605AF/M, p. 152; 6102AF, p. 83; 5506AF, p. 79.

15. 5503AM, p. 90; 5007AF, p. 62; 6702AF, p. 93; 5101AM, p. 108.

16. 5007AF, p. 64; 5302AM, p. 79; 5507AF, p. 63; 5204AM, p. 45.

17. 6904AF, p. 58; 5003AM, p. 57.

18. 6501AM, p. 60; 5404AF, p. 105; 6802AF, p. 65.

19. 5206AM, p. 62.

20. 6502AM/F, p. 121.

21. 6902AF, p. 65; 5605AF, p. 138.

22. 5401AF2, pp. 148–51.

23. Itzin 1986b:2; Hunt 1976; Tinker 1984.

24. 5206AM, p. 59; 5006AF, p. 52; 5503AM, p. 90.

25. 5404AM, p. 74, 103, 106.

26. 5501AF, p. 143; 5409AM, p. 42.

27. 5413AM, p. 82; 5003AM, p. 60; 5401AF2, p. 149; 5409AM, p. 45.

28. 5413AM, p. 86; 5003AM, p. 55.

29. 6902AF, p. 66; 5201AF2, p. 96; 5101AM, p. 106.

30. 5302AF, p. 77; 5208AF, p. 77; 5204AM, p. 44; 5504AF, p. 63; 5506AF, p. 125; 5505AF, p. 107; 5201AM, p. 93.

31. 5202AF/M, p. 48; 5208AF, p. 82.

32. Another reason why some old people may be reluctant to join old people's clubs is because of the extent to which they are class-segregated and overwhelmingly aimed at the working-class elderly.

33. 5503AM, p. 92.

34. 5208AF, p. 53; 5302AF, p. 84; 6902AF, p. 62; 5101AM, p. 105; 5006AF, p. 51; 5007AF, p. 61; 5302AM, p. 77.

35. 6904AF, p. 57; 5502AF, p. 143; 6102AF, p. 81; 5401AM, p. 82.

36. 6501AM, p. 59; 6902AF, p. 64.

37. 5202AM, p. 100.

38. 1981 Census.

39. 5505AM, p. 106; 6501AM, p. 58; 5412AM, p. 133; 5614AF, p. 83; 5504AF, p. 61.

40. 6502AM, p. 117; 5401AF, p. 147; 5206AM, p. 63; 5302AF, p. 52; 5412AM, p. 133; 5401AF, pp. 147–8.

41. 5504AF, p. 65; 5412AM, p. 62; 5003AF/M, p. 87.

42. 6001AF, p. 89; 5410AF, pp. 63, 66; 5401AM, pp. 79–80.

43. 5501AF, p. 121; 6904AF, p. 56; 5503AM, p. 94.

44. 5605AF, p. 133.

45. 6102AF, p. 80; 5003AM, p. 58; 5401AM, p. 63.

Chapter 7

1. 5410AF, p. 18.

2. 5413AM, pp. 2–3, 6–7, 10–12, 17–23, 53, 87.

3. 5001AM, p. 19; 5401AF2, p. 118; 6502AM, pp. 75–6; 5505AM/F, pp. 35, 79, 81.

4. 5502AF, pp. 11–12; 5401AM/F, pp. 156–7; 5401AM, pp. 54–5.

5. 5407AF, p. 24; 5605AM, pp. 27, 112. On the shock of unwanted retirement, cf. Phillipson 1982:42–4; Townsend 1957:159–60.

6. Abrams found 10% of men and 7% of women aged 65–74 were earning (1980:54); Hunt reported that in the whole group over 65, one in six men and one in twenty women were still at work (1976:71). Of our informants over 65, one-fifth had a regular job, and another tenth were earning through irregular or home-based work.

7. At the time of the research only £4 a week could be earned before benefits were deducted. Beyond this earnings over £50 a week were needed before significant gains in total income could be made. Since 1981 men aged 60–4 out of work for more than one year could claim the higher rate of Supplementary Benefit previously only available for pensioners over 65 and the long-term sick, thus reducing the financial incentive for continuing to seek work after 60 (Lyon 1987:14). 5003AM, pp. 58, 61; 5101AM, p. 52; 5502AF, p. 10; 5405AF, pp. 79–80; 5201F2, p. 106; 5007AF, p. 57.

8. 5505AM, p. 81; 6502AM, p. 108; 5405AF, p. 57.

9. 5501AF, pp. 104, 115.

10. 5201AM, pp. 77–9; 5101AM, pp. 83, 87.

11. 6501AM, pp. 7–8, 24, 47–8, 62.

12. 5502AM, p. 117; 5202AM, p. 36; 5502AF, pp. 11–12; 6001AF, pp. 35–6.

13. 5101AM, p. 79; 5206AM, p. 53; 5204AM, p. 4.

14. 5007AF, p. 55; 6001AF, p. 54.

15. 6101AF, pp. 58–9; 6902AF, pp. 43–4; 5207AF, pp. 72–3; 5408AF, p. 33. A former nurse regretted giving up voluntary meals on wheels work at 70 because of transport difficulties—'I miss the old people' (5607AF, p. 68)

16. 6102AF, pp. 56, 60, 62.

17. 6702AF, p. 73.

18. 5404AF, pp. 45–7, 50, 53–9, 67–8, 74, 77, 80, 110.

19. 6902AF, p. 40.

20. 5605AM/F, pp. 120–3.

21. 5407AF, p. 55; 5409AM, pp. 41–2, 54; 5605AF/M, pp. 48, 107, 117, 130.

22. 6502AM/F, pp. 12, 35, 41, 69–70, 72–3, 76, 79–80, 94.

23. 6502AM/F, pp. 110–11.

24. 5406AF, pp. 31, 46.

25. 6802AF, pp. 43–5, 49.

26. 6702AF, pp. 46–9, 64–5, 68, 71 (cf. 5607AF, who brought up her grandchildren for five years (p. 54), and 5405AF, who brought hers up for six years, also after a divorce: 'I think that's why they're so close really.' When they left 'it was terrible. It was like losing them'). Susan Yeandle's recent study of 'Married Women at Midlife' in South Wales also cites examples of acute distress at children leaving home: one mother could not get out of the habit of making her son's unused bed daily (in Allatt *et al.* (eds.) 1987:126–8).

27. 5506AF, p. 72; 5607AF, p. 57.

28. 6902AF, p. 38.

Chapter 8

1. 5505M/F, p. 109; 5401AM, p. 83; 5504AF, p. 49; 5506AF, p. 101.

2. 5505AM/F, pp. 82–3, 89, 91, 5405AF, p. 48; 5302AF, p. 70.

3. 5410AF, p. 54; 6902AF, p. 53; 5502AF, p. 17, 5201AF, p. 109;

5405AF, p. 84; 5302AF, p. 71. Abrams (1980:7) also reports the dominance of television, followed by reading. So does Hunt (1976:127), and again like ourselves, she found gardening and knitting or sewing next in popularity. Some of these estimates depend on what is included, and for reading ours are lower than hers, but for gardening we both report a quarter. Jonathan Long found similar patterns among Edinburgh men 42% of whom had taken up a new leisure activity on retirement (Bytheway, Keil, Allatt, and Brynan 1989:58–9).

4. 6904AF, p. 40; 5506AF, pp. 54, 77.

5. 5506AF, pp. 40–1, 77; 5503AM, p. 61; 6802AF, p. 55; 5413AM, p. 60; 5409AM, pp. 43, 47, 61.

6. 5409AM, p. 62; 5401AM, p. 77; 5408AF, p. 32; 5401AF2, p. 149; 5206AM, p. 58; 5607AF, pp. 61, 65; 5401AF2, p. 129; 5503AM, pp. 58–9, 64.

7. 5202AF/M, p. 91; 5207AF, pp. 89–99; 5201AF/M, p. 130.

8. 6001AF/M, pp. 32, 67; 6904AF, p. 36.

9. 5501AF, pp. 57–61, 75–6, 107.

10. 5502AF, p. 3; 6501AM, p. 34.

11. 5507AF, p. 61.

12. 5406AF, pp. 25, 56–62, 66, 68, 70, 77, 85, 87, 90–1.

13. 5003AM, pp. 35, 59–60, 73; 5101AM, pp. 49, 79, 90; 6102AF, pp. 53, 60; 6904AF, p. 40.

14. 5507AF, pp. 50–1; 5007AF, p. 53.

15. Clubs and societies: political 3; charitable 3; professional and service 6; sports 9; church 9; OAPs 7.

16. 6502AM, p. 91; 5412AM, p. 3; 5409AM, p. 51; 5003AM, p. 72; 5605AF, p. 115; 6505AM, p. 50; 5410AF, p. 54; 5412AM, p. 112.

17. 5502AF, pp. 22–3; 5614AF, p. 63; 5202AM, p. 96. C. C. Harris reports similar hostile attitudes from Swansea (in Jerrome 1983:23). The proportion of our informants who were club members is typical: Abrams found 13% of those over 75, of whom half were widowed or single, were members, and a much lower proportion among those under 75 (1980:25); Hunt found 8% belonged to pensioners clubs, 13% to churches, and 46% altogether to some kind of organization (1976:126).

18. 5001AM, pp. 15, 31; 6904AF, p. 37; 5409AM, p. 34.

19. 5401AM, pp. 48, 56–8, 69, 76–7.

20. 6102AF, p. 81; 5007AF, p. 63; 6001AF, p. 72; 6502AM, p. 120; 5405AF, p. 75; 6802AF, p. 65.

21. 5506AF, p. 126.

Chapter 9

1. Ben Turner, p. 361.
2. Hess and Waring 1978; Cherlin and Furstenberg, jun. 1985.
3. 5413CF, p. 4; 5403CF, p. 1; 5409BF, p. 114.
4. Vorse, pp. 54, 59, 61.
5. 5403CF, p. 2; 5409BF, p. 114; 5413BF, p. 69.
6. 5508BF, p. 3; 5503CF, p.4.
7. 5405AF, p. 99.
8. 5404AM, p. 97; 5403BM, p. 137.
9. 5506BM, p. 84; 5502BF, p. 118; 5402BF, p. 111.
10. Vorse, p. 60; 5410BM, p. 86; 5413AF, p. 73.
11. Cherlin and Furstenberg, jun 1985; Cunningham-Burley 1984*a*:p. iii.
12. 5407AF, p. 37.
13. 5401AM, p. 57.
14. 5409BF, p. 111.
15. 5501AF, pp. 88–9.
16. 5508BF, p. 3; 5503AM, p. 4.
17. 5405AF, p. 94.
18. Neugarten and Weinstein 1964. Possibly contemporary fears of abuse have been a countervailing inhibiting influence.
19. 5404AF, p. 102.
20. 6001AF, p. 70.
21. 5507BF, pp. 6 and 9; 5507AF, p. 38.
22. 5407BF, pp. 85.
23. 5404BF/M, p. 97.
24. 5505BM, p. 94; 5506AF, p. 117.
25. 5505AM/F, p. 99
26. Hagestad 1985.
27. 5002CF, p. 10; 5503CF, p. 8.
28. 5508CF, p. 8.
29. 5401AM, p. 73.
30. 5411BF, p. 119.
31. 6001AF, p. 20.
32. 5002CF, p. 4.
33. 5412AM, p. 127; 5505AM/F, p. 105.

34. 5401CF, p. 3.

35. 5411CM, pp. 2–3.

36. 5502AF, p. 33; 5410AF, p 24; 5503AM, p. 72.

37. 5408AF, p. 36.

38. 5407AF, p. 60.

39. 5406AF, p. 83.

40. 5501AF, p. 62; 5501BM, p. 6.

41. 5508CF, p. 3; Cherlin and Furstenberg, jun. 1986:132; Adams 1964:327–31.

42. 5410AF, p. 22.

43. 5504BF, p. 4.

44. 5505BF, p. 70.

45. 5407AF, p. 38; 5407BF, pp. 3–4; 5502BF, p. 115.

46. 5409BF, p. 72; 5506AF, p. 116.

47. 6001BF, pp. 52 and 72; 6001CF, p. 1; 6001AF, p. 74.

48. 5503CF, p. 1.

49. 5403CF, p. 9.

50. 5508BF, p. 101; 5508CF, p. 5.

51. 5413BF, p. 66; 5413CF, p. 1.

52. 5507BF, p. 61.

53. 5502BF, p. 117.

54. 5407AF, pp. 56 and 62.

55. 5506BM, p. 121.

56. 5504AF, p. 57.

57. 5406BM, p. 109.

58. 5408AF, p. 36.

59. 5411BF/M, p. 107.

60. 5508CF, p. 9.

Chapter 10

1. Townsend emphasized especially the Bethnal Green wives who resented their husbands in the house—'I couldn't stand him here all day'—although noting that some older couples grew 'more matey together' (1957:89–90, 167). Phillipson also describes divergent patterns among retired car workers: the minority of men who were

contented with retirement were now more home-centred, helping more in the house (1978:254–61). Time budget studies suggest that on average retired men do spend twice as much time as working men on domestic work of all kinds, although still substantially less than women: Miles 1984:61–5.

6303AF, p. 26; 5404AF, p. 76; 5405AF, p. 112.

2. 5503AM, p. 41; 5206AM, p. 64.

3. 5404AF, pp. 25, 70, 76, 107; 5405AF, p. 50; 5201AF, p. 75; 6001AF, pp. 64, 88; 6303AF, p. 26.

4. 5404AF, p. 26; 5001AM/F (b. Cyprus; words of interpreting relative), p. 34; 6303AF, p. 25.

5. 5505AF/M, pp. 86–7; 5507AF, pp. 53–4; 6702AF, pp. 69, 74; 5405AF, pp. 47–8, 76–7, 108, 113.

6. 5505AM/F, p. 87; 5507AF, p. 62; 6303AF, p. 26 (cf. 5404AF, p. 108, same phrase); 5405AF, p. 49; 6802AF, p. 31; 6001AF, p. 88; 6702AF, p. 92; 5404AM, p. 109.

7. 5504AF, pp. 26, 51; 6502AM/F, pp. 79–81; 5302AF, p. 57; 5606AF, pp. 114, 151; 6102AF, pp. 60, 64.

8. 6102AF, p. 79; 5504AF, p. 61; 6502AF/M, pp. 116, 120.

9. 5202AF, pp. 93–4; 5204AF, pp. 33, 37.

10. 5407AF, p. 31; 5506AF, pp. 47, 102, 124.

11. 5605AF, p. 41.

12. 5413AM, p. 58; 5208AF, p. 60; 5405AF, pp. 2–3.

13. 5101AM, p. 59; 6501AM, pp. 14, 63.

14. 5410AF, pp. 63, 66; 5207AF, pp. 107–8. Another nurse similarly kept the secret from her dying husband (5607AF, p. 59). Marris found that the majority of widows at first suffered from sleeplessness, loss of contact with reality (especially seeing their husbands as if still alive), social withdrawal, and apathy (1958:22). On the social desolation of widowhood, see also Gorer 1965:96–102.

15. 5006AF, pp. 36, 56; 5208AF, p. 72; 5410AF, pp. 20–1, 72.

16. 5503AM, pp. 27, 56; 5101AM, p. 51; 6904AF, pp. 20, 56.

17. 6904AF, p. 57; 5409AM, p. 34; 5401AM, p. 65 (cf. 6904AF, p. 42: a widow and friends).

18. 5207AF, p. 109; 5101AM, pp. 98, 100.

19. 5604AF, p. 34; 5607AF, p. 59; 5101AM, p. 52; 5007AF, p. 65; 6902AF, p. 48; 6904AF, pp. 37, 42, 57.

20. 6501AM, pp. 42, 47.

21. 6904AF, p. 43; 5614AF, p. 82.

22. 5409AM, pp. 24, 65.

23. 5607AF, p. 60.

24. 5603AF, pp. 12, 66; 5207AF, pp. 105–6; 6902AF, pp. 50, 63, 67.

25. 5501AF, pp. 35, 116–30, 135–6, 143.

26. 5408AF, pp. 2–3, 5, 11–12, 17–19, 21–5, 27–32, 37–8.

27. 5401AM, p. 79.

28. 5101AM, p. 100

29. 5412AM, pp. 39, 44, 59, 61–2, 107, 134–6.

30. 5101AM, pp. 51, 81, 94.

31. 5503AM, pp. 54–6, 73.

32. 6502AF, p. 102; 5408AF, p. 36; 6904AF, p. 44.

33. 5201AF2, p. 75.

34. 5201AF2, pp. 74, 78–9; 5503AM, p. 49. The age of starting second marriages could be the most important single factor: see Table 3.

35. 5413AF, p. 81; 5003AM, p. 61.

36. 5502AF, pp. 12, 36–7.

37. 5401AF2, pp. 18, 23–8, 86, 117–17, 132, 149.

Chapter 11

1. Bytheway, Keil, Allatt, and Brynan 1989:37, 115–16.

2. Murphy, Smith, Lindsay, and Slattery 1988; Antonovsky 1979:8, 162; and more recently, his *Unravelling the Mystery of Health*, where he identifies 'meaningfulness' as its crucial component (1987:49); Fennell, Phillipson, and Evers 1988:106; Sixsmith 1986; Coleman 1986; Kanfman 1986:162. Other recent studies of meaning and the self in later life include Breytspaak 1984; Le Blanc 1987; and Whitbourne 1987. There is of course a longstanding tradition of 'healing through meaning' in psychotherapy: e.g. Frankl 1978:1988.

3. Marris 1958; Bowling and Cartwright 1982; Taylor and Ford 1981:331; Clark and Anderson, 1967:382.

4. Letter from Elspeth Bristow to Marion Thompson, 10 Dec. 1985.

5. Phillipson and Walker (eds.) 1986:58.

6. *New Statesman and Society*, 16 Dec. 1988, p. 27.

7. Cherlin and Furstenberg, jun. 1986:189–91.

8. 5607AF, pp. 78–9; 5603AF, pp. 38, 71, 75.

9. Tunstall 1966:91: over 65-year-olds who did *not* sometimes or often feel lonely:

Married		Widowed	
Men	Women	Men	Women
86%	78%	67%	57%

Abrams 1978:39: over-75-year-olds who do *not* feel lonely and remote from others:

Not living alone		Living alone	
Men	Women	Men	Women
94%	87%	64%	71%

Tables

Note: Totals in Table 1 are based on one individual from each household; in Table 2 on households; in Tables 7–10 and 13 on each marriage, past and present; Tables 3–6 and 11–12 on individuals. Class definitions are as follows: middle class— husband non-manual, wife also non-manual or not working after marriage; intermediate—one spouse non-manual, the other manual; working class—both in manual occupations.

Table 1. *Sources of contentment*

	Contented	In between	Unhappy/depressed	Total
All	16 (36%)	18 (40%)	10 (23%)	44
Middle class	3 (25%)	8 (67%)	1 (8%)	12
Intermediate	4 (44%)	4 (44%)	1 (11%)	9
Working class	9 (39%)	6 (26%)	8 (35%)	23
In first marriage	3 (16%)	9 (47%)	7 (37%)	19
In second marriage	4 (80%)	1 (20%)	0 (0%)	5
In widowhood	9 (47%)	7 (37%)	3 (16%)	19
Under 70	4 (20%)	9 (45%)	7 (35%)	20
70–9	8 (47%)	7 (41%)	2 (12%)	17
Over 80	4 (57%)	2 (28%)	1 (14%)	7
Men	6 (40%)	7 (47%)	2 (13%)	15
Women	10 (34%)	11 (38%)	8 (27%)	29

Table 2. *Frequency with which children were seen*

	Daily/weekly	Fortnightly or less	Not known	Total
Middle class	5	6	1	12
Intermediate	6	3	0	9
Working class	16	6	1	23
TOTAL	27	15	2	44

Table 3. *Wife's Mean age at marriage*

	Type of relationship		
	Close	Not close	Unhappy
Surviving first marriages	24	24	23
Second marriages	51	36	(none)

Table 4. *Wife's age of marriage and fertility, by class*

	Working class	Middle class and intermediate
Mean age at first marriage	23	25
Completed family size (incl. second families)	3.2	2.4

Table 5. *Family and non-family social leisure*

Saw children:	Weekly or more	Fortnightly or less	Not known
Some non-family social leisure	18	12	
No non-family social leisure	15	7	3
TOTAL	33	19	3

Table 6. *Age and non-family social leisure*

	Aged under 70	Aged over 70
Some non-family social leisure	13	17
No non-family social leisure	17	8
TOTAL	30	25

Table 7. *Types of marriage and satisfaction: current first marriages*

	'Traditional' marriage	'Joint' marriage	(Adjusted to 'joint')	All
Close	1	4	(2)	5
Not close or unhappy	9	5	(4)	14
TOTAL	10	9		19

Table 8. *Types of marriage and satisfaction: retrospective first marriages*

	'Traditional' marriage	'Joint' marriage	All
Still in first marriage:			
All categories	16	3	19
Divorced:			
Unhappy	2	0	2
Widowed:			
Close	8	9	17
Not close or unhappy	7	0	7
Unclassified	7	1	8
TOTAL	22	10	32

Table 9. *Types of marriage and satisfaction: remarriages*

	'Traditional' marriages	'Joint' marriages	All
Close	3*	2*	5**
Not close or unhappy	2	0	2
TOTAL	5*	2*	7**

* includes one since widowed
** includes two since widowed

Table 10. *Proportion of those in various marital groups whose marriages can be classified as 'traditional' or as 'close'*

	'Traditional' marriages (%)	'Close' marriages (%)
First marriage (in past, as remembered by those still married)	84	*
First marriage (as remembered by widowed)	69	53
First marriage (now)	52	26
Second marriage (now)	71	71

* information insufficient

Table 11. *Recovery from widowhood, by age and sex*

	Age when widowed				Total
	Under 60		Over 60		
	Men	Women	Men	Women	
Fully recovered (single or remarried)	4	3	1	6	14
Not fully recovered	1	4	3	4	12
TOTAL	5	7	4	10	26

Table 12. *Recovery from widowhood, by degree of recovery*

	Still depressed	Functioning, but empty heart	Single, but full recovery	Second marriage	Total
Men	0	4	2	3	9
Women	3	5	6	3	17
Average age when widowed	66	63	63	44	

Table 13. *Attitude to sex in different types of marriage*

	Active	Passive	Hostile	Not known
Close	6	2	0	2
Not close	1	2	4	2
Unhappy	0	0	5	2
TOTAL	7	4	9	6
Average age	72	61	68	

Bibliography

Place of publication is London unless otherwise noted.

1. The Autobiographies

With the exception of Stott and Vorse, all are part of the sample born between 1830 and 1879; those quoted are asterisked.

* AIRLIE, MABEL, COUNTESS OF, *Thatched with Gold*, 1962
ARMSTRONG, CHESTER, *Pilgrimage from Nenthead*, 1938
ASQUITH MARGOT, *Autobiography*, 1920; *More Memories*, 1933
BALDRY, GEORGE, *The Rabbit Skin Cap*, 1939
* BALFOUR, LADY FRANCES, *Ne Obliviscaris*, 1930
BARBER, GEORGE, *From Workhouse to Lord Mayor*, Tunstall, 1937
BARCLAY, THOMAS, *Memoirs and Medleys*, Leicester, 1934
* BARNES, GEORGE, *From Workshop to War Cabinet*, 1923
BARNETT, WILL, *Life Story of the ex-Jockey*, Congleton, 1911
BARR, DAVID, *Climbing the Ladder*, 1910
* BELL, JOHN JOY, *I Remember*, 1932
BENSON, EDWARD FREDERICK, *Our Family Affairs, 1867–1890*, 1920; *As We Were*, 1930
* BIRCH, JOHN THOMAS, *Shop Boy*, 1983
BLATCHFORD, ROBERT, *My Eighty Years*, 1931
* BONFIELD, MARGARET, *A Life's Work*, 1949
BROADHURST, HENRY, *The Story of his Life from a Stonemason's Bench to the Treasury Bench*, 1910
BULLEN, FRANK, *Confessions of a Tradesman*, 1908
BURGESS, JOSEPH, 'Nineteenth Century Lancashire Textile Operatives Tribulations, 1800–95', Labour Party Archives, London
* BURT, THOMAS, *Pitman and Privy Councillor*, 1924
* CARBERY, MARY, *Happy World*, 1941
* CARNEGIE, ANDREW, *Autobiography*, 1920
CHOLMONDELEY, MARY, *Under One Roof*, 1918
CHRISTIE, ELLA, and STEWARD, ALICE [sisters], *A Long Look at Life*, 1940
* CLARKE, ALLEN (as Adhem, Ben), *Liverpool Weekly Post*, 24 Feb.–29 Dec. 1934
CLYNES, JOHN ROBERT, *Memoirs*, 1937; *When I Remember*, 1940
COCKING, GEORGE, *From the Mines to the Pulpit*, Cincinatti, 1901

* COMPTON-RICKETT, ARTHUR, *I Look Back*, 1932
COWARD, SIR HENRY, *Reminiscences*, 1919
DAVIES, MARGARET LLEWELYN (ed.), Co-operative Working Women, *Life as We Have Known-it*, 1931: Mrs Layton and Mrs Wrigley
* DESART, HAMILTON CUFFE, EARL OF, *Page for the Past*, 1936
DUNN, JAMES, *From Coal Mine Upwards*, 1910
* EDWARDS, GEORGE, *From Crow-scaring to Westminster*, 1922
* ELSON, GEORGE, *The Last of the Climbing Boys*, 1900
FANE, LADY AUGUSTA, *Chit-chat*, 1936
* FARNINGHAM, MARIANNE, *A Working Woman's Life*, 1907
* FLETCHER, MARGARET, *O, Call Back Yesterday*, 1939
* FOX, JOHN, *Life and Poems*, Bingley, 1914
FRANCIS, W. J., *Reminiscences*, 1926
* FRASER, JOHN, *Sixty Years in Uniform*, 1939
FREER, WALTER, *My Life and Memories*, Glasgow, 1929
* FRISBY, MINNIE, 'Memories', transcript, Brunel University Library
GALTON, FRANK, 'Autobiography', manuscript, British Library of Political and Economic Science
* GELL, EDITH, *Under Three Reigns*, 1927
GORING, JACK, manuscript, Brunel University Library
* GOSLING, HARRY, *Up and Down Stream*, London, 1927
GOSSE, EDMOND, *Father and Son*, 1907
* GOWER, SIR GEORGE LEVESON, *Years of Content*, 1940; *Years of Endeavour*, 1942
GREENWOOD, JOSEPH, 'Reminiscences of Sixty Years Ago', *Co-partnership*, 1909–11, pp. 177–200
* GWYER, JOSEPH, *Sketches of the Life: with his Poems*, Penge, 1877
HADDOW, WILLIAM, *My Seventy Years*, 1943
HAGGARD, HENRY RIDER, *The Days of My Life*, 1926
* HAGGARD, LILIAS RIDER (ed.), *I Walked by Night*, 1935
* HALDANE, LOUISA, *Friends and Kindred*, 1961
* HARBORD, CHARLES, Lord Suffield, *My Memories, 1830–1913*, 1913
* HARDY, EMMA, *Some Recollections*, 1961
* HARE, AUGUSTUS, *The Years with Mother*, 1952
* HARVEY, BASSIE, 'Youthful Memories', Suffolk Record Office
HOBHOUSE, STEPHEN, *Margaret Hobhouse and her Family*, 1934
HODGE, JOHN, *Workman's Cottage to Windsor Castle*, 1931
HOLLOWAY, HENRY, *A Voice from the Convict Cell*, Manchester, 1977
HORNER, FRANCES, *Time Remembered*, 1933
HOUSEMAN, LAURENCE, *The Unexpected Years*, 1937
* HUGHES, EDWARD, manuscript, Clwyd Record Office
HUGHES, MARGARET VIVIAN, *A London Family*, 1946
HUNT, T. J., *Life Story*, 1936
IRESON, ALFRED, 'Reminiscences', typescript, Brunel University Library

* JERMY, LOUISE, *The Memories of a Working Woman*, Norwich, 1934
* JERSEY, COUNTESS OF, *Fifty-one Years of Victorian Life*, 1922
* JOHNSTON, ELLEN, *Autobiography, Poems and Songs*, Glasgrow, 1867
* JONES, SIR HENRY, *Old Memories*, 1922
* KENDALL, S. G., *Farming Memories*, 1944
  KENNEY, ANNIE, *Memories of a Militant*, 1924
* LANSBURY, GEORGE, *My Life*, 1928
* LAX, WILLIAM HENRY, *Lax: His Book*, 1937
* LAYTON, MRS, 'Memories of Seventy years', in Davies (ed.), *Life as We Have Known it*, pp. 1–55
* LEE, JOHN, *The Man They could not Hang*, 1908
  LIPTON, SIR THOMAS, *Leaves from the Lipton Logs*, n.d. c.1930
* LOCKWOOD, FLORENCE, *An Ordinary Life*, 1932
* LONSDALE, SOPHIA (ed. Violet Martineau), *Recollections*, 1936
  LUCK, LUCY, 'A little of My Life', *London Mercury*, 13 (1925–6), 354–73; reprinted in John Burnett, *Useful Toil*, 1974, pp. 68–77
  MABEY, WILLIAM, 'History of the Life', manuscript, Dorset Country Record Office
  MACE, JEM, *Fifty Years a Fighter*, 1908
* MACKENZIE, JAMES, 'Strange Truth', manuscript, Brunel University Library
* MACLELLAN, ANGUS, *The Furrow behind Me*, 1962
* MALLOCK, W. H., *Memoirs of Life and Literature*, 1920
* MARSH, GEORGE, 'A Sketch of the Life of a Yorkshire Collier', Barnsley Reference Library
  MARSHALL, MARY PALEY, *What I Remember*, 1947
  MEAD, ISAAC, *The Life Story of an Essex Lad*, Chelmsford, 1923
* MEEK, GEORGE, *Bath Chair-Man*, 1910
* MEYNELL, LADY MARY, *Sunshine and Shadows over a Long Life*, 1933
  MITCHELL, ALEXANDER, *Recollections of a Lifetime*, Aberdeen, 1911
* MITCHELL, HANNAH, *The Hard Way Up*, 1968
* MUMFORD, EDITH READ, *Through Rose-coloured Spectacles*, 1952
* MURISON, ALEXANDER, *Memoirs of 88 years*, Aberdeen, 1935
* NEVILL, RALPH, *Unconventional Memories*, 1923
  NEVISON, MARGARET WYNNE, *Life's Fitful Fever*, 1926
  PEEL, LADY GEORGIANA, *Recollections*, 1920
  PLUMMER, JOHN, *Songs of Labour*, Kettering, 1860
* POINTER, THOMAS, Manuscript, Broadstairs Library
* POLLOCK, ALICE, *Portrait of My Victorian Youth*, 1971
  POWELL, JAMES HENRY, *Life Incidents and Poetic Pictures*, 1865
  PUGH, ALBERT, 'I Helped to Build Railroads', in Charles Madge (ed.), *Pilot Papers: Social Essays and Documents*, 1 (1946), 75–98
  RADNOR, HELEN COUNTESS OF, *From a Grandmother's Armchair*, 1927
* RAGLAN, ETHEL, *Memories of Three Reigns*, 1928

RHYS, ERNEST, *Wales England Wed*, 1940

* RIBBESDALE, LORD, *Impressions and Memories*, 1937
* ROBERTS, ROBERT, *Life and Opinions*, Cardiff, 1923

ROBINSON, MAUDE, *A South Down Farm in the Sixties*, 1938

ROGERS, FREDRICK, *Labour, Life and Literature*, 1913

* ROSS, JANET, *Fourth Generation*, 1912

RYMER, EDWARD ALLEN, *The Martyrdom of the Mine*, Middlesborough, 1898

* ST HELIER, LADY, *Memories of Fifty Years*, 1909
* SANUNDERS, JAMES, *A Glance at the Past*, 1922
* SEXTON, SIR JAMES, *Agitator: The Life of the Docker's M. P.*, 1936
* SHAW, CHARLES, *When I was a Child, by an Old Potter*, 1903 (originally anonymous)

SHERVINGTON, JESSE, 'Autobiography of an Agricultural Labourer', from the *Baptist Banner* (1896), manuscript, Worcester Record Office

* SICHEL, WALTER, *The Sands of Time*, 1923

SILVESTER, SUSAN, *In A World That Has Gone*, Loughborough, 1968

SMITH, CORNELIUS, *Life Story*, 1890

SMITH, RODNEY, *Gipsy Smith*, 1902

SNELL HENRY, *Men Movements and Myself*, 1936

STANLEY, HENRY MORTOR, *Autobiography*, 1909

STRACHEY, JOHN ST LOE, *The Adventure of Living*, 1922

STELL, FLORA ANNIE, *The Garden of Fidelity*, 1929

STEEL, FRANK, *Ditcher's Row*, 1939

* STIRLING, ANNA MARIA WILHELMINA, *Life's Little Day*, 1924
* STOTT, MARY, *Before I Go . . .*, 1985
* SUFFIELD, CHARLES HARBORD LORD, *My Memories*, 1913
* SWAN, ANNIE S., *My Life*, 1934
* TAYLOR, JOHN, *Poems, Chiefly on Themes of Scottish Interest*, Edinburgh, 1875

TAYLOR, PETER, *Autobiography*, Paisley, 1903

* THOMPSON, FLORA, *Lark Rise to Candleford*, 1945

THORNE, WILL, *My Life's Battles*, 1925

TILLETT, BENJAMIN, *Memories and Reflections*, 1931

* TURNBULL, JAMES (Anonymously), *Reminiscences of a Stonemason, by a Working Man*, 1908
* TURNER, BEN, *About Myself, 1863–1930*, 1930

TURNER, JAMES, *Hard up Husband*, Orwell, 1981

* VORSE, MARY H., *The Autobiography of an Elderly Woman*, New York, 1911
* WARWICK, FRANCES, Countess of, *Life's Ebb and Flow*, 1929
* WATSON, LEWIS, 'Autobiography', typescript, Stalybridge Library
* WAUGH, ARTHUR, *One Man's Road*, 1931
* WILLOUGHBY DE BROKE, LORD, *The Passing Years*, 1924

WILSON, JOHN, *Memories of a Labour Leader*, 1910

WILSON, JOSEPH, *His Life and Work*, n. d. c.1910

* WILSON, JOSEPH HAVELOCK, *My Stormy Voyage through Life*, Newcastle, 1925

WRIGLEY, MRS, 'A Plate Layer's Wife', in Davies (ed.), *Life as We Have Known it*, pp. 56–66

WRIGLEY, AMMON, *Rakings Up*, Rochdale, 1949

2. *References: Later Life And Ageing*

ABRAMS, MARK, 1978 and 1980: *Beyond Three Score and Ten*, 2 vols.

ACHENBAUM, W. ANDREW, 1978: *Old Age in the New Land: the American Experience since 1770*

ADAMS, BERT N., 1964: 'Structural Factors Affecting Parental Aid to Married Children', *Journal of Marriage and the Family*, 26. 327–31

ALLATT, P., *et al.* (eds.) 1987: *Women and the Life Cycle*

ANDERSON, MICHAEL, 1971: *Family Structure in Nineteenth Century Lancashire*, Cambridge

—— 1988: 'Households, Families and Individuals in 1851', *Continuity and Change*, 3. 421–38

ANTONOVSKY, ARON, 1979: *Health, Stress and Coping*, San Francisco

—— 1987: *Unravelling the Mystery of Health*

ARENSBERG C. M. and KIMBALL S. T., 1940: *Family and Community in Ireland*, Cambridge, Mass.

BEAUVOIR, SIMONE DE, 1972: *Old Age.*

BLYTHE, RONALD, 1979: *The View in Winter: Reflections on Old Age*

BOOTH, CHARLES, 1894: *The Aged Poor in England and Wales*

BORENSTEIN, AUDREY, 1983: *Chimes of Change and Hours: Views of Older Women in Twentieth Century America*

BORNAT, J., PHILLIPSON, C., and WARD, S., 1985: *A Manifesto for Old Age*

BOWLING, ANN, and CARTWRIGHT, ANN, 1982: *Life after a Death*

BREYTSPAAK, L. M., 1984: *The Development of Self in Later Life*, Boston

BROMLEY, D. B. 1988: *Human Ageing: An Introduction to Gerontology*, 3rd edn.

BUTLER, ROBERT N., 1975: *Why Survive? Being Old in America*, New York

BYTHEWAY, BILL, KEIL, TERESA, ALLATT, PATRICIA, and BRYNAN, ALAN, 1989: *Becoming and Being Old: Sociological Approaches to Later Life*

CARVER, VIDA, and LIDDIARD, PENNY, 1978: *An Ageing Population*, Open University (includes Johnson, Rosenmayer, Sontag, Laslett)

CASTELLS, M., and GUILLEMARD, A. M., 1971: 'La Determination des pratiques sociales en situation de retraite', *Sociologie du travail*, 13. 282–307

CAVAN, RUTH, 1962: 'Self and Role Adjustment during Old Age', in ARNOLD M. ROSE (ed.), *Human Behaviour and Social Processes*, Boston, pp. 526–36

CHERLIN, A., and FURSTENBERG, F., Jun., 1985: 'Styles and Strategies of Grandparenting', in U. Bengstrom and J. Robertson (eds.), *Grandparenthood*

—— and —— 1986: *The New American Grandparent*, New York

CLARK, MARGARET, and ANDERSON BARBARA, 1967: *Culture and Ageing: An Anthropological Study of Old Americans*

COLEMAN, PETER, 1986: *The Ageing Process and the Role of Reminiscence*

COMFORT, ALEX, 1977: *A Good Age*

CRAWFORD, MARION, 1971: 'Retirement and Disengagement', *Human Relations*, 24. 255–78

—— 1981: 'Not Disengaged: Grandparents in Literature and Reality: An Empirical Study in Role Satisfaction', *Sociological Review*, 29. 499–519

CRIBIER, FRANÇOISE, 1968: *Une génération de Parisiens arrive à la retraite*, CNRS, Paris

—— 1971: 'La Retraite au bord de la mer et les relations avec enfants', *Gerontologie et société*, 21. 44–69

CUMMING, M. E., and HENRY W. H., 1961: *Growing Old: The Process of Disengagement*, New York

CUNNINGHAM-BURLEY, SARAH, 1984a: 'The Meaning and Significance of Grandparenthood', Aberdeen Ph.D.

—— 1984b: ' "We Don't Talk about it . . . ": Issues of Gender and Method in the Portrayal of Grandfatherhood', *Sociology*, 18. 325–38

DAVIDOFF, LEONORE, and HALL, CATHERINE, 1987: *Family Fortunes: Men and women of the English Middle Class, 1780–1850*

DAVIES, ALAN, SCHWER, KEVIN, WALL, RICHARD, and LASLETT, PETER, 1987: 'Family and Living Arrangments', Conference Paper, Beijing, October

FENNELL, GRAHAM, PHILLIPSON, CHRIS, and EVERS, HELEN, 1988: *The Sociology of Old Age*, Milton Keynes

FINCH, JANET, and GROVES, DULCIE, (eds), 1983: *A Labour of Love: Women, Work and Caring*

FONER, NANCY, 1984: *Age in Conflict*, New York

FORD, JANET, and SINCLAIR, RUTH, 1987: *Sixty Years On: Women Talk about Old Age*

FRANKL, V. E., 1978: *The Unheard Cry for Meaning: Psychotherapy and Humanism*, New York

FRAZIER, E. FRANKLIN, 1939: *The Negro Family in the United States*, New York

GAUNT, DAVID, 1983: 'The Property and Kin Relationships of Retired Farmers in Northern and Central Europe', in R. Wall (ed.), *Family Forms in Historic Europe*, Cambridge, pp. 249–79

GERARD, JESSICA, 1982: 'Family and Servants in the Country-House Community in England and Wales, 1815–1914', London Ph.D.

—— 1988: *The Country House Society, 1815–1914*, Oxford

GIBSON, MARY JO, 1984: 'Sexuality in Later Life', *Ageing International*, 11.1 (Spring), 8–13

GOODY, JACK, THIRSK, JOAN, and THOMPSON E. P. (eds), 1976: *Family and Inheritance: Rural Society in Western Europe, 1200–1800*

GORDON, C., 1986: 'Patterns of Support for the Elderly', LSE M. Sc. Thesis

GORER, GEOFFREY, 1965: *Death, Grief and Mourning*

GREEN, HAZEL, 1985: *Informal Carers*, General Household Survey, 15, Supplement A

GREENWOOD, WALTER, *c*.1935: *How the Other Man Lives*

HABER, CAROLE, 1983: *Beyond 65: The Dilemma of Old Age in America's Past*

HAGESTAD, G., 'Older Women in Intergenerational Relationships', in M. Haug *et al.* (eds.), *The Physical and Mental Health of the Aged Woman*, New York

HANNAH, LESLIE, 1986: *Inventing Retirement: The Development of Occupational Pensions in Britain*, Cambridge

HAREVEN, TAMARA, and ADAMS, KATHLEEN, (eds), 1982: *Ageing and Life Course Transitions: An Interdisciplinary Perspective*

HEMMINGS, SUSAN, 1985: *A Wealth of Experience*

HENDRICKS, J. and C. D. 1977: *Ageing in Mass Society*

HESS, B., and WARING J., 1978: 'Parent and Child in Later Life', in R. M. Lerner and A. B. Spanier (eds.), *Child Influences on Marital and Family Interaction*, New York, pp. 241–68

HOULBROOKE, RALPH, 1984: *The English Family, 1450–1700*, pp. 189–210

HOWELL, CICELY, 1983: *Land, Family and Inheritance in Transition: Kibworth Harcourt, 1280–1700*, Cambridge

HUNT, AUDREY, 1976: *The Elderly at Home*

ITZIN, CATHERINE, 1986a: 'Ageism Awareness Training', in C. Phillipson, C. Bernard, and P. Strang, *Dependency and Interdependency in Old Age*

—— 1986b: *Elderly People in the Community: Screening, Support and Services*, Newham Health Authority

JACOBS, JERRY, 1974: *Fun City An Ethnographic Study of a Retirement Community*, New York

JERROME, DOROTHY, 1981: 'The Significance of Friendship for Women in Later Life', *Ageing and Society*

—— (ed.), 1983: *Ageing in a Modern Society* (includes Thane, etc.)

JOHNSON, MALCOLM, 1976: 'That was Your Life: A Biographical Approach to Later Life', in J. M. A. Munnichs and W. J. A. Van den Heuvel (eds.), *Dependency or Interdependency in Old Age*, The Hague, pp. 148–61

JOHNSON, SHEILA, 1971: *Idle Haven: Community Building among the Working Class Retired*, Berkeley

KARN, VALERIE, 1977: *Retiring to the Seaside*

KAUFMAN, SHARON, 1986: *The Ageless Self: Sources of Meaning in Later Life*, Madison

KEITH, JENNIE, 1982: *Old People as People*

KENDALL, M., and ROWNTREE, B. S., 1913: *How the Labourer Lives*

KERR, MADELINE, 1958: *The People of Ship Street*

KOMAROVSKY, MIRRA, 1962: *Blue Collar Marriage*, New York

LASLETT, PETER, 1977: *Family Life and Illicit Love in Earlier Generations* pp. 174–81

—— 1976: 'Societal Development and Aging,' in Robert Binstock and Ethel Shanas, *Handbook of Aging and the Social Science*, New York, pp. 87–116

LeBLANC, D., 1987: 'Case Studying the Philosophy, Integrity, and Emotional Health of the Elderly', *Educational Gerontology*, 13. 387–402

LEVIN, J. and W. C., 1980: *Ageism: Prejudice and Discrimination against the Elderly*

LEWIS, OSCAR, 1970: *A Death in the Sanchez Family*

LYON, PHIL, 1987: *Nearing Retirement*

MAAS, HENRY, and KUYPER, JOSEPH, 1974: *From Thirty to Seventy*, San Francisco

MACFARLANE, ALAN, 1986: *Love and Marriage in England, 1600–1840*, Chapter 6

MARKSON, E. W. (ed.), 1983: *Older Women: Issues and Prospects* (including Braito and Anderson, 'The Ever Single Elderly Woman', and M. E. Szinovacz, 'Beyond the Hearth: Older Women and Retirement')

MARRIS, PETER, 1958: *Widows and their Families*

MASON, JENNIFER, 1987: 'Women, Marriage and Inequality in Later Life', in Patricia Allatt *et al.* (eds.), *Women and the Life Cycle: Transitions and Turning Points*, pp. 90–105

MATTHEWS, SARAH, 1979: *The Social World of Older Women: Management of Self-Identity*

MILES, IAN, 1984: 'Work, Non-work and Ageing', draft report to ESRC

MISHLER, ELLIOT, 1986: *Research Interviewing*, Cambridge

MITTERAUER, MICHAEL, and SIEDER, REINHARD, 1983: *The European Family*

MURPHY, ELAINE, SMITH, RAE, LINDSAY, JAMES, and SLATTERY, JIM, 1988: 'Increased Mortality Rates in later-Life Depression', *British Journal of Psychiatry*, 152. 347–53

MYERHOFF, BARBARA, 1979: *Number our Days: A Triumph of Continuity and Culture among Jewish Old People in an Urban Ghetto*, New York

NEUGARTEN, BERNICE, and WEINSTEIN, KAROL, 1964: 'The Changing American Grandparent', *Journal of Marriage and the Family*, 26. 199–204

PHILLIPSON, CHRIS, 1978: 'The Experience of Retirement: A Sociological Study', Durham Ph.D.

—— 1982: *Capitalism and the Construction of old Age*

—— and WALKER, ALAN, (eds.), 1986: *Ageing and Social Policy*, Aldershot Plummer, Ken, 1983: *Documents of Life*

PULLING, JENNY, 1987: *The Caring Trap*

QUADAGNO, JILL, 1983: *Ageing in Early Industrial Society: Work, Family and Social Policy in nineteenth century England*

RAPOPORT, RHONA, and RAPOPORT, ROBERT, 1975: *Leisure and the Family Life Cycle*

RILEY, M. W., 1972: *Ageing and Society*, especially John Clausen, 'The Life Course of Individuals', pp. 457–514

ROBERTS, ELIZABETH, 1984: *A Woman's Place*, pp. 170–91

ROSENMAYER, LEOPOLD, 1981: 'Objective and Subjective Perspectives of Life Span Research', *Ageing and Society*, 1. 29–50

ROSS, JENNIE-KEITH, 1977: *Old People, New Lives*, Chicago

ROSSER, C., and HARRIS, C. C., 1965: *The Family and Social Change: A Study of Family and Kinship in a South Wales Town*

ROWNTREE, B. SEEBOHM, 1901: *Poverty: a study of town life*

RUSSELL, CHERRY, 1981: *The Ageing Experience*, Sydney

ST PHILIP'S SETTLEMENT, 1919: *Equipment of the Workers*

SEABROOK, JEREMY, 1980: *The Way We are Now: Old People Talk about Themselves*

SHANAS, ETHEL, TOWNSEND, PETER, WEDDERBURN, DOROTHY, FRIIS, HENNING, PAUL, MILHOJ, and STEHOALWER, JAN, 1968: *Old People in Three Societies*

SIXSMITH, ANDREW, 1986: 'The Meaning of Home: An Exploratory Study of Environmental experience', *Journal of Environmental Psychology*, 6. 281–98

SMITH, DANIEL SCOTT, 1979: 'Life Course, Norms, and the Family System of Older Americans in 1900', *Journal of Family History*, 4. 285–98

SMITH, HUBERT LLEWELYN, 1930–5: *The New Survey of London Life and Labour*

SMITH, S. R., 1976: 'Growing Old in Early Stuart England', *Albion*, 8

SONTAG, SUSAN, 1978: 'The Double Standard of Ageing', in Vida Carver and Penny Liddiard (eds.), *An Ageing Population*, Sevenoaks, pp. 72–80

SPUFFORD, MARGARET, 1974: *Contrasting Communities: English villages in the 16th and 17th Centuries*, Cambridge

STEARNS, PETER, 1977: *Old Age in European Society: The Case of France*, 1977

—— 1980: 'Old Women: Some Historical Observations,' *Journal of Family History*, 5. 44–57

SZINOVACZ, MAXIMILIANE, (ed.), 1982: *Women's Retirement*

TAYLOR, REX, and FORD, GRAEME, 1981: 'Lifestyle and Ageing', *Ageing and Society*, 1. 329–45

THANE, PAT, 1987: *Economic Burden or Benefit*, Centre for Economic Policy Research, Discussion paper 197

THOMAS, GEOFFREY, 1947: *The Employment of Older Persons*

THOMAS, JEANNE, 1986: 'Age and Sex Differences in the Perceptions of Grandparenting', *Journal of Gerontology*, 41. 417–23

THOMAS, KEITH, 1976: *Age and Authority in Early Modern England*

THOMPSON, PAUL, 1978, 2nd edn. 1988: *The Voice of the Past: Oral History*

THOMSON, DAVID, 1980: 'Provision for the Elderly in England, 1830–1908', Cambridge Ph.D.

—— 1983: 'Workhouse to Nursing Home: Residential Care of Elderly People in England since 1840', *Ageing and Society*, 3. 43–69

—— 1984: 'The Decline of Social Security: Falling State Support for the Elderly since Early Victorian Times', *Ageing and society*, 4. 451–82

TINKER, A., 1984: *Staying at Home: Helping Elderly People*, Department of Environment

TOWNSEND, PETER, 1957: *The Family Life of Old People: An Inquiry in East London*

—— 1964: *The Last Refuge*,

—— 1965: 'The Effects of Family Structure on the Likelihood of Admission to an Institution in Old Age', in Ethel Shanas and Gordon Streib, *Social Structure and the Family*, Englewood Cliffs, NJ,

TUNSTALL, JEREMY, 1966: *Old and Alone*

UNGERSON, CLAIRE, 1987: *Policy is Personal: Sex, Gender and Informal Care*

WHITBOURNE, S. K., 1987: 'Personality Development in Adulthood and Old Age: Relationships among Identity style, Health, and Well-being,' *Annual Review of Gerontology and Geriatrics*, pp. 189–216

WALL, RICHARD, 1984: 'Residential Isolation of the Elderly: A Comparison over Time', *Ageing and Society*, 4. 483–503

—— 1989 'The Living Arrangements of the Elderly in Europe in the 1980s', in Bytheway *et al.*, pp. 121–42

—— and Grundy Emily, forthcoming: *The Elderly and the Family: A Review of the Living Arrangements of the Elderly since Pre-industrial Times*

WILLIAMS, RICHARD, and WIRTHS, CLAUDINE, 1965: *Lives through the Years*

YOUNG, MICHAEL, and WILLMOTT, PETER, 1957: *Family and Kinship in East London*

Index